THE
LIVING
CITY

THE LIVING CITY

Why CITIES DON'T NEED to Be GREEN to Be GREAT

DES FITZGERALD

BASIC BOOKS
NEW YORK

Basic Books
Hachette Book Group
1290 Avenue of the Americas, New York, NY 10104
www.basicbooks.com
Printed in the United States of America
First Edition: November 2023

Published by Basic Books, a subsidiary of Hachette Book Group, Inc. The Basic
Books name and logo is a trademark of the Hachette Book Group.

The Hachette Speakers Bureau provides a wide range of authors for speaking
events. To find out more, go to hachettespeakersbureau.com or email
HachetteSpeakers@hbgusa.com.

Basic books may be purchased in bulk for business, educational, or promotional
use. For more information, please contact your local bookseller or the Hachette
Book Group Special Markets Department at special.markets@hbgusa.com.

The publisher is not responsible for websites (or their content) that are not owned
by the publisher.
Print book interior design by Sheryl Kober

Some sections in Chapter 1 appeared previously in "A Gigantic Vertical Zoo:
Madness and the Green City/Un Gigantesque Zoo Vertical: Folie et Ville Verte,"
published in *Terrain: Anthropologie & Sciences Humaines*, Volume 76, in 2022.
Small sections from Chapters 1, 2, and 3 have appeared in "A Forest, a Maze,
a Garden, a City: Psychiatry's Architectural Turn," in *Cultural Politics* (Duke
University Press), Volume 18, Issue 3, also in 2022. For another version of the Jonas
Salk story, see "A City is Not a Park," an episode of The Essay for BBC Radio 3, also
by Des Fitzgerald, first broadcast in 2019.

Library of Congress Cataloging-in-Publication Data

Names: Fitzgerald, Des, author.
Title: The living city : why cities don't need to be green to be great / Des Fitzgerald.
Description: First edition. | New York, NY : Basic Books, [2023] | Includes
    bibliographical references and index.
Identifiers: LCCN 2023013076 | ISBN 9781541674509 (hardcover) | ISBN
    9781541674516 (ebook)
Subjects: LCSH: Cities and towns. | City and town life. | Urban policy. | City planning.
Classification: LCC HT151 .F5155 2023 | DDC 307.76—dc23/eng/20230515
LC record available at https://lccn.loc.gov/2023013076

ISBNs: 9781541674509 (hardcover), 9781541674516 (ebook)
LSC-C
Printing 1, 2023

CONTENTS

INTRODUCTION

In September 1868, forty-six-year-old Frederick Law Olmsted, already the most prominent landscape designer and conservationist of his day, sat down at his desk in New York City to compose a report on a suburb proposed for the banks of the Des Plaines River, about nine miles outside Chicago—a site to which the developer, E. E. Child, had just given the deceptively bland name Riverside.[1] To understand the possibilities for this site, in Olmsted's account, you had to understand not so much the environmental but rather the social conditions that would encourage people to live in it. You had to understand, he wrote, that the middle of the nineteenth century was a period of what today we would call urbanization. People were coming together in booming towns and cities. They had developed a taste for the luxuries and refinements that they could only get from city life. And yet, from the vantage point of his desk in New York, Olmsted sensed something new in the air. "There are symptoms of a change," he wrote to Riverside's financial backers, who had contracted his and his partner's firm, Olmsted, Vaux & Co., to design the site from scratch—"a countertide of migration" away from the city and back toward a different kind of life. This phenomenon was becoming visible, he said, in the common desire to live near parks. It could be detected, similarly, in people's desperation to plant rows of trees, "little enclosures of turf and foliage," in every newly laid street. Indeed, he went on, a certain Dr. Rumney of the British Association for the Advancement of Social Science had recently established that simply *living near other people* could make a person ill, even manifesting a kind of "nervous feebleness." It was therefore the suburb, according to Olmsted, that was truly the city of the future. And not just any suburb, but rather one that could successfully re-create that very particular feeling of not being in the city at all—that could re-create the feeling of being in the countryside, with its pure air, its shade, its open spaces, its "distance from the jar, noise, confusion and bustle of commercial thoroughfares."[2] A realization was dawning: there was something just a bit off about city life. The city was not, in fact, a very good place to live at all. Some new way of living, somewhere between the urban and the rural, now loomed on the horizon. As Olmsted put it the following year in a letter to the author and journalist Edward Everett Hale, the key thing now was to create a space for living that was not quite the city and not quite the country. "[I] urge principles, plans and measures," Olmsted wrote effusively, "tending to the ruralizing of *all* our urban population and the urbanizing of our rustic population."[3]

Olmsted was neither the first nor the only person to have such thoughts. The fantasy of the city that was not really a city at all, of the landscaped park that still maintained the rugged virtues of the open frontier, had become a guiding theme of American public life in the nineteenth century. It was a fantasy, indeed, the historian Dorceta Taylor reminds us, that was held on to with special fervor by urban elites, such as Olmsted, anxious, among other things, about what city life was doing to their own waning sense of racial superiority.[4] Through different, often overlapping waves of urbanization across the globe, this idea has never fully disappeared. My interest in this book is in following its contours into the present day, as a new kind of urban anxiety, and a new kind of desire for the countryside, begins to rise again. This desire is, of course, in many ways very different from the racialized anxieties of Olmsted's day. And yet also maybe not so different.

Things ultimately went south for Olmsted and Vaux at Riverside—their plans were not exactly followed, Child went bust, and Olmsted had to take payment in lots, which quickly collapsed in value. And yet somehow, Riverside, a surprisingly sturdy green village on the banks of an unloved river, began to take shape. Olmsted was by then out of the picture. But there was another figure, living in obscurity in Chicago at that time, who may well have seen Riverside under construction and who would carry this urge articulated by Olmsted much further in the decades that followed.[5] This was Ebenezer Howard, the unlikely founder of the Garden City movement, who would go on to establish two urban centers on his return to his birthplace in England—first there was Letchworth Garden City, founded in 1904, and then the new town of Welwyn Garden City, which followed in 1920.

———

On an unseasonably warm day in mid-September 2021, I caught a train at King's Cross Station in London, admired the station's spectacular new glass-and-steel dome—now arced over the frantic concourse like an upturned glass over an ant colony—and traveled twenty miles north to the sleepy commuter county of Hertfordshire, and into a different world entirely. My destination was Welwyn Garden City—England's second and last true "garden city," once part of a great international movement to shift twentieth-century urban planning toward new, medium-sized satellite towns surrounded by green space. Just as Frederick Law Olmsted had dreamed, these towns were to be new places for living that were not quite urban and not quite rural, with decent housing and work for all, and underpinned by an economic system (this part was not Olmsted's dream) that would reinvest the proceeds from increasing land values for everyone's benefit. Though it never really worked out that way, and the broader movement has long since faded away, the busy and prosperous town of Welwyn was nonetheless happily celebrating its one hundredth anniversary, as well as its small but critical role in the history of urban planning. So I went along, curious to see what the onetime city of the future looked like, now that the future had, unambiguously if rather unceremoniously, arrived.

Having founded Welwyn with his collaborators in 1920, Ebenezer Howard quickly appointed a Montreal-born architect, Louis de Soissons, to create the town's master plan. De Soissons, who had just graduated from university, would end up spending his life as chief architect at Welwyn Garden City and died there in 1962. In his original plan, de Soissons laid out the green heart of the town a bit like a T where the vertical bar, Parkway, is longer than the horizontal bar, Howardsgate. At the north end of Parkway, de Soissons added a small, bulbous park, rather pompously known as "the Campus." From overhead, the whole thing looks a bit like a gun—or a penis.

The idea behind Welwyn, and behind garden cities more generally, was not simply to remake urban space around green and healthy country life. It was an attempt to reform how land was owned and who made money from it—to stop increases in land value going solely to private owners and instead use that increase for the collective good of the residents. But the movement was also about creating a new kind of person, or at least it was a serious attempt to return the benighted inhabitants of industrial cities to some more natural state. "Men," Howard wrote, quoting the eugenicist philosopher Herbert Spencer, "are equally entitled to the use of the earth." What they want is the "practical life," the fruits of their toil, an equal share, a short commute, a patch of grass to call their own, neither rural simplicity nor urban drudgery but something somehow in-between. If planners would just use "the resources of modern science," Howard wrote, "Art may supplement Nature, and life may become an abiding joy and delight."[6]

Today, though, I realized, exiting the ugly 1990s shopping mall that somehow contains the train station, if central Howardsgate is still a lush, green, formally landscaped city-center park, it's also more or less a taxi stand. A line of cars creeps around the edges like flies on a cake, collecting passengers from the station and the nearby chain shops. Mutual ownership, meanwhile, disappeared in the 1980s. Today, all the houses are available on the open market—many of them, I saw in estate agents' windows as I walked around, going for well over a million British pounds. Welwyn Garden City might still represent a kind of utopia, I reflected, trying not to be run over by speeding commuters in their SUVs, but *whose* utopia, exactly, was not quite so clear.

I had come to Welwyn because, for some time, I'd been thinking a lot about urban planning and the future of the city. I wanted to know why so many people in that field were convinced that there was something about our cities that was simply bad for us, and especially that there was something about them that was psychologically or even morally bad for us. I was trying to imagine what this future would look like, and how it might be different from previous attempts to fix these problems. I was also trying to figure out why it was that so many planners and architects and policy makers were so fixated on *nature* as the solution to all of the city's problems—why they seemed to think that treating the city as if it were a kind of organism, a living thing, would finally bring planning and architecture into the twenty-first century. As I traipsed around international events on future cities, healthy cities, green cities, and so on, it began to feel as if there were no issue in city life, from air quality to mental health, that couldn't be fixed by a line of trees, a green roof, a biomimetic office block, a forlorn plant growing through the cracks in some derelict wall.

But by the time I arrived in Welwyn, I was starting to find the whole "green city" rhetoric extremely unconvincing. Too often, it seemed to me, an urban park was just a nice-looking taxi stand in waiting. Carefully tended green space was maybe just another way of pushing up house prices and creating exclusive communities where the lush trees act as pretty effective symbolic gates. Maybe the reality is that, however the rest of us feel about it, lots of people find their joy not in digging vegetables or caressing the bushes, but in driving ugly cars at high speed through exclusive commuter towns.

It seemed to me, too, that what a place like Welwyn or Riverside symbolized was perhaps not really an attempt to transform urban space. Rather it was an attempt to do away with the city altogether. In the late 1920s, just as the first streets in Welwyn were taking shape, a quarter of a century after Olmsted's death in an asylum for the insane in Hartford, Connecticut, another American architect, Frank Lloyd Wright, was starting to sketch his "broadacre city." This, too, was a new kind of urban space that was, in fact, no kind of urban space at all. It was an endlessly rolling suburb without a center, dotted throughout with little prairie homesteads, each standing proudly alone and connected only by a hot, strangling mesh of twentieth-century freeway. "To look at the cross section of any plan of a big city," Wright wrote in *The Living City*, "is to look at something like the section of a fibrous tumor." A city like New York is really a kind of "vampire"—a monster that "must renew itself from our farms and villages."[7] What had once been a simple desire for green suburbia had become a decidedly *anti*urban philosophy. This philosophy, which was powered by the eugenic pastoralism and frontier "individualism" of the nineteenth century, had been partly held at bay by the urban-focused modernist tide that had swept through the mid-twentieth century. But now it was returning, with more and more force, in the queasy opening decades of the twenty-first.

Here's an example: one very boring afternoon, not long after I got back from Welwyn, I saw a tweet from the hugely successful Danish architecture firm, BIG, announcing its participation in a major new project.[8] A US billionaire called Marc Lore—who had made a good part of his fortune through his co-ownership of the baby accessories website diapers.com—announced that he would finance the building of a new city, called Telosa, somewhere deep in the Arizona desert. Telosa, I found out from a link in the tweet, was an attempt to reform capitalism around a philosophy that Lore called "equitism."[9] The core of this notion belongs to the Victorian economist and reformer Henry George, who, in a much earlier period of rapid urbanization, argued for using the increasing value of residential land for community benefit rather than private gain (it was George's ideas that had also inspired Ebenezer Howard).[10] To design his own utopia around these principles, Lore had hired the celebrity Danish architect Bjarke Ingels, BIG's founder, who had made his name in the early 2000s by building a housing block in Copenhagen called VM, modeled on Le Corbusier's Unité d'habitation. The idea behind VM was that the twisting angles of two buildings (one in the shape of a V, the other more like an M), added to skillfully cantilevered balconies, meant that instead of simply gazing into each other's windows, all the residents could look out onto green fields. In a book setting out his design philosophy, Ingels spoke of work such as this in grand Darwinian terms. "Human life evolved through adaptation to changes in the natural environment," he wrote. "With the invention of architecture and technology we have seized the power to adapt our surroundings to the way we want to live…as life evolves, our cities and our architecture need to evolve with it."[11]

When I googled Telosa, I saw, okay, many of the urban futurist clichés that you might expect, but I saw something else, too. In the promotional materials, people were shown hanging out in parks, surrounded by trees, lazily dipping their feet into pools. In busy street scenes, the artists were careful to show that the pavements were lined with local Arizona plants (or my possibly problematic idea of Arizona plants; anyway, they looked like really big cactuses) and that there would always be clear views of the distant mountain range. The website assured would-be residents that they would "always be connected to nature" and that abundant "city parks" would "host carefully managed reservoirs which store water for the city and provide all residents with open space within minutes of where they live."[12]

Things began to escalate. In July 2022, a video popped up in my social media feed showing an artist's rendering of *another* new city, to be built this time in the desert northwest of Saudi Arabia. It was called the Line, and in the video, it just kind of looked like a giant night-club corridor: two enormous mirrored walls, each 500 meters high and 170 kilometers long, were apparently going to be erected 200 meters from one another. In the space between, the designers imagined a hyperfuturistic urban space filled with trees and flowers with—here and there—a few modern-looking buildings peeking out. In the publicity material, the Line is described as "the future of urban living…a civilizational revolution that puts humans first, providing an unprecedented urban living experience while preserving the surrounding nature."[13] This place will eventually be home, says the Saudi government, to nine million people. There will be no roads or cars, no emissions of any kind; the city will operate wholly on renewable energy; nature will be fully integrated throughout. In one sense, this all seems like pie in the sky—something that can be easily dismissed. But the Line is just one part of a new urban megaproject underway in Saudi Arabia called NEOM, a giant new smart city to be built from scratch, including not only the Line but also a floating octagonal port city, an airport, and a ski resort.[14] There may also be, according to the *Guardian*, "a huge artificial moon, glow-in-the-dark beaches, flying drone-powered taxis, robotic butlers to clean the homes of residents and"—this final flourish seems to tempt fate somewhat—"a Jurassic Park–style attraction featuring animatronic lizards."[15] Since the project began, despite reports that it is being built on empty land, Indigenous people have claimed that they have been violently evicted from the area. In October 2022, it was reported that three members of a tribe who refused to leave their land had been sentenced to death.[16]

If Telosa and NEOM are visions of the future, they are nonetheless both oddly familiar. From the parks to the tree-lined streets, from the references to Henry George to the weird concern with civilization, from the interest in Darwin to a violent relationship with Indigenous people, these two places seemed to offer a vision of the future city—the future *green* city—wholly rooted in the ideologies and anxieties of the nineteenth century. What if this connection between the past and the present, I wondered, between the not quite urban and the not quite rural, held up for green urbanism more generally? And also, in thinking about billionaires and superstar architects and the autocratic leaders of petrostates, what if we were importing not just the urban and environmental aesthetics of the nineteenth century but also the social and political structures that those aesthetics were very explicitly designed to convey? Were we, in fact, returning to the premodern city in more ways than one?

This book is written *against* green cities. It's also more or less against the idea of the urban future—not least because, as is becoming clear in Saudi Arabia, visions of the future city are almost always violent for someone. I'm writing against these things not because I'm skeptical about the positive effects of green space or about the need for some kind of environmental transformation as climate change starts to really bite. In what follows, I'll talk to scientists and architects; I'll meet people doing meditation work in forests and activists trying to protect city trees. These are all *good* people. And yet there's something else going on in the background—something in the grand, overarching visions of the urban future with which we are ceaselessly bombarded. Despite the science-fiction visual rhetoric that purveyors of the green urban future so often trade in, despite the critical work that many activists and planners are doing in cities today, I'm worried that what is really at stake, ideologically as well as aesthetically, is a decidedly nineteenth-century vision—a vision in which the primal urges of grasping city dwellers need to be tamed by the stern hand of nature, in which social elites, once anxious about the lively and convivial mass of urban humans that surrounds them, have suddenly become interested in covering streets with forests, in turning bustling neighborhoods into sterile parks. What I realized, in the course of researching and writing this book, is that the future of the city looks weirdly like its past. I realized, too, that there was something worth valuing and protecting about the city as it is now. The city can be messy, unequal, often violent for sure. But it's still a space, and maybe the only space, in which the moral and political goods of the late-modern world are not only available but even imaginable in the first place. There is something worth protecting about the city as it is now, about our ability to think and build and plot collectively, our drive to improve our situation materially, our capacity to actually *impose* ourselves, and our ideas, and our homes, and our lives, on the material world around us.

I emailed Bjarke Ingels's office to see if someone might talk to me about all of this. They sent back a polite response thanking me for reaching out but regretting to inform me that they weren't doing interviews right now. Maybe I could circle back in six months? Maybe. In the meantime, I decided to start with an architect who had inspired Bjarke Ingels, surely the most interesting, most influential, most problematic, and simply *strangest* person to take the problem of nature and the city seriously in the century just gone. I decided to start with Le Corbusier.

CHAPTER 1

City Life

In the late summer of 1933, a group of architects and planners boarded a steamship, SS *Patris II*, at the port of Marseille. The passengers were all members of the Congrès Internationaux d'Architecture Moderne (CIAM), a movement founded in 1928 to create a new architecture, one better attuned to the forms and rhythms of the machine age.[1] The 1933 congress—CIAM's fourth—had been planned for Moscow, where the Communist Party had once shared the group's revolutionary approach to remaking the built environment. By the early 1930s, however, Stalin had his own ideas about what the monumental architecture of the new century should look like. Spurned, CIAM decided to make for Greece by boat—for what would become one of the most influential urban planning meetings of the century.[2]

On board was the great modernist architect and planner Le Corbusier, who was then becoming CIAM's most visible figure.[3] Le Corbusier was at a creative high point: having made his name—and a great public scandal—with his "Plan Voisin" to more or less level the center of Paris in 1925, he had at this point proposed a similar plan for the rebuilding of Algiers. This would have meant, among other things, surrounding the city's world-famous Kasbah with a forest of skyscrapers and a fourteen-story-tall highway (alas, the mayor of Algiers went in another direction).[4] Also on board was the Finnish designer and architect Alvar Aalto, who had just completed his Paimio Sanatorium in southwest Finland, a hugely influential modernist intervention in hospital design, where the hospital building itself was designed to be part of the healing equipment.

These were serious times for modern design. Two weeks before the ship left Marseille, the Bauhaus School in Berlin, then the world's most famous design institute, had voted to dissolve itself following raids by the Gestapo and increasing pressure from the Nazi government. László Moholy-Nagy, the Hungary-born photographer, filmmaker, and designer who had taught at the Bauhaus in the 1920s, was also traveling on the *Patris II*. Moholy-Nagy had even brought a 16-mm camera, shooting footage that he later edited into a twenty-nine-minute silent film, *Architect's Congress*. The film still floats around online today, a remarkably watchable yet deeply melancholic document of the voyage. In wavering, silent images, earnest planners paste schemes for cities such as Detroit and Zaandam to the ship's heaving bulkheads; serious young men crowd the sunny decks for talks by Le Corbusier and CIAM's chair, the Dutch planner Cornelis van Eesteren; excitement overcomes the passengers as the ship approaches the Isthmus of Corinth, and then we see Moholy-Nagy himself, smiling warmly as he greets the Greek delegation; the ship docks at port and, finally, there is the grand opening of the congress, with 1,500 hopeful people in attendance. Hovering overhead, we see the acropolis of Athens, lit for the occasion and brightening the night sky—like a promise, from history, of great things to come. Within a decade, both the city that these architects set sail from and the one they had just arrived in would be under fascist occupation.

In 1933, the future of Europe and the future of the city seemed like two halves of the same equation. CIAM had been founded on the idea that in the age of the machine, architecture could no longer be neatly separated from political and economic realities. Now more than ever, thinking about what buildings should be like, about how towns should work, meant confronting the starkest political, ethical, and even biological questions of how humans would make their lives in the century to come.

This was, to say the least, a politically ambiguous and awkward project. In the years to come, Le Corbusier—a longtime fascist and anti-Semite despite being widely associated with the left—would move to Vichy, the capital of occupied France, and collaborate actively with its Nazi-backed puppet government.[5] In 1943, he anonymously published his *Athens Charter* in occupied Paris—formally recording the findings of the 1933 meeting in his own inimitable style.[6] The cities that CIAM had examined, he

15

argued, were pictures of total chaos, leading to nothing but misery for their poor citizens. Modern cities are failures; they "do not fulfil their purpose, which is to satisfy the primordial biological and psychological needs of their populations." The urban citizen is even "molested" by the machine age—they are stifled, crushed, trodden underfoot; green space is devoured by the unplanned growth of the suburbs; the air is foul and the transport makes no sense.

The solution, Le Corbusier said, summarizing the findings of the congress, is to divide the functions of work, play, housing, and movement. With high-speed motorcars, you can keep factories and offices far from houses, with green open space (and a multilane highway) in between. That also means building upward, making the city vertical but doing so, perhaps counterintuitively, to preserve vast tracts of open land for rest and play, to make a pleasant vista, even to grow vegetables.

For the members of CIAM, the hypermodern city is not—as it was so influentially caricatured in the filmmaker Fritz Lang's 1923 masterpiece *Metropolis*—a place of endless speed, efficiency, production, and toil. As the historian Peder Anker points out, avant-garde architecture in the 1930s was deeply concerned with biological science and humans' place in nature.[7] The delegates in 1933 were interested in leisure, good living, and what we might today call "well-being." They were bothered about sunlight and green spaces, and play areas, and what a person might do for entertainment when they got home from work. "A town is a tool," Le Corbusier had written in 1924. In the modern age, we are confronted with an "immense step in evolution, so brutal and so overwhelming" that we will either grip that tool firmly and put it to use or we will perish. No more rustic pastoral. No more thatched roofs. We have to "burn our bridges," Le Corbusier declared; we must "break with the past."[8]

Almost a century later, we still somehow find ourselves deeply concerned with the future of the city. We are unsure of its ideal form, and the kind of life we want it to shape, in the midst of yet another period of political and economic crisis. But one thing that *has* changed is the central ambition that animated so much of the modernist movement—its radically negative relationship to the past. Thinking about the future city today, by contrast, often means not only being more open to older architectural and environmental arrangements. It means, sometimes, an ambition to entirely reproduce them from the ground up.

Exactly eighty-five years after the delegates of CIAM set sail from Marseille, I traveled in less elegant fashion to Athens for another congress on the future of the city in troubled times. Amazingly, I had booked a flight without it having occurred to me that Athens is quite far from London. I landed, deeply confused, at an empty, smoke-smelling terminal at 4 a.m. and took a taxi at great speed down the deserted motorway before arriving at an alarmingly fancy hotel, where I briefly collapsed. I woke, three hours later, bleary-eyed, to an open-air breakfast deck filled with sun, yogurt, cold meat, and Americans. The morning heat was up, the magpies had started to circle—and there, overlooking the city as if nothing at all had happened, was the same acropolis that had been lit in hope for Le Corbusier, Moholy-Nagy, and the other architects of CIAM all those decades ago.

I was in Athens for the first-ever meeting of a new group that was also interested in urbanization, well-being, and the good life: the World Congress on Forests for Public Health. I had tagged along because I wanted to see, up close, a loosely organized "movement" that I had been following for a while—a movement that, it seemed to me, was also rethinking the shape and fabric of modern life, albeit with more subtlety, and perhaps a little less bombast.

This was still a movement of architects and planners, but psychologists, public health people, and politicians were also now involved. They, too, saw something potentially catastrophic in the modern city, but not because of bad planning. I was following people who were convinced that living in cities was perhaps, *in itself*, fiercely bad for us, that the literal brick and stone and speed of urban life were making us stressed, lonely, depressed, *ill*. And their vision for remaking the city wasn't one of skyscrapers, helipads, ten-lane highways, and the latest synthetic materials. It was the opposite: a vision of the city remade as a *forest*—a pastoral space of parks, streams, and hedgerows, of otters in the river and trees on the streets.

Le Corbusier once wrote that we should think of the city as "the grip of man upon nature"—even as a "human operation directed *against nature*."[9] A century later, the ambitions of architects and planners seemed to be very different. Instead of exalting the city as a kind of triumph over nature, here was a vision of urban space as a kind of *anti*city, a place that hides its own basic *citiness*, embarrassed, beneath a canopy of trees.

In the weeks and months surrounding the congress, London formally declared itself a park. A week or so after that, there was a story in the news about wild boars taking over parts of Barcelona. Singapore announced that it was turning its airport into a botanic garden, complete with orangutans. Indonesia said that it would rebuild its new capital as a forest city. What was happening here? What was this shrubby, green urban future that seemed to be coming into a global existence—and doing so almost without notice? How and why was the fabric of city life being transformed before our eyes?

Here's the thing that surprises you about Athens: it's very modern. Ancient ruination is everywhere obviously. There's still the agora and the library; there's the temple of Athena Nike and the theater of Dionysus; here and there, you can even find a still functioning Byzantine temple, and if you stand in the right place for long enough, you will hear the low, uncanny hum of Greek Orthodox chant, the distant sound of a premedieval world that can gently unhook your bones from your nerves. So the slightly rickety, jerry-built air of the twentieth-century city takes you by surprise—hastily bolted together over the decades, without much planning regulation, as people came in from the countryside seeking work and a better life.

More incongruous are the great monumental modernist constructions that dot the Athens skyline—the serene US Embassy by the Bauhaus founder, Walter Gropius; the Hilton Hotel, with its reliefs by the Greek artist Yiannis Moralis; the great hulking passenger terminal at the ancient port of Piraeus, built in the early 1960s by Ioannis Lapsis and Elias Scroumbelos.[10] Athens is a city where the ancient and modern slide over one another in sometimes eerie ways. On a day off, I tried to take a photo of the ruined Temple of Olympian Zeus—a row of colossal fifty-foot columns, standing in rigid formation against the sky—and my phone, mistaking the giant pillars for a close-up of a barcode, began frantically searching the internet to find me a better deal. It was a strange reminder that our symbols move around, but the visual grammar they reply upon has surprisingly long roots.

The congress was meeting at one of these great symbols of modernist Athens, the Hellenic War Museum—a square-looking building topped by a thick overhanging rectangle of concrete, like a giant stone mushroom. I had come early to see the keynote speaker and main attraction, a scientist and author whose name has become synonymous with the idea that getting out of the city to "bathe" in the forest is vital for your psychological and emotional health, Dr. Qing Li from the Nippon Medical School in Tokyo and the then president of the Japanese Society for Forest Medicine.

"People like forests" Dr. Li told the assembly as the room gradually filled with foresters, planners, and public health people from all over the world. The air, he said—I am paraphrasing from my notes—the atmosphere, the sense of calm, all of it, produces a preventive effect against the diseases produced by our modern lifestyle. The practice known in Japanese as Shinrin-yoku—literally, forest bathing—reduces the amount of adrenaline in the body, thus bringing down stress and ultimately making us less prone to depression, anxiety, and anger. "Forest medicine," Dr. Li told us, is a "new science."

As images of ancient Japanese forests flashed up behind him, he described the role of "phytoncides," organic compounds found in the natural oils that trees sometimes use as a defense against insects and fungi.[11] Releasing phytoncides into the air, he told us, is also how trees communicate with one another—in fact, this is often what you smell when walking through the forest. In his book extolling the virtues of Shinrin-yoku, Dr. Li describes a study in which he took twelve volunteers and slipped phytoncide oil into a diffuser as they slept but changed nothing else about their lives; all of them slept better, had lower stress hormones, and had higher levels of some immune-system cells.

Li has been interested in this topic since 1982 and has been collecting data in earnest since 2004. In his best-selling book, *Into the Forest*, he talks about how modern humans have become estranged from nature as we have moved toward life as an urban species. We live, he writes, in dense, overcrowded cities, packed onto subways, crammed against footpaths, corralled in our offices and air-conditioned houses. We've allowed ourselves to become overworked, stressed out, tied to screens in small rooms. The city might be an exciting place, he concedes, but it's a stressful one, too, and that stress plays a role in heart attack, stroke, and cancer.[12]

Even more insidious is the effect of this urban mode of life on our mental health—on loneliness, isolation, and depression. "A two-hour forest bathe," writes Li, "will help you to unplug from technology and slow down. It will bring you into the present moment and de-stress and relax you." It'll boost your energy, improve your mood, bring down your blood pressure, and help your immune system, he asserts. Simply being in the atmosphere of the forest—breathing in the organic compounds emitted by the trees—can have major effects on your health.

Shuffling in my beautifully designed but strikingly uncomfortable 1970s seat, I was skeptical. What would the utopian skyscraper architects on the *Patris II* have made of it all? And yet speaker after speaker came to the podium and told a similar story. Groups of people with mental health problems are led into the woods in Poland, Ireland, Serbia, South Korea; with the help of trained guides, they're taken on structured walks through the trees; they breathe in the phytoncides; they touch the trees. And over and over again, stress goes down, mood goes up.

Several other speakers outlined plans for giving city dwellers more opportunities to experience nature in their daily lives. There were discussions of the mental health benefits of increasing tree cover in cities, of creating the conditions for more birdsong, of producing "microforests" in otherwise forlorn pockets of urban space, of the psychological benefits of people simply tending to their own gardens, and so on and on. Overwhelmed by it all, I skipped the conference dinner and went out for sausages and *bifteki* on my own, flicking through the scientific literature and brooding over what seemed to be an unavoidably green, leafy future for the modern city.

The thing is, none of this can be dismissed, even if, like me, you're inclined to dismiss it. It's true that the scientific literature is still quite new and it hasn't really settled down yet, but generally it does seem to support these conclusions—fairly consistently showing the positive effects of being around green space for health, and especially for mental health. In one striking study, a group of Danish researchers used historical satellite images to track the amount of green space around the childhood homes of current Danish adults; they were able to show, remarkably, that the more green space around your house at age twelve, the less likely you were to be admitted to a psychiatric hospital as a grown-up.[13] Another study, reported in many newspapers, showed that taking just twenty minutes out of your day to be around nature—strolling through a park on your lunch break, say—is enough of a "nature dose" to measurably reduce your stress levels. Scientists even suggest that doctors should write prescriptions for this, instructing their stressed-out, city-dwelling patients to take twenty-minute "nature pills" and improve their mental health.[14]

There's something incredibly seductive about all this. When I got home, I moved into the back bedroom of our house and opened the big window wide—when I woke, I was no longer looking at the gray slate of my neighbor's roof but had a view onto the thick canopy of trees and bushes that our small row of terraced houses hides behind its back. And it's true: I slept better. I *felt* better.

It's that feeling that I want to try to understand—that sense of calm and stillness that comes from looking out of a bedroom window onto a slowly waving set of trees. For a lot of influential people, that feeling is hugely important, even vital for our physical and emotional well-being. Some environmental scientists have shown that your body heals itself more quickly when you can see some trees. Others argue that being around nature is such a core part of our evolutionary inheritance that in its absence, many of us will entirely lose our reason.[15]

Such claims have now found their way into the worlds of architecture and urban planning and so into the political and financial institutions that ultimately decide how cities take shape. In London, leading architectural theorists are now trying to design buildings that function like biological organisms to be more in tune with our natural rhythms and preferences. In Shanghai, city authorities have approved an enormous residential and retail complex in the city center that is literally built into an entirely new tree-covered hill (the designer is Thomas Heatherwick, who once designed a grand new "garden bridge" in London. This project, alas, controversially ran aground due to cost overruns and a growing realization that what had been sold as a new "floating paradise" for the city was in reality a privately owned gated space, to be hired out for corporate events among other activities).[16] All of this seems at odds with what—until very recently—everyone assumed the future of the city would look like. From the most avant-garde science fiction to the most banal planning documents, a shared agenda has emerged: for the good of humanity, the future of the city must be woody and green.

It is no coincidence that this is happening as we are living in one of the greatest periods of urbanization in human history. The much-cited UN statistic is that nearly seventy percent of the world's population will be urban dwellers by 2050[17]; make of that what you will. It's certainly true that there are more cities in the world today than there have ever been and that the sizes of some—the twenty-four million people of Shanghai, the eighteen million of Karachi—have grown at scales that would have been unimaginable until quite recently. A bit of me wonders if a lot of this desire to entirely reimagine the city as a green space doesn't also reflect a kind of cultural anxiety about that—a growing fear that we have perhaps pulled ourselves out of reach of our natural roots, that we have wandered too far from the garden.

This is perhaps a good moment to remember that ours is not the first point in history when there has been, at the same time, a great movement of population to the cities *and* a large official anxiety about what that movement means for the minds and bodies of the people who move—*and* a large cultural turn toward greenery, trees, and wilderness. In fact, there is a striking historical correlation between romantic ideas about nature, on the one hand, and periods of mass urbanization, on the other. In the early 1860s, during the violent displacement of Indigenous North American people from the central Sierra Nevada, travelers into the western part of the still-expanding American empire were reportedly struck by the awe-inspiring beauty of the area we now call Yosemite. Reports filtered back to the cities of the East, and so the first white tourists started to come—and with them the early stirrings of a tourist infrastructure, with major consequences for the ecology of the area.[18]

This was also a time when hundreds of thousands of people were arriving every year in the exploding cities of the northeastern United States, cramming into the manky streets of New York, Boston, and Philadelphia, making a new life as best they could in unsanitary, overcrowded cities. The historian Dorceta

Taylor argues that at the meeting point of these simultaneous developments—rapid urbanization in the East, colonial conquest in the West—the *idea* of wilderness emerged in North America. So too did a new kind of person with a new kind of aim—a self-consciously robust man or woman given to wandering westward, away from the dank of the metropolis into what they thought of as a pristine, natural landscape. This ideology of North American wilderness, needless to say, was reliant on erasing Indigenous people from both the territory and history of the landscapes that were then being settled.[19]

Yosemite was declared a national park by Abraham Lincoln in 1864. A commission was then appointed to study the ecology of the new park and make plans for its effective management, with Frederick Law Olmsted as the chair. Olmsted, who we already met in the introduction, is known to many today as the "father" of American landscape architecture. In 1864, he was already the codesigner of New York's Central Park, a prolific writer and anti-slavery campaigner, and a decorated former head of the US Sanitary Commission during the Civil War.[20] But Olmsted was also a journalist (he cofounded the magazine *The Nation*) and a hugely influential writer about nature. He was someone who not only shaped natural spaces; he also shaped how we think about those spaces in the first place and what we think they are for.[21]

Olmsted wrote his first report on Yosemite the following year. It was vitally important, he argued, for Congress to secure the area before some rich individual acquired it for himself and, in pursuit of personal gain, spoiled this "union of the deepest sublimity with the deepest beauty of nature." Olmsted made two arguments for governments acquiring spaces such as Yosemite. One argument was purely financial: people were already coming from Europe to see the area, and it would be an enormous advantage to the finances of the new state of California, and to its enterprising citizens, to preserve the thing that these travelers were coming to see. But the other argument was more psychological in nature. "It is a scientific fact," Olmsted wrote in the report,

> that the occasional contemplation of natural scenes of an impressive character, particularly if this contemplation occurs in connection with relief from ordinary cares, change of air and change of habits, is favorable to the health and vigor of men and especially to the health and vigor of their intellect beyond any other conditions which can be offered them, that it not only gives pleasure for the time being but increases the subsequent capacity for happiness and the means of securing happiness.

In other words, without the opportunity to contemplate nature, there could be no happiness—and this in a nation founded on precisely the notion that achieving happiness is the central object of human existence. But it gets worse: urban people do not have the opportunity to contemplate natural scenes, Olmsted wrote, and the result is "a class of disorders, the characteristic quality of which is mental disability, sometimes taking the severe forms of softening of the brain, paralysis, palsey, monomania, or insanity, but more frequently of mental and nervous excitability, moroseness, or irascibility, incapacitating the subject for the proper exercise of the intellectual and moral forces."

What we see here is a key moment in the cultural production of the great outdoors as, specifically, a *psychological* object—a moment in which influential figures are cementing a deep connection between the human psyche and the environment. This isn't any kind of deliberate plot—Olmsted, I am certain, is wholly sincere. But there's nonetheless something in the air as he and his fellow commissioners tramp through the valleys and caverns of Yosemite. They are simply very ready to see a deep relation between mind, body, and nature; they are ready to believe that being immersed in nature might have a profound effect on a person's nervous system.[22]

In Olmsted's writing, then, we can begin to grasp some of the deep roots of the cultural connection between nature, urbanization, and the psyche—to understand that what may look to us like a finding from recent science goes well back into the nineteenth century.[23] And it goes back into not only early versions of scientific research but also landscape design, architecture, conservation, and government bureaucracy. It was a collective anxiety about the mental states of immigrants—from Ireland, Italy, and what were certainly seen as the less "civilized" parts of Europe—that Olmsted was partly channeling when he wrote about Yosemite and what it might mean for America; a sense that being deprived of nature was bad for these weak urban dwellers' general character; that a lack of what the feminist theorist Donna Haraway once called a "prophylactic dose of nature" would produce nervous disorder, anxiety, and a general sense of degeneration; that the new nation had to act—and it had to act fast.[24]

On the other side of the Atlantic, at more or less the same time, an identical concern had already manifested—with a strikingly similar solution. In London in 1833—one hundred years before the delegates of CIAM set sail from Marseille—a parliamentary committee was set up to investigate the lack of green space in the United Kingdom's rapidly expanding industrial cities.[25] "We are convinced," the committee wrote in its first report, "that some Open Places reserved for the amusement (under due regulations to preserve public order) of the humbler classes would assist to wean them from low and debasing pleasures...it must be evident that it is of the first importance to their health on their day of rest to enjoy the fresh air."[26] In other words, parks should be provided for the benefit of the lower classes on Sundays. And the committee was very frank about what the purpose of such parks would be—the control of the burgeoning working classes: "A man walking out with his family among his neighbours of different ranks, will naturally be desirous to be properly clothed, and that his Wife and Children should be so also...this desire duly directed and controlled, is found by experience to be of the most powerful effect in promoting Civilization, and exciting Industry."

Anxieties about urbanization, green space, and the proper conduct of man had been circulating in Britain even before the Indigenous people of Yosemite were being torn from their land. In fact, it was an 1850 visit to Britain's first urban park, at Birkenhead in Merseyside, that partly inspired Olmsted's later work: "This magnificent pleasure ground is entirely, unreservedly, and forever the People's own," he marveled in an article for the

Horticulturalist the following year. "The poorest British peasant is as free to enjoy it in all its parts as The British Queen."[27]

Birkenhead Park had been designed by Joseph Paxton and opened to the public in 1847. An improvement initiative by the wealthy merchants of Liverpool, Birkenhead was a small-scale intervention in the grand scheme of things, and was aimed more at the wealthy classes than at the slothful day laborer. But it was also the tipping point of a movement that had begun to grow and swell as the century proceeded: a movement to bring more green spaces into Britain's exploding cities and to do so not for aesthetic reasons, nor particularly from the munificence of urban authorities, but rather as an intervention in the health—including, to use a term that didn't exist then, the mental health—of the urban poor.[28]

The city park, in this sense, should be understood as one thread within the thick weave of moralism, reform, and improvement that characterized the great public institutions of the age.[29] The rapid expansion of green space in the city was born partly from a genuine sense of patrician duty, it's true, partly from a moral objection to the base pursuits of drinking and dogfighting (and thus the desire to provide a healthy alternative), and partly, in this era of revolutions, from an attempt to channel any insurrectionary feeling into more tranquil, and indeed—where appropriate—amorous, even reproductive pursuits. It was also simply about getting people out walking and breathing in the fresh air, keeping them physically healthy and rejuvenated so that they would be all the more ready for the week's work when their day of rest was done.

All of this is well and good. But the history of England's great nineteenth-century parks—Victoria Park in East London, Moor Park in Preston, Stanley and Sefton Parks in Liverpool, Philips Park in Manchester, Peel Park in Bradford—is then also the history of an attempt to mold and create a new urban citizen, to intervene in and even alter the "character" of that citizen, to affect what we might today call their mental state. We should think of the urban park in Victorian England not as a neutral space but as a technology for soothing people, for calming them, even for *civilizing* them in quite explicit terms.[30]

This attempt to use the city park to intervene in the body and the mind—to keep the humble urban citizen both physically fit and morally good—is perhaps best seen in the work of the National Health Society, a philanthropic and reformist health promotion society formed in London in 1871. The historian Clare Hickman, drawing on the society's archive, shows how its members' wide-ranging interests in public health became embroiled in the growing "open space" movement, which promoted the creation of urban parks among other kinds of healthy spaces—even turning into a kind of early environmental activism.[31]

The urban park, Hickman says, was thus where two anxieties about the new class of urban worker came together. In one sense, the desire to get people out walking in the park came from a *medical* concern to keep the urban worker fit and well (not least so they could keep working without the inconvenience of illness or death). But the same development can also be seen as a *moral* concern that the worker be a person of good character, that they not be brought low by a nervous agitation, a melancholy, or an insanity. And this was the case not only for the park but also for the allotment, the vegetable patch, the domestic garden, the arboretum, and so on. This was an age marked by a generalized concern with the "social question"—the question of how to keep booming industrial capitalism on the road, despite the enormous and highly visible violence and injustice it produced, and to do so without creating the conditions for revolution. For many among the governing classes of the day, the urban park was a major part of the answer to this problem.

These developments had grown at least partly out of a connection between green space and the mind that had been established, Hickman again tells us, a half century earlier—in the then new practice of asylum architecture.[32] As asylums for the insane had gradually stopped being spaces of confinement and punishment, they had morphed into restorative, therapeutic retreats, generally in rural areas—where interaction with nature was at the heart of the new system of treatment. In Britain, this development was pioneered by the Quakers William Tuke, who established the York Retreat in 1796, and his grandson Samuel, who popularized the method with a book he published in 1813. Frederick Law Olmsted also worked on plans for a number of mental institutions in Hartford, Buffalo, and western Massachusetts. His plan for the last of these—the McLean asylum in Belmont, which is still functioning today—was thrown into relief when he became a patient there himself at the end of his life.[33] Who knows how much of Olmsted's own agitated thinking was soothed by the woody calm of his new surroundings? By the time he died there, in 1903, the debate about nature, the city, and the mind had barely gotten started.

———

A few months after I left Athens, I was in Paris. I hate Paris. It's something about the mix of imperial pomp and saccharine cutesiness in the streetscape. It's also the terrible food, I think. And though quite a few European cities confuse rudeness with personality, in Paris there is just something about the sheer *frequency* of interpersonal unpleasantness that, over time, becomes wounding to the human spirit. Mostly my hatred of Paris is a reaction to a very dull and conventional city's vastly inflated reputation. I'm broadly with Le Corbusier here: raze the center, build a highway and some skyscrapers, then fill the space between with gardens and vegetable patches. That at least would be interesting.

I was in Paris, nonetheless, for a gathering of global "thought leaders" interested in the benefits of making the modern city more green. It was, in fact, an auspicious location. The mayor of Paris had just announced a plan to surround the city's major landmarks with trees, creating an "urban forest" to help meet a goal of being 50 percent covered by trees by 2030. This was no small endeavor: "The city imagines turning the square in front of city hall into a pine grove," wrote the journalist Feargus O'Sullivan, "while future springtimes will see the opera house's back elevation emerge from a sea of cherry blossom. The paved plaza at the side of the Gare de Lyon will become a woodland garden."[34]

The conference I was attending—a self-described global "movement," in fact—was a forum for scientists, planners, political leaders, and others to come together around a shared green city agenda. It was big: several hundred attendees from around the world at the Sorbonne, including many major figures from the world of urban ecosystems, with an art program, an accompanying book of "flash fiction," and a "farm-to-table" banquet. For an event happening on a university campus, it was slickly choreographed—with a rolling program of public "dialogues," "microtalks," and "seed sessions," ranging from how to finance green infrastructure to how to meditate with plants. There were speeches from various French political and business figures, a wordless performance about street trees that I didn't understand, and lots of talk about biodiversity and the psychological benefits of nature. I went to one session where you got to wear a VR headset to see what your green roof might look like and one where you had to pretend to be a place and then be psychoanalyzed as if you were that place. An artist gave a talk on how she likes to dance with nature in the city, and later I saw her weaving her body, with great deliberation, through the array of small potted plants that lined the meeting's entranceway.

There was something very charming but also oddly *evangelical* about all of this—like a weird mix of Silicon Valley and Christian revivalism. "Your project is so sacred and so wonderful," said one speaker to another. Someone else said to a panel of presenters, "Your talks are so beautiful and poignant." A planner told the crowd, with great seriousness, "My job is to be a healer." You get the idea. At the beginning of each day, everyone had to stand up, look around, and introduce themselves to the people nearest to them—it was *that* kind of conference.

Amid the fervor and the enthusiasm and the—I wrestle with my own cynicism here—basically *good* desire to fill the city with trees and birds, to plan in a more ecologically sustainable way, and so on, I was struggling with a larger problem—a problem that runs through the work of the great park designers of the nineteenth century, the revolutionary modernists of the twentieth, and, as we will see, a whole host of other major urban movements and philosophies. That problem explains a lot of my own suspicion about this entire scene and is one of the major issues I want to help myself understand as I move around this world.

The problem is that everyone in Paris basically seemed to think more nature was good. But no one ever actually said what they meant by "nature" in the first place. What they meant by this term was, I guess, what most people mean by it: green things, trees, parks, birds, open space, clean air. This was never actually said, though, and so I was left wondering. We're all convinced that there's something wrong with contemporary city life. We're equally all convinced—I think—that much of what's wrong has to do somehow with an absence of nature. And that absence seems to go in two directions. On the one hand, there's not enough natural *stuff* in cities—too few trees, not enough otters. On the other hand, a kind of unnatural *way of living* has taken hold among city people—too much sitting in air-conditioned buildings, too much concrete, too much stress and speed. All of this, I think, is fairly uncontroversial.

But it was unclear to me then—it still isn't clear to me now—what it is, exactly, that makes the city so unnatural in the first place. Maybe this seems like hairsplitting, but truly, if put on the spot, I don't think I know what "nature" actually is. And while we're at it, I'm not even sure I know what counts as "the city" and what doesn't. Walk as far as you can in a city such as London or Shanghai. Walk through Swansea, even. Where does the city actually end? At what point—exactly—do you enter the great "outside" of modern urban life?

In an influential essay in 1938, Lewis Mumford, perhaps the greatest American critic of urban planning, defined a city as that place where "the diffused rays of many beams of life fall into focus."[35] Cities, said Mumford, are the culmination of human-kind's domination of the earth; they're where the need for industry and cooperation have come together. Cities are the great sites of monumental and public life—they are living museums of themselves, cathedrals to their own glory and to the forms of life they make possible; cities are where vastly different kinds of people can come together with different functions, and desires, and needs, that somehow are orchestrated into the great four-dimensional fold of human social life.

This seems like a fine description of Rome in the fourth century or London in the nineteenth. But it tells us more or less nothing about daily life in a midsized regional city in the early twenty-first century—which is to say, it tells us nothing about the mundane, unremarkable, badly planned, and more or less ugly places where almost all urban life plays out today. "The future of the city" sounds like a fine topic for discussion until you realize that we are talking about a category that includes Beijing, Poughkeepsie, Byzantium, Atlantis, and Limerick.

Airy talk tells us little about what actually counts as "the city" and what doesn't—about what is urban space, what is a natural environment, and what actually marks the break between these categories. This really matters. In Paris, lots of people were convinced that the future of the city inevitably meant bringing healthier, greener, more natural, noncity things into it, even reshaping and replanting the city itself around those things.

But take a concrete tower block—for many people the epitome of unnatural urban living and the great icon of modern, nature-conquering architecture and planning. There's nothing obviously unnatural about concrete. Even the raw *béton brut*, the concrete that gives its name to the distinctive style we call brutalism; the chalk, clay, and various chemical admixtures that make up a cement; the sand, gravel, and slag of aggregate; the water that binds it all together . . . all of these things are unambiguously of the earth. All of them are found in, and harvested from, the wild outdoors. All of them have been bobbing around the surface gloop that covers this planet at least as long as we have, and likely longer. To rub one's face against a concrete wall and to rub it against a leaf is, no doubt, a different sensory experience—but it is not a difference that is obviously marked by contact with "nature." Yes, someone might say, but surely there is something in the *processing* of these raw materials that somehow shifts the end product into the category of the unnatural. This does not seem convincing. Just as with moral panics around "processed food," the act of mixing, processing, and combining is complex, but it is not doing any metaphysical work. There is no process that can make things unearthly, no churn that lifts them out of the same chalky, debased realm that humans, along with every other living creature on the planet, have always inhabited. "The dams of beavers and the webs of spiders are presumably natural," says the environmental philosopher Steven Vogel—then, "why are the dams built by humans or the polyester fabrics they weave not so?"[36] If we feel things to *be* unnatural—if on principle we dislike a modern art gallery, say, or a Cup-a-Soup—well, we are entitled to our moralism, but no one is obliged to grant this feeling any philosophical or scientific status.

And anyway, as much as urban things don't seem obviously unnatural, so natural things are not necessarily unurban. The languid mother fox who took over a tire yard next to a flat where I lived in South London, and who would raise her head, cautious but unafraid, whenever the outside light hit her rubbery throne—she was no less a creature of the city than I was. I once lived in Cardiff, the capital city of Wales, which, like many cities near the sea, is regularly terrorized by roaming packs of gulls. You'd see them strutting in groups around town, angrily guarding chips and pizza. Or you'd go home to find them screaming angrily from behind your chimney. I hated those gulls. But still I could recognize that they were not only city creatures—they had even adopted a specifically urban mode of life. They were urban*ists*, those gulls, as fiercely identified with that status as any bearded gentrifier. These kinds of awkward urban cohabitations are only going to become more common: a new wildlife ordinance in Los Angeles, for example, means you might just see a mountain lion hanging out at your country club.[37] In Asheville, North Carolina, the local population of black bears knows which day is the city's trash day and behaves accordingly.[38]

When we think about how life has developed in the city—especially when we think about that development in relation to nature or our own place in nature—we are often thinking about a set of material traces, traces that seem to lead us back to an artificial turn in the development of human society. At such moments, the city appears to us as a synthetic density of concrete, glass, and medium-density fiberboard; of slate, chrome, and liquid crystal; of synthetic fabric, industrial carpet, air-conditioning, high-pressure sodium, rubber, petrol, polyester—all the human things of the late-modern world, all of which seem to have carried us very far from a more innocent age of trees, birds, otters, air, wood, water, and soil. The problem is that the distinction between these sets of things is not obvious. Medium-density fiberboard is held together by a wax that comes from palm trees. The town is already full of otters. "Nature," it turns out, is not necessarily a natural category.

Go back about 250 years, the environmental historian William Cronon wrote once, and there's no such thing as "wilderness."[39] No one's going off wandering around pristine lakes and canyons in 1700—and any traveler encountering Yosemite in this period would most likely have understood it as a deathly space of horror and fear. It was the Romantic poets and their contemporaries in the eighteenth century who came up with the idea that untouched nature was a way to encounter the "sublime"—to have a sort of religious experience, even to attain full personhood, in an increasingly industrial and urban age. This romantic ideal, as it flowed into what became the environmental movement, is at least partly embedded in a suspicion of—even a hostility to—the modern, urban world as such. Nature is the central symbol of this hostility—it comes to signify the things and objects that are furthest from human development. Nature, according to Cronon, is in this sense a fundamentally negative concept; it describes "the places where humans are not." We might say that nature, for many urban thinkers today, is only the place where the *city* is not.

And this is a big part of my problem: I'm worried that we're overinvesting in nature as a panacea for what are actually fairly mundane urban problems—that we have mistaken what is really only a historically specific malaise, or a sideshow to the wider sense of melancholy that has often accompanied the modern world, for some kind of biological or psychological problem. And it's not that the biology or psychology is meaningless—it isn't. As this book goes on, nonetheless, I'm going to think in a slightly different way about the relationship between humans, well-being, and the urban environment. I'm going to suggest that whether and how we live well in some place might not have much to do with the relative artificiality or naturalness of that place; that in fact (and here we can learn something from the twentieth-century modernists), there are ways of thinking about planning and design in which natural, organic things and high-tech, industrial things do not move in different spheres.

I'm also worried that we have given too much weight to people who don't actually like cities very much and probably never did—people who maybe don't even like the modern world itself very much. But I *do* love that world. I love its unromantic insistence on always looking forward, always moving on, always going *somewhere*—even with all its jaggedness, its hardness, and its capacity for awfulness. I love the cities that absolutely embody that sensibility. I spent my first seven years living in remarkable proximity to an actual bog, and I have never had great time for pastoral scenes.

Before I left Paris, I walked down to the river, to the cathedral of Notre Dame—which had been wracked by fire only a few months earlier. The cathedral was cordoned off then and closed to visitors. And yet the ruined structure was still a tourist landmark—people crowded the temporary fence, trying to get a good angle for a photo of the gaping hole in the roof, snapping away at the empty space where the spire used to be. There the cathedral stands now, like the acropolis of Athens, a melancholy tribute to the urban mode of life—a monument to the glorification of the city but also to its ruination as time, hubris, and—yes—nature take their inevitable toll.

Following a general invitation from President Emmanuel Macron for ideas to repair the structure, a well-known French architect, Vincent Callebaut, proposed not simply rebuilding the cathedral's roof but transforming it into a garden, complete with a park, a contemplation space, and an aquaponic farm producing its own energy and twenty-one tons of fruit and vegetables every year. The cathedral, if it were to follow such a design, wrote Callebaut, "would become an exemplary eco-engineering structure, and the church a true pioneer in environmental resiliency."[40]

This is a purely speculative design that seems unlikely to be realized, in this space at least—the French senate has since insisted that the cathedral be rebuilt exactly as it was, despite Macron's grandiose vision. And yet even just as an idea or a wish—to remake the cathedral as a park—this proposal makes clear just how much that tree has become an object of both psychological and spiritual repair in the contemporary city. If we can recognize the cathedral as an iconic symbol of the city in previous centuries, with the spire

41

as its towering sign of authority and transcendence, then today we just might see the richly landscaped rooftop garden as playing a similar role. It's no longer towering Gothic stonework, but rather a little copse of waving trees, a raised vegetable garden looking over the grimy streets below, that today offers the urban citizen a promise of moral purity, spiritual repair, and even something like eternal life.

CHAPTER 2

The Garden Bathed in Sunlight

I n May 1984, the Indian architect Charles Correa arrived in London to attend an event celebrating the 150th anniversary of the Royal Institute of British Architects (RIBA). Correa was regarded as among the most important architects of independent India, which was not a minor accolade. Ever since Jawaharlal Nehru—India's first prime minister—had invited Le Corbusier to design a new capital for the Indian portion of the partitioned territory of Punjab, architecture had been central to the projection of twentieth-century Indian identity.[1] And the MIT-trained Correa, who had returned to practice in Mumbai in 1958, was perfectly suited to this task: his signature blend of contemporary and "traditional" materials demonstrated, as one obituary put it, "an authentic Indian modernity."[2] In fact, so well recognized was Correa by this time that he not only was attending the RIBA gala as a guest but also was to be awarded the institute's highest prize, its Royal Gold Medal. The medal is a big deal in the architecture world. It is—as RIBA puts it rather pompously on its website—"approved personally by the Monarch" and can be given, once a year, to "a person or group of people who have had a significant influence either directly or indirectly on the advancement of architecture."[3]

The event was to be held at Hampton Court Palace on the bank of the River Thames. Given its various royal entanglements and desires, RIBA had invited the then Prince Charles to give the keynote address. What was required of Charles, we might imagine, was the issuance of some standard royal emollient—a general blessing of the occasion, its fine attendees, the noble profession of architecture, etc., etc. When Charles stood up, however, it was quickly apparent that he had other ideas. "For far too long, it seems to me," he began, "some planners and architects have consistently ignored the feelings and wishes of the mass of ordinary people in this country."[4] The delegates must have stirred in their seats. *What?* What indeed, Charles asked, had they done to the fine historical city of London with their ugly modern buildings? He described one winning design to extend the National Gallery in Trafalgar Square as looking "like a municipal fire station, complete with the sort of tower that contains the siren." The building, he said, in a now famous phrase, would end up looking "like a carbuncle or a wart on the face of an old friend." One can almost hear the vol-au-vents and thick slices of quiche Lorraine catching in people's throats. One observer later said that the RIBA president's face froze into "a glazed mask."[5] Warming to his theme, Charles described another proposal for a tower near the Mansion House in the city of London as "a giant glass stump." And anyway, he went on, why has everything these days got to be straight and vertical and functional? Why not use curves or those nice arches that you see on old buildings?

Consider London before the war, he went on (which was to say, before his audience had gotten their hands on it). Building to his speech's highest rhetorical moment, Charles asserted that it was at this time that "the affinity between buildings and the earth, in spite of the City's immense size, was so close and organic that the houses looked almost as though they had grown out of the earth." To ensure that his audience would not misunderstand the insult, Charles closed by quoting Goethe, to the effect that there was no point in having imagination without taste. He acknowledged that the association probably regretted having asked him to speak. Still, he concluded, he hoped the next 150 years would see some improvement. And then he sat back down. As someone put it in RIBA's journal some years later, Charles "might as well have dropped the mic as he walked off."[6] That other Charles who had traveled from Mumbai—somewhere still in the room, we have to assume—was by now wholly and entirely forgotten.

From the moment of this speech, and up to the present day, the now King Charles has been one of the most influential and widely discussed figures in architecture and town planning in England. The guiding points of his vision have remained much the same—a kind of jocular but still biting hostility toward twentieth-century building materials; a sly fetish for not only the physical but also the social order of the premodern city; and a loosely theological idea that anything not built in his own lifetime probably grew out of the soil. But, this being England and he having been the longest-serving heir apparent, Charles had many opportunities to air and expand upon these notions. In particular, along with many institutes and writers who have followed in his wake, Charles developed the idea that this vision of the city, as a sort of premodern, organic, human-scale construction, is simply *better* for the people who live in it, including for their health—that there is something in the built fabric of late modernity that has jolted people out of the social and biological groove that they had been squatting happily in for some centuries and that we now need to put this right.

A few years after his speech, Charles expanded on his views in a paranoid and—for the son of a monarch—rather self-pitying volume, *A Vision of Britain.* "For a long time," Charles wrote, opposite a picture of a watercolor he had painted at his mother's Balmoral estate, "I have felt strongly about the wanton destruction which has taken place in this country in the name of progress; about the sheer, unadulterated ugliness and mediocrity of public and commercial buildings, and of housing estates, not to mention the dreariness and heartlessness of so much urban planning." Modern architecture, he suggested, is the obsession of a shadowy, powerful group of architects that had captured key institutions and produced "deformed monsters which have come to haunt our towns and cities, our villages and our countryside." He went on, "We have ended up with Frankenstein monsters, devoid of character, alien and largely unloved, except by the professors who have been concocting these horrors in their laboratories."[7]

King Charles is well known in Britain for his strong architectural views. He is understood by many in the profession to simply be a kind of idiot dilettante. For others, no doubt—perhaps for people with more conservative leanings—he represents a rare voice of reason and sanity on urban design. But there is something more interesting—more troubling—about the king's view that is often less noticed, which is his idea that the modern cityscape is not simply ugly or badly constructed; rather, it is unnatural; that, unlike the buildings of previous centuries, the architecture of our age has somehow become confected and artificial. Charles looks at Georgian doorways and little stone cottages like a farmer might approvingly regard his soil or his vegetable patch—the rich and loamy stuff of natural growth and replenishment.

There is a history here. In fact, Charles is reanimating some quite old and distinctive ideas—found in garden cities, hygienic cities, and weird utopian cities built by wealthy industrialists—about the relationship between humans and the urban environment. In this view, cities are not simply the places we make to live in; rather, cities are environments for making and growing humans. From this perspective, the town is a kind of ecology, the street a sort of petri dish. Once you start thinking like this, of course, the question of the city and its design becomes transformed: we are no longer faced with an aesthetic question of what kind of city we do or don't like. We are confronted instead with a moral and political question of how cities can best be adapted to human life—and of what *kinds* of humans, exactly, we want our cities to produce.

———

In the late 1980s, the town of Dorchester in southwest England wanted to expand to the west. The land that Dorchester wanted to expand *into*, however, was owned by the Duchy of Cornwall—a territory, with accompanying title, that had been inherited, as it happens, by the then Prince of Wales. Fresh from the popular success of his book and accompanying BBC program, Charles took the opportunity to "work with the council to create a model urban extension to this ancient market town," as the website of that new extension, now called Poundbury, delicately puts it.[8] He immediately appointed the Luxembourg architect Léon Krier, a well-known opponent of modernist town planning and a noted expert on the work of Hitler's architect, Albert Speer.[9] Krier was the man for the job. Having once worked for the modernist architect James Stirling, Krier, says the writer Owen Hatherley, "became fixated by the existentialist, rural-romantic philosophy of Martin Heidegger and increasingly disenchanted with the results of postwar reconstruction."[10] Thus, against the clearly zoned modernist city—where there is one space for living, another for industry, a third for retail, and so on—in *traditional* urban planning, wrote Krier in 1987, one finds instead "the totality of urban functions within a comfortable and pleasant walking distance."[11] The traditional city in his vision is "a complete and finite urban community, a member of a larger family of independent urban quarters, of cities within the city, of cities within the country. The traditional city is economical in the use of TIME, ENERGY and LAND. It is by nature ECOLOGICAL." Drawing on these principles, Krier delivered his master plan to Prince Charles the following year, and construction of the first phase of the new town began just four years later.

Look, it's easy to make fun of all this and easier still to read it as a very conservative, reactionary kind of vision, a squeak of aristocratic terror at the jostle and possibility promised—however ephemerally—by the twenty-first-century city. But what does it actually look like? To find out, I went to Poundbury for the first time on a Sunday with my wife and son, as well as my father, who, unexpectedly, had decided to visit for the weekend. So we took his rented car on the scenic route toward Dorset, and somewhere in the Mendip Hills, my then one-year-old son vomited all over his child seat, himself, and the back of the rental. We brushed him down at the side of the road, pulled half-digested porridge from his hair, and made a collective decision to press on. It was Remembrance Sunday, a day when melancholy and nationalism get weirdly entangled in the English psyche, and I had been worried about taking my father—a socially awkward Irishman—out for lunch in what was, after all, still very much the domain of the then Prince of Wales.

The day was gray, and Dorset grayer still; from Dorchester, where elderly men with Union flags were already heading for the pub and a Vera Lynn sing-along, we drove up Bridport Road and into Poundbury itself. We carried on through the heart of the new town toward the recently completed Queen Mother Square, all four of us staring at the bleakly empty streets like teenagers in a zombie movie. Whatever you think about Poundbury, its aesthetics or its politics, it is an undeniably *weird* place. The shape of the main bit of the town is a bit like a human kidney split into four quadrants; in each, there is a mix of housing, a few shops here and there, and even some small industry. The houses themselves are all "traditional," meaning in most cases that they follow an aesthetic caught somewhere between the eighteenth and nineteenth centuries. But they're also all pretty new and well-kept, so the effect is less like being in a well-worn Georgian street in, say contemporary London, and more like being transported to the historical moment when these styles were new. The effect is a bit uncanny.

That's not the architects' fault, in fairness. But it struck me, as we walked up and down the empty residential streets, that much of what people find so charming about old houses is that they're *old*; it's not so much the design of a Georgian house that people like specifically; it's just that we live in an age when Georgian houses happen to be old. Not in Poundbury, though. Here, old and new are pressed awkwardly together, rather like a couple skipping the period of getting to know one another and just getting straight down to some very public sex. There's a coffee shop in a brand-new area called the Butter Market, where the coffee is sold in a round, commercial-looking building, as if some part of an old butter market had indeed been repurposed for twenty-first-century tastes. I don't know if anyone ever actually sold butter in this area, but it feels like someone created a "repurposed" space in the absence of the original purpose, and then named the area after the purpose that may or may not have existed. That's the Poundbury vibe.

Queen Mother Square, though, is where the town goes full Las Vegas. Elizabeth Bowes-Lyon herself is resplendent on an enormous plinth at its center, a large protruding feather in her hat giving her, from a distance, the unexpected form of a defiant figure holding up a fist. The public and commercial buildings around the square abandon the English vernacular of the surrounding streets and offer something more like Imperial Russia in one of its less self-effacing moments. The square itself, Hatherley again noted, is now "a free car park, to encourage visitors to the town so that they can inject some life into a rather eerie place, and maybe look at some real estate." There's a Waitrose, a pub, and, nearby, a rather forlorn little playground. Above it all, the Queen Mother gazes benignly down on the Range Rovers and SUVs. "It's what she would have wanted, really," said my father.

It seems hard to deny that Charles's urban vision, whether one admires these qualities or not, is thoroughly Ruritanian, anti-modern, nostalgic, and often strikingly vicious for all the king's image of doddery amiability. At one point in *A Vision of Britain*, he presents an image of himself actually demolishing a block with the caption "I am told that crushed tower block, mixed with soil, makes a very good basis for growing roses." Later, he waxes lyrical about N. M. Lund's 1904 painting of the Bank of England, *Heart of Empire*—a "painting," says Charles, "that says everything about the harmony and scale of a City of London where the Lord Mayor's Mansion House and the houses of God were given appropriate prominence—all finding their place comfortably in the landscape." God, empire, and capital, in other words, all nestled together, as unchanging—and unchangeable—as the very soil in which they are grounded. In his writing, Charles emphasizes "hierarchy" in design and describes how the scale of buildings should reflect the hierarchy of "our social organisations." He likes "harmony" and "enclosure" and emphasizes "our indigenous roots." Some of the ideas in this book—and we might recognize, in Charles's defense, that the book is more than thirty years old—are almost comically reactionary. The things that he values (hierarchy, enclosure, order) are like a paean to feudal privilege—to the point that it seems hard to sustain the idea that we are talking only about buildings here. All I'm saying is, if I was the undeserving heir to a rich and influential monarchical institution, I, too, would spend a lot of time talking about the virtues of hierarchy, and God's wishes, and the natural order of things.

This idea of soil, though, or of urban space as potentially *organic*—the idea that the modern city is a problem precisely because it is *not* organic, that the past is to be preferred not so much for aesthetic but rather for biological reasons—is what drew me to Poundbury in the first place. The week before I visited, I had been to an online conference on traditional architecture and had seen a talk by the well-known mathematician and architectural theorist Nikos Salingaros, who argued that humans' relationship to older-style buildings is neurological and subliminal. Beauty isn't about aesthetics, Salingaros suggested; it's about healing. Old-fashioned buildings draw the eye and engage the attention; natural materials are encoded with fractal patterns that human beings are attracted to; evolution drives us to seek out the deep symmetries that classical architecture offers. More modern buildings, he went on, with their minimal look and their synthetic design, actually repel people at the neurological level (this is an argument we will see in more detail in the next chapter).

What are we to make of all this? I don't find this argument particularly compelling, but I do get why people might be convinced that the modern built environment is...at least at something of a remove from human beings' evolutionary origins or our general biological inclinations. Personally, I don't think it's interesting or useful to say that Trump Tower, for example, is objectionable because its sheer brute ugliness offends our instinctive desire for trees, water, or open space, but okay—I get it. The extension of this argument into a claim that, on the other hand, there *are* some buildings that are somehow closer to nature, and better for *our* nature, is where I come unstuck.

"Buildings," says Charles at one point in *A Vision of Britain*, "should look like they belong." And then, later, "There is no need for London to ape Manhattan, we already possessed a skyline. They had to create one." What could this possibly mean? Does he truly imagine that St. Paul's Cathedral or the Bank of England sprang from the earth? Does he think buildings from before the twentieth century have somehow always been there without any intervention from humans—that the premodern skyline of London has some kind of affinity with the landscape or even *belongs* to that landscape? The classical column, Charles says at one point, began life as a tree trunk propping up a roof; in this sense, the column-as-trunk offers "a mysterious sense of well-being and a kind of contentment." In Charles's fantasia, in other words, classical design elements are not simply more biologically appealing to humans; they actually fade back into the earth itself, as if classical buildings are only minor elaborations on already existing natural forms.

What's at stake here is an idea that the modern cityscape is not bad simply because it's ugly or because lots of people just don't like the look of modern buildings but because it is *inherently* bad. The claim is that disliking the minimal steel and glass of modern construction is not only an aesthetic judgment but in fact a kind of biological repulsion, an aversion encoded in one's very genome, passed down from generation to generation as humans became increasingly displaced from their natural habitats. A person does not dislike downtown Manhattan, in this logic, in the same way that they might dislike a book or a film, but rather as they would dislike a snake or a stinging plant.

"There are two principal things that appeal to me about classical architecture," George Saumarez Smith said to me over lemon tea in his office at the back of a beautifully restored sixteenth-century manor house in Winchester. I had come to see Saumarez Smith partly because he's one of the most lauded and well-known architects working in the classical tradition in Britain, and I thought he might help me understand its appeal. But I had also come to Winchester because Saumarez Smith, along with the designer Ben Pentreath, is the architect behind a good deal of what's been built in Poundbury over the last ten years or so. Saumarez Smith's work ranges from art galleries in London's swish Bond Street to rather grand villas in the country as well as streets of more ordinary-looking homes. Much of his work centers on an appreciation of what classically minded architects call the five orders, derived from architectural treatises first published in renaissance Italy that formalized the different "orders" of classical architecture (Doric, Ionic, and so on). These were principally focused on the design of columns but also on the precise relationships between the different elements: the correct ratio of width to capital height and so on. This kind of architecture, Saumarez Smith said, has "essentially been made irrelevant in [today's] architectural education." Classical architecture, he said, "by which I mean something that has its roots in Greek and Roman antiquity, had its expression originally in temples but was developed into other sorts of building types and is bound up in its architectural expression in the orders."

I nodded as he rather beautifully sketched some column types on a napkin in front of me. "But it also originates," he went on, "in the way that society is organized and the way that cities are designed and built as well." We talked about architectural education and how, as a student in Edinburgh, he had tried hard to reconcile his interest in the city's more traditional buildings with the rather fixed twentieth-century training he was getting from his university tutors. "The people that I was being taught by," he said, "I guess had probably been trained in the '80s. And the people they were trained by would be, as it were, first-generation modernist. And so I think that they would have received an extremely dogmatic training in which classical architecture simply would have been . . . it would have been deliberately excluded."

I asked him what made these older, more traditional styles still relevant today, then. "One thing is that it has its roots in the natural world," he replied, sipping his tea. "And wherever you look, whether it's the shape of molding on a glazing bar"—he tapped the very nice wooden sash windows next to where we were sitting—"or the way that materials throw water off them or the way that shadows are cast on architectural forms…it's all to do with a symbiotic relationship to the natural world. Light, and the effects of weather, and the passing of seasons and all of those sorts of things, are programmed into the classical vocabulary." Right, I said. Huh. "And the second thing," he continued, "is that classical architecture is able to organize buildings and places in cities in a way that has a civilizing effect on society. Ultimately, I just think that it's much more humane than the alternatives."

We talked about his work in Poundbury and about Krier and the then Prince Charles, who I was surprised to learn were still very much involved. "Right from the outset," Saumarez Smith said suddenly, "Poundbury was an experiment. The Prince of Wales had written *Vision of Britain* and had come under fire from the architecture profession. And he said, well, the best thing to do is to try and put these ideas into practice. The Duchy of Cornwall own a huge amount of land in the southwest of England and other places as well. And they had been selling off land for development for years. And that parcel of land on the west side of Dorchester was going to be developed at some point. Had the Prince of Wales not intervened, the duchy would probably have done a deal with one of the major house builders, and it would have been developed with very little design oversight. And it would be a completely bog-standard housing estate by now; it would have probably been built in half the time that it has been built, and all the houses would be essentially the same. There would be no mixed use. No attempt at something out of the ordinary. And nobody would bat an eyelid at all. It would just be…"

"Unremarkable?" I said.

"Like any other modern suburb in any other market town any-where else in the rest of Britain," he replied. "So I think one ought to approach Poundbury within that context, that it is an experiment of trying to do a whole lot of things which are out of the ordinary. And if that is the point by which one measures success, then I think it has been very successful. There are as many workplaces in Poundbury as there are houses. That is quite incredible. Find another develop-ment anywhere in the country in the last fifty years that you can say that about."

He talked about how so much housing and so many cul-de-sac estates were essentially guided by housing regulations, and how Poundbury had worked around these to create a permeable, walkable space. "There's no signage," he said. "There's no street parking regulation. And all of the services are put through the rear courtyards so the streets don't get dug up for getting at the services. And the whole development benefits from an anaerobic digestion plant nearby in order to make it as off grid as possible. And all of those are really extraordinary pioneering things to have done. And amazingly difficult to achieve. A measure of how hard they are to achieve is you just see that it hasn't been done elsewhere despite the fact that many people have attempted it. You know? But Poundbury really goes to extremes."

We were finishing up by now. Despite my misgivings about the place, I found myself oddly moved by Saumarez Smith's defense of what Poundbury was trying to do and sympathetic to his light sense of frustration that people wouldn't take it seriously—treat-ing Poundbury as a kind of Georgian Disneyland, cut off from the world. "I was in Poundbury last week," he said as I was leaving, "just walking around. And somebody opened their front door and said, 'Are you George? Did you design our house?' And I said yes! They said, 'Oh, come in. We'd love you to see what we've done with the house.' And then I got sort of attacked by the family dog in the kitchen, and they were telling me how much they love living there, and how everybody has great pride in their gardens, and how it's really nice on a Sunday morning. Everybody walks their dogs and has a chat to one another. And how there's a residents' association, and you walk past the school and the children are out in the playground, playing. And you kind of think, architects say that Poundbury is make-believe but you know, *it's all real life.*"

Let's go back a little over a century before the Prince of Wales got up to speak in Hampton Court Palace. It's October 1875, and a noted physician and writer, Benjamin Ward Richardson, has been asked to give an address on urban planning to the annual meeting of the Social Science Association at Brighton. Now more or less forgotten, at the time, the association was one of the UK's largest and most influential civic organizations. It wasn't interested in "social science" as we might understand it; the association was really a vehicle for social reformers, politicians, journalists, and the civic-minded bourgeoisie more generally to think publicly about the problems of the day, establish commissions and reports on them, and then try to influence the government. Who should be allowed to vote? What are effective deterrents to petty crime? How can we clean up cities? How can public health be improved? These were among the topics analyzed by five well-regulated "departments." The association's annual congress, meanwhile, went around the country like a traveling circus of liberal reform. People attended in thousands, while what was actually said at the meetings was lavishly reported in the newspapers.[12]

Richardson's address to the 1875 meeting covered two topics close to the heart of many Victorian reformers: the condition of the city and the problem of public health. By the middle decades of the nineteenth century, the sanitary situation in cities in England had become so bad that in Liverpool, about 3.5 percent of the city's population (roughly one person in every twenty-eight) died each year.[13] Most of this was a product of the sheer dirt of everyday life in the industrial Victorian city and people's inability to access basic sanitary facilities: families lived more or less on top of one another with no ventilation or space, limited access to laundry or hot water, sewage floating in the streets, no separation of living and working spaces, and the chemical by-products of heavy industry hanging in the air. All of this produced a public health disaster that was so bad that even the urban rich were no longer insulated from it. In 1875, Parliament finally passed the Public Health Act, which tried to alleviate the appalling urban mortality rate by at least mandating the use of sewers, creating new housing controls and regulations, and setting up a public health bureaucracy made up of medical officers and sanitary inspectors.

Such was the scene when Benjamin Ward Richardson got up to speak in Brighton. He didn't offer a proposal for new sanitary techniques, any medical theories about why urban living might be bad for people, or even a polemic against the complacent urban bourgeoisie. Instead, Richardson offered science fiction. With vivid, often hyperreal detail, he described a future city that he had invented called "Hygeia."[14] Hygeia, in Richardson's mind, is a city of 100,000 souls built across 4,000 acres of land (roughly the size of the London Borough of Islington, current population about 240,000). No building in Hygeia is higher than sixty feet, which allows for the free movement of air. In fact, water and air are critical to Richardson's construction. He imagines his city on a slope, like a gently subsiding house, with an angled subway running the full length underneath so that all water and waste flow down to a gravel layer at the southeastern edge of town. At street level, the pavements are also tilted, with slits every few yards for dirt and water to fall through. "Gutter children" are thus nowhere to be seen, Richardson points out, because—one can almost feel him beaming—there is no gutter. "Instead of the gutter," indeed, "the poorest child has the garden; for the foul sight and smell of unwholesome garbage, he has flowers and green sward."

Elsewhere, the gridded streets are built wide to maximize sunlight; shrubs and trees line each side, with gardens to the rear of every house; the city is mostly silent at street level because there's an underground railroad ferrying everyone and everything around; all sewage and power, all slaughterhouses and sanitary works, all refuse dumps and mortuaries are built at a distance from the city; animals are kept away from places of human habitation and killed humanely; in the residential areas of town, houses are glazed in gray brick to keep the water out, prevent damp, and rest the eyes; inside, chimneys go through a central furnace to remove the carbon before smoke is released; kitchens are always built on upper floors, which gives light so you can quickly detect dirt and also disperses cooking smells out of the house; rubbish goes through a hidden slot in the wall; every room has hot and cold water, while the roofs, which are flat, are all covered in flower beds; clothes are washed and disinfected at large public laundries; nothing is dried indoors; there are pools, gymnasia, libraries, and lecture halls but no alcohol for sale, and no tobacco either.

Above all of this, watching with a kindly but unblinking eye, Richardson imagined a system of total medical supervision under the command of a principal sanitary officer, who receives reports from town doctors, records all births and deaths, keeps an eye on animal disease, inspects samples of food, and conducts chemical analyses. For those who—in spite of all these measures—still insist on dying, burial takes place outside the city. The corpse is placed in the earth with only a shroud. Vegetables are grown in the fertile soil left by the city's decomposing former residents.

This sounds mad—and of course it *is* mad. But Richardson was deadly serious. If you build Hygeia, he argues, you remove the conditions for cholera, typhus, diarrhea, croup, rheumatic fever, and smallpox. There will be no deprivation, hunger, or scurvy. Liver disease, kidney disorders, and delirium tremens will become the stuff of fairy stories. Parasites will be eradicated and insanity virtually unknown. Tuberculosis will simply float away through open windows and down well-ventilated streets. Sure, it might not be a very *joyful* place—but death rates will plummet, at least.

It may tell us something about the anxious climate at the time, and the real deep fears around unhealthy urban environments, that Richardson's talk was an enormous public success. Newspapers at home and abroad reported on it, and the whole speech was published as a pamphlet the following year. "Rich old ladies," wrote the historian James Cassedy in 1962, "began to build 'Hygeian residences'; tradesmen advertised Hygeian goods."[15] Early ideas for a national health service, meanwhile, began to draw on Richardson's arguments for public medical infrastructure. The pamphlet was taken up particularly enthusiastically in the United States as cities like Chicago and San Francisco entered a wave of enormous growth. But then, Cassedy reported, just as *Hygeia* was reaching the height of its fame, it disappeared. In 1876, the same year Richardson's pamphlet was published, the German physician and biologist Robert Koch discovered the bacteria that cause cholera and tuberculosis. With the growing acceptance of germ theories of disease, public health tilted on its axis. Who cared about huge, costly schemes of urban design when laboratory scientists could simply eradicate these newly discovered microorganisms? There was no need for a contentious social reorganization—people could still enjoy beer and tobacco; they didn't need to be ruled by medical superintendents, and, okay, landlords could continue to exploit people, but at least now with fewer fatalities. Richardson's triumph ended almost before it began.

The dream did not quite die, however. One person in Chicago who certainly *did* read *Hygeia* was Ebenezer Howard, a British-born clerical worker and stenographer who had arrived in that city five years earlier; in the building boom that came in the wake of the great fire of 1871, Howard might well have seen something of Frederick Law Olmsted's planned suburb of Riverside. This was, as we saw in the introduction, a landscaped utopia of colonial houses surrounded by parks and greenery.[16] When

Howard returned to England later the same year, he began to formulate the plans that would not only bring *Hygeia* closer to reality than anything else, but would have a transformative effect on urban design and planning, and their relationship to health, for at least the next century.

Back in London, Ebenezer Howard found a job at Hansard—the organization that makes the official record of UK parliamentary debates—and began to move in reformist and dissenting circles. He met figures as diverse as the playwright George Bernard Shaw; the anarchist Russian dissident Peter Kropotkin; and Beatrice and Sidney Webb, the founders of the Fabian Society. He read J. S. Mill on new cities, Henry George on urban economics, and Herbert Spencer on biology and eugenics. From this array of influences, Howard distilled an assortment of political and quasi-biological ideas, a mélange of notions about good health and proper morals, and he crystallized it into the new discipline of city planning—something he had neither experience nor expertise in.

In 1898, Howard published *To-Morrow: A Path to Peaceful Reform.* What he would propose as the "garden city" in that now famous text is strikingly close to Richardson's Hygeia. It is a mixture of town and country—a dream city built in a garden, surrounded by green space, well governed, with light industry and reasonable rents, a kind of city without the city, brought together within a similarly weird spatial fantasy.

It is *land*, said Howard, a renewed relation of people *to* the land, that will solve "the problems of intemperance, of excessive toil, of restless anxiety, of grinding poverty" that characterize modern urban life.[17] Think of the city, he said, as a kind of magnet and human beings as so many tiny needles drawn toward it. The force of the magnet, or what attracts people to the city, is made up of high wages, a good social life, better living conditions than in the countryside. At the same time, that force is weakened by the downsides of city life—long hours, bad air, noise, and so on. The countryside has attractive powers—low rent, decent air, sunshine. But here, too, the force is weakened, and perhaps fatally so, by isolation, lack of work, and social stagnation. To the extent that people end up in one place or another, it is through the balance of these forces of attraction and repulsion.

But what if, said Howard, there was a *third* magnet—one that would hold together all the advantages of the city (stuff! friends! a job!) but do so while also holding on to the attractions of the countryside (fields! cheap things! air!). This "third magnet" is what Howard called the Garden City: "Human society and the beauty of nature are meant to be enjoyed together," he said. "The two magnets must be made one. As man and woman by their varied gifts and faculties supplement each other, so should town and country." This weirdly heteronormative sex imagery is a constant in Howard's writing, and it is no mere metaphor. The capacity of the town and country to come together and reproduce, and in the process to make healthy new people, is central to his vison and, indeed, to the generally reproductive and eugenic urges that guide it. "Town and country *must be married*," he said elsewhere, with the emphasis included, "and out of this joyous union will spring a new hope, a new life, a new civilisation." One can almost see him standing approvingly over the conjugal couple, encouraging them here and there in their movements.

What Howard was trying to create was a new kind of environment—something completely different from the "crowded, ill-ventilated, unplanned, unwieldy, unhealthy cities" that were like "ulcers on the very face of our beautiful island." What would it mean to make a city that had all the "natural healthfulness of the country"? For Howard, remember, health is not only physical, it is *moral*, and it is *beautiful*. A man of his time, he was in conversation not only with eugenicists and agriculturalists but also with vegetarians, biologists, and racists. He wanted the city to be a petri dish for physically fit people and also good people and also beautiful people, and he equated physical fitness *with* beauty and *with* goodness. Immersion in natural surroundings, in Howard's view, is unique in its capacity to produce all three. You might see the garden city as a sort of fusty aesthetic object—a boring, very white suburb with some extra trees and a kind of inchoate hostility toward whatever its inhabitants imagine urban life to be. In all fairness, this is often what places calling themselves "garden" cities, suburbs, villages, and so on actually are. But this is not how Ebenezer Howard imagined it. His was a much stranger, much more radical, and much more troubling vision.

In 1902, the Garden City association held a meeting in the planned community of Bourneville, near Birmingham, sponsored by the Quaker chocolate magnate (and Bourneville founder) George Cadbury. As well as Cadbury, the delegates included George Bernard

Shaw, Earl Grey (later the governor general of Canada and grandson of the prime minister for whom the bergamot-scented Chinese tea blend is named)—and, of course, Howard himself. From this meeting, the Garden City Pioneer Company and then the First Garden City Ltd. emerged, with £300,000 in authorized share capital; a site at Letchworth, in Hertfordshire, England, was selected and ultimately purchased by the company, with capital provided by its directors. In 1904, Raymond Unwin and Barry Parker, devotees of William Morris, were appointed as architects and master planners of the new city. By 1905, two thousand people had moved to Letchworth, and the population grew slowly but steadily thereafter.

The movement, too, continued to grow, if in similarly unspectacular fashion. In 1919, with World War I over and the scent of bolshevism in the air, there was a widespread political interest in providing better living conditions for returning soldiers. Howard, who by this time was at the margins of events in Letchworth, raised money to buy 1,500 acres near Lord Salisbury's estate in Hertfordshire; Salisbury sold the newly formed Second Garden City Company another seven hundred acres, and in 1920, Welwyn Garden City was born. A few years ago (I mentioned this already in the introduction) I attended an event to mark the town's centenary, but after a dispiriting morning tramping around faux-pastoral laneways with some of the well-heeled residents, I abandoned the second half of the tour and instead went around taking photos of the town's weirdly eroticized statuary, which gave the place a kind of harvest-bacchanalia, *Wicker Man* vibe. Suffice it to say that if I'd stayed the night—I did not—I'd have made sure the door of my room was well locked.

Later, though, as I was reading through the history of the movement's early days, one of the names at the 1902 meeting in Bourneville leaped out to me. It wasn't Earl Grey or George Bernard Shaw—it was William Lever, later Lord Leverhulme, who in addition to being a director of the First Garden City Company was a cofounder of the Lever Brothers soap operation. This highly successful company would eventually join with a Dutch margarine conglomerate to form Unilever—the global corporation that today produces a truly wild array of toothpastes, breakfast cereals, toilet cleaners, ice creams, and laundry detergents. It's also still the world's number-one manufacturer of soap.

Having been born into a successful family grocery in Bolton, Lancashire, Lever became a partner in his father's firm, which he significantly expanded, before leaving to set up his own soap manufacturing concern.[18] Though the soap had some genuine advantages—Lever's chemist used vegetable rather than animal fats—Lever's real gift was for branding. His soap was the first to be sold in prewrapped standardized tablets, covered in the company's distinctive insignia and bearing the brand "Sunlight." When he eventually left Bolton, Lever established his new soap works on the banks of the River Mersey, a few miles downstream from Liverpool. From the beginning, Lever's plan for his factory included a town for his workers and their families. He called the town Port Sunlight, literally buttressed by the walls of his factory. By 1907, it was home to nearly four thousand people.

Port Sunlight was hardly the first architecturally ambitious company town. In the 1850s, the remarkably named Sir Titus Salt, an industrialist and Liberal member of Parliament, founded the village of Saltaire in West Yorkshire, intended as an improved environment for workers at his textile mills.[19] The picturesque stone houses that he built remained in the gift of Salt's Mill well into the 1930s (the mill itself is today a rather spectacular shopping center and art gallery, the latter much associated with the work of David Hockney, who was born nearby). In the early 1800s, the radical social reformer Robert Owen, having married into a cotton-milling family in New Lanark on the River Clyde, began to plan improvements to the dire living conditions of the workers who lived next to the mill. By the 1820s, Owen's model town was attracting thousands of curious visitors from all over Europe, while Owen himself spent much of the rest of his life founding rather beautiful-looking but generally disastrous utopian communities in the United States. Indeed, as early as the 1760s, the potter Josiah Wedgwood's model town, Etruria—named rather fancifully for the home of the ancient Etruscans, a pre-Roman civilization noted for its terra-cotta pots—began to fan out from Wedgwood's rapidly growing pottery at Stoke-on-Trent.

But Port Sunlight was distinctive—not only for its size and success but also because of how it worked as a material elaboration of its founder's social and moral philosophy. This wasn't exactly the same as Howard's, but it shared with him the vision of making a new kind of urban space, and a new kind of urban person, through a mix of architecture, natural materials, and social order.

To be honest, the reason Lever's name stood out to me was because I had a personal interest in his legacy. The research that I was carrying out, which resulted in this book, was funded by the Leverhulme Trust, which had generously given me a prize, and a significant amount of money for research expenses, in 2017. The trust was formed from a bequest from William Lever's will in 1925, and today it funds a wide range of academic research. It's an independent charity, and yet nonetheless, as its website puts it, it "continues to own Unilever stock and, as per the terms of Lever's will, its Board is largely drawn from Unilever past and current executives." More pointedly, though, the trust has also recently faced questions about how it handles its historical relationship to Lever Brothers' colonial plantations and settlements in the Congo and in the Solomon Islands. In 2020, the trust funded a four-month scoping project[20] to sketch the state of current knowledge of this history and said that it was funding research to further explore these legacies.[21] In the meantime, I decided to do some exploring of my own.

I finally arrived in Port Sunlight, on the banks of the River Mersey, quite late on a cold evening in November 2021 after a disturbingly long and creaky train ride from my home in southwest England. I had spent the journey, and its many stops, with Jules Marchal's extraordinarily grim book, *Lord Leverhulme's Ghost*, in which Marchal, a historian and former Belgian diplomat—the book was originally published in French and has only recently been translated into English by a small left-wing press—doggedly traced the details of Lever's activities in the Congo. At first glance, as the train nears its destination, the location of Port Sunlight seems inauspicious for an experiment in urban living. This is, after all, the marshy edge of a peninsula in England's unglamorous northwest. But as soon as you see the wide expanse of the Mersey, as well the monumental financial and trading buildings that still line the Liverpool side of the river, you get it instantly: this once was, after all, as the historian Amy Sergeant reminded us, the second most important port of the British empire.[22] Port Sunlight might have been designed as a sedate garden village, but Lever placed it quite precisely. The town and its factory are not at all in some bucolic hinterland. Though it hides these qualities well, Port Sunlight was from its inception a cosmopolitan, high-tech, and *global* place. But perhaps not, as we will see, very much for the good.

A thing that perhaps separates Port Sunlight from many other model or company towns, I realized, as I walked around, is that it actually *is* quite beautiful and charming. The houses, originally built for workers in the factory (today anyone can buy one) are mostly arranged in short terraces. But what makes the place attractive is its sheer variety—many different architects, including major figures like Edwin Lutyens, were involved in designing houses in Port Sunlight. And yet there's a family resemblance in the quasi-medieval, William Morris–influenced aesthetic. Though mostly terraced, the houses are still notably cottagey, with large gables and big wooden beams; there are many half-timber houses and Dutch-style ornament and patterning. Though Port Sunlight is technically not a "garden city," as you walk around it's plain that green space is everywhere. A proper architectural historian would probably talk about the town's debt to the Arts and Crafts movement, but a more modest visitor might just think Port Sunlight has a kind of Bilbo Baggins energy—and why not?

Sometimes, too, it gets a bit monumental. At the center are two intersecting expanses of park that, from overhead, form a shape something like a crucifix. If you stand at the war memorial on one end, with the Union Jack fluttering plaintively over your head, you can look straight down past a long expanse of flowerbeds to the neoclassical art gallery that Lever commissioned for his own collection in 1922. Directly to its left is the memorial erected after his death just three years later: an Expressionist figure with her arms up stands on top of a sixty-foot pillar, and at her feet is a set of full-sized human figures representing Lever's preferred virtues: industry, education, and (this last symbolized by a woman suckling an infant, for some reason) charity. Okay, at this point, it's maybe all gone a bit Albert Speer. But still. There's a charm.

Port Sunlight is supposed to look like a picturesque garden. But it's also a place of business. Across the town's southern edge, a redbrick factory wall still runs for some distance—its carefully sealed doorways reminding you that Unilever, successor to Lever's soap company, still manufactures bathroom-adjacent products here. These include the shower gel Dove and also a bleach called Domestos, which is generally used to clean toilets. This association of the town with cleanliness and hygiene is not accidental. As you walk through the neat rows of modest houses, set respectfully back from the place of busy manufacture, the shared desire for a certain kind of physical as well as moral purity is palpable. This is, in many ways, not a bad thing. Without question, Port Sunlight offered significant material improvement for the factory workers who once lived here, in terms of not only working and living conditions but also general health outcomes as well as education.[23] There was firm discipline, it's true—for the worker who stepped out of line, not only his job but his home was at stake. But for those willing to play by Lever's rules, a level of social and physical comfort was available in Port Sunlight well beyond what was available elsewhere—which included facilities for recreation, for self-improvement, even for growing your own vegetables if you really wanted to. Such was his pride in it that Lever even used images of the town in his soap advertisements. It captured the clean, healthy, morally good life he wanted both his customers and his employees to imagine for themselves. Indeed, his goal, said the historian Amanda Rees, was to "produce a distinctive visual ideology to shape the behaviour and attitudes of factory workers and their families."[24] The idea was to provide a healthy environment for workers—with not just pretty houses, but also good temperate bourgeois activities: gardening, communal dining, debate, and so on.

As you walk around, there is something extraordinarily peaceful about Port Sunlight—but something kind of jarring, too. At one point, not long after I arrived, with the evening closing in on the mostly empty streets, I took a wrong turn and ended up in a kind of hollow in no-man's-land, still filled with crisp autumn leaves and a stream[25] running through, crossed at the end by a very small, cute arched stone bridge. I took a bunch of photos. But honestly, it was too much. There's a point in landscaping where things take on the uncanny quality of a Thomas Kinkade painting or start to look like something generated by artificial intelligence. You get the feeling that if you look too hard, you might spot a computer-rendering error—a disembodied hand, say, or half a human face, hovering glitchy and ghostlike in the background. That faintly sinister sense of glitch—the feeling that at any moment, the scene might break, a curtain might drop—never left me in Port Sunlight. I came to be grateful that the only hotel I could find, which was really more of a pub with rooms, was just outside the town's boundaries. As I passed through a set of hedges and onto a main road to get to it, there was just an *instant* and really kind of welcome transportation back to the everyday ugliness of provincial modernity. That evening, not really wanting to sit in the pub, and looking for some supermarket wine, I trudged a couple of miles down a barely lit path, in the opposite direction from Port Sunlight itself, until I came to an anonymous strip mall on the Wirral Peninsula, with a cinema, some fast-food places, teenagers in cars, and a branch of the slightly upmarket British chain store, Waitrose. It could have been anywhere, and I could have died from happiness. Port Sunlight isn't gated, certainly. But its symbolic and moral edges are clear. The town wouldn't be more tightly closed off from the petty bourgeois everyday of the Wirral if Unilever's factory wall simply curled itself around the place entirely—pulling the residents gently away from the hustle, strife, uncertainty, and low-key alienation of twenty-first-century capitalism.

Walking out the next morning, I realized that, in daylight, you get a sense of the specificity and deliberation of Lever's plan for his people-shaping environment: he had delineated ten to twelve houses per acre, the road to be at least forty-five feet in width, with a strip in its center paved for cars; around this, Lever imagined a gravel pathway, then grass, and, "if possible," an avenue of trees. Houses should be minimally fifteen feet back from the road, with space for a vegetable garden at the back and open space for recreation within easy reach. There is no room for extravagance here—or at least this is a vision in which extravagance is produced not by elaborate decoration or style but by the simple provision of open space and nature. "A few sprays of ivy," wrote Lever, "and a greensward in front of the house, a shrub here and there, and the plainest and most economical cottage, architecturally, becomes more beautiful than a more costly and elaborate one, built right on the edge of the footpath without any intervening fringe of greensward."[26]

Throughout his writing, indeed, it becomes clear that Lever's urban vision has two central themes: race and nation. The cottage home, he told a visiting housing conference in 1907, is "the unit of a nation." The more comfortable and happy the home, the healthier its inhabitants and, in turn, the more efficiently productive the nation. The early twentieth century, Lever argued, was a period of competition between nations, governed not by armies of soldiers but rather by armies of industrial workers. The nation that would be declared "the fittest to survive" would be the nation that best prevented the "deterioration of the race" though "physical fitness." And it was the home and its surrounding environment that would play the determining role. Even if "the strain of modern life is ever increasing," Lever went on, "this should not necessarily tend to the deterioration of the race"—a "healthy home life and environment," he declared, will "produce a healthier, stronger, and more virile race."

But look, on one level, you might say, strip away the eugenics, which was broadly characteristic of people of Lever's class and background; ignore, if you can, the fantasy of imperial domination lurking in the background of his anxious paean to vigor and virility; and honestly, it's hard to object to many of the specifics of his urban vision. Lever wanted "proper air space and good planning" as well as "the provision of large open spaces and recreation grounds outside the home." For adults, he wanted "healthy relaxation from toil when strenuous work is done" and for children, a careful calculation of residents per hectare so as to reduce infant mortality. He even showed that the average height and weight of a child in a Port Sunlight school was higher than that of a child in the equivalent council school. All of this (and I will quote this passage at length because it captures a vision of the relationship between life and environment that came to the fore in Lever's day and remains deeply influential in our own) proves that

> given regularity and permanency of employment to the parents, and consequently also of feeding and clothing of the children, reasonable and proper housing conditions, plenty of surrounding land for healthy, open-air recreation, provision of Parks, Swimming Baths, Gymnasia, Football Field, Cricket Field, Clubs, and all that makes for healthy out-door life, and the children of our artisans and labouring people became equal in physique to those of the better classes.

Port Sunlight was a machine for producing the future of the imperial nation. Drawing on the statistics of a Mr. Fraser from his firm, Lever went into quite weird, exhaustive detail about the number of children born to the different grades of employee at his firm before concluding, with great approval and satisfaction, that by far the largest families were those of the higher-grade workmen, "the most intelligent of the working classes," and thus, "Port Sunlight shows the way to the rest of England."

Lever is often read as a somewhat benign paternalist of his age—sure, his ideas were odd and a bit patronizing, goes the thinking, but there is at least a concrete vision for making a better life for his employees and their families. All of this is true enough. But it's also the case that for Lever, a better life for his own employees, in the form of a healthy town, was not an end in itself. It was part of a competitive colonial endeavor, a white supremacist strategy to maintain British domination. As the historian David Jeremy points out, Port Sunlight was an attempt to demonstrate that sharing prosperity, and not profit, was the path to social peace.[27] The planned town, in this sense, is an engine of social harmony at home and imperialism abroad. Its hastily planted greenswards were spaces for the production of good, docile British workers—and, if need be, good, violent British soldiers.

The main ingredient in William Lever's soaps was vegetable oil, chiefly palm oil. Palm oil is extracted from the oil palm tree, a species native to West Africa, among other places. To serve the needs of his booming soap business, Lever first tried to obtain exclusive rights to extraction from oil palms in what was then British West Africa—a space that today covers much of Ghana, Nigeria, Sierra Leone, and the Gambia. This request was refused by Britain's colonial office on the ground that such an exclusive right might foment local unrest. Lever began to look elsewhere.

In 1908, the Belgian state took control over the so-called Congo Free State, a space that had hitherto been a private possession of the country's genocidal king, Leopold II. In Leopold's wake—he died the following year, but not before burning all archival evidence of his own atrocities—Belgium tried to promote the newly annexed Belgian Congo as a cleaned-up *"colonie-modèle"* in which, among other advancements, forced labor would be forbidden. With supplies of rubber and ivory exhausted by Leopold, but anything other than continued exploitation seemingly unimaginable to the European authorities, the Belgians turned to the groves of oil palms that made up much of Congo's interior. They actively tried to interest Lever in extracting the oil, and in 1911, Lever Brothers and the Belgian government finally formed a company called Huileries du Congo Belge (HCB). This company was ceded vast amounts of space in Belgian Congo (more territory than actual Belgium) with the idea that it would build infrastructure, including towns, to house and educate workers while creating conditions for the exploitation of the palm. The largest such settlement was called Leverville. It was built on the banks of the Kwilu River across from an existing village called Lusanga.

The surface logic of Leverville was the same as that of Port Sunlight: that humane conditions—decent homes, schools for children, and recreation facilities—make better workers. The town was again said to be an engine for making the kinds of people, in this case a Congolese middle class, who would share the moral outlook and bearing of their counterparts on the banks of the Mersey. Lever's international reputation as a humane capitalist was a major selling point for the Belgians, who were keen to see the kinds of physical and moral improvements in Africa's interior that Lever had modeled with the British working classes at Port Sunlight. In reality, though Lever sank a great deal of his company's money into developing infrastructure and saw little profit, and though he undoubtedly was driven, at least in the abstract, by the same paternalistic desires that had motivated him on the banks of the Mersey—which were, yes, a desire to extract the surplus labor of his workers for his own private benefit, under at least implicit threat of immiseration, but to do so in a nice way—this never came to pass.

As the historians Reuben Loffman and Benoît Henriet carefully documented, wages at HCB were bad, and forced labor persisted well into Lever's era; there were accusations of corruption among HCB agents and feeble attempts to inculcate "European" values among the Congolese workforce (essentially, this meant trying to turn the Congolese into good, desiring consumers through a money economy and a network of company-owned enterprises).[28] But really, this was all a smoke screen. From the beginning, according to the retired Belgian diplomat Jules Marchal, who spent decades excavating Lever's Belgian activities, Leverville was about forced labor, monopoly capital, and brutally low wages maintained by coercion as well as, where necessary, by violence.[29]

One of the major aims of HCB's leaders throughout this period, as convincingly evidenced by Marchal, was to be allowed to simply move the workers—which is to say, move their entire villages—nearer to the place of work. The Belgian Department of Colonies, still at least loosely committed to the *colonie-modèle*, resisted; the Congolese would simply become serfs, these officials said, essentially the property of the company. In May 1926, Lever's company sent a memorandum in response—if it was allowed to move whole villages near the land containing palm groves, these would not be just any new villages but might even become *garden villages.* Sure, the memorandum said, this would make the natives extremely economically dependent on the company. But after all, this was already the case in many European towns and villages built near large industrial facilities. It was, it pointed out, what the company had already achieved in Port Sunlight.

Perhaps the comparison goes too far. But here, in the end, is the only way I can make historical and political sense of King Charles's idea—and he is far from the only one to hold it—that buildings and cities should grow naturally, as from the soil. The idea is not only to freeze the physical and social form of the city in time; it is to insist, in the same breath, that a particular utopian vision of urban function and shape—a vision of the city as beautiful, ordered, rigidly hierarchical—is the obvious and natural state of things. And the people produced by such an urban space—people who are bright and well rested, people who eat carefully and rest quietly, people who are ready for nearby work, people who keep their bodies and minds scrubbed clean of impurity—are also, in this vision, in their natural condition. Of course there are critical differences marked by racism and colonialism, but still a similar kind of logic holds in England, North America, and West Africa. Because the green and living city is not, in this imaginary, a heterogeneous and unpredictable space of human creativity and culture. Rather, it is an organized and well-oiled machine for the production of new kinds of people, people ready to take up the place already assigned to them under conditions of both colonialism and monopoly capitalism.

The garden city, from this perspective, is no benign relic of Victorian reform. It was—and it remains—a deeply influential experiment for the transformation of urban space and urban citizens.

In the decades after Lever's death, his ideas about urban space fell out of favor and became impossible to realize. However, some of the general principles that guided people in Lever's time, in particular ideas about how space can shape moral character, were to receive something of a new lease on life from a surprising quarter many years later. Shorn of the racist and imperialist underpinnings of Lever's ideas, this new lease on life nonetheless came from the natural sciences, and in particular from psychology. If in Lever's era the garden city was intended to cultivate people's eternal souls and their moral characters, soon it would have a new, but not wholly different, object. By the end of the twentieth century, we would be focused instead on what the modern city was doing to people's minds and brains.

CHAPTER 3

A Rat in a Maze

In the middle decades of the twentieth century, a polio epidemic that had been simmering for fifty years exploded into one of the century's most devastating outbreaks of infectious disease. Poliomyelitis, the infectious disease better known as polio, is caused by the poliovirus. The virus moves from person to person mostly through human feces spread by poor hand hygiene. The resulting disease affects mainly young children; the effects range from a short illness lasting a week or so to life-altering paralysis and ultimately death by suffocation as the respiratory muscles cease to function. The historian Dora Vargha records that at the peak of the global polio pandemic in the 1950s, rates of the disease were about eighteen per hundred thousand people in England

and Wales, twenty-four per hundred thousand in Hungary, and, by 1952, a devastating thirty-seven per hundred thousand in the United States. Between 1950 and 1954, about twenty-two thousand people each year were paralyzed by polio in the United States; in 1950 alone, three thousand children died from it.[1] To most people in the world today, polio is a half-known ghost disease of their parents' or grandparents' era, but its midcentury Euro-American iconography—roomfuls of children encased in iron lungs; starched, matronly nurses; wheelchairs, stiff leg braces, and large wooden crutches—still offers a potent visual shorthand for the horrors of pandemic infectious disease.[2]

Jonas Salk was, in the late 1940s, a young virologist working at the University of Pittsburgh. Having moved to Pittsburgh from New York City to start his own laboratory, Salk was one of many people working desperately on a vaccine that would prevent infection by the poliovirus. But then something important changed for Salk, which altered the course both of his own life and of the pandemic he was immersed in. The story—maybe "myth" is a better word—goes like this: Salk found Pittsburgh—hardscrabble, industrial, dirty Pittsburgh—not to be the most conducive environment for the delicate mental labor of vaccinology. So he left and made his way to the small town of Assisi in Umbria, central Italy. Dug into the slopes at the foot of Mount Subasio, Assisi is famous among Christians mostly as the birthplace of St. Francis, the medieval ascetic and founder of the Franciscan monastic order. In Francis's wake, and also that of St. Clare, founder of the Order of Poor Ladies, Assisi became a center of medieval monasticism and a site for significant architectural projects. One of the most prominent of these projects was the Basilica of

St. Francis, whose distinctive Gothic half (the basilica actually forms two churches) is lined from floor to ceiling with frescoes by Giotto and members of his school. In fact, today the entire medieval town is a UNESCO world heritage site, including the famous Eremo delle Carceri—a semihidden complex of caves and outbuildings located in a forest gorge some distance outside the city, where Francis was said to have come to pray, often staying for some time in the caves. In some versions of the myth, Jonas Salk spent his time in Assisi at the basilica; in others, he even spent significant time in the caves. Either way, he returned to noisy, industrious Pittsburgh not only refreshed and renewed but having made the crucial intellectual breakthrough that would deliver the world its first successful polio vaccine. Salk intuited that a technique he had already used in developing an influenza vaccine, where researchers used a dead version of the virus to induce an antibody response, might work with polio, too. He returned to Pittsburgh, began successful field trials of his dead-virus vaccine in 1952, and licensed it in 1955; a mass vaccination campaign began the same year.[3]

The history of both polio and polio vaccination is, of course, much more complex than this. Despite the mythmaking around Salk, an oral vaccine developed by his contemporary Albert Sabin, which was a good deal easier to administer to children and was initially used with great success in the Soviet Union, quickly became the vaccine of choice in many countries.[4] Still, I want to stay with the story for a moment—and I want to stay in Assisi, perhaps sitting contemplatively in one of the shaded quadrangles of the Basilica San Francesco, for just a bit longer. In the 1960s, having finally received funding to establish his own biological institute in La Jolla, California, on the edge of the Pacific Ocean, Salk engaged the modernist architect Louis Kahn to design an ideal space for the production of scientific knowledge. The Salk Institute, the complex that Kahn ultimately designed, is a set of strong but modest-looking buildings that appear, for all the world, like rows of fiercely concreted monastic caves. Working explicitly with ecclesiastic and contemplative history, as well as the more prosaic demands of Salk, Kahn built a machine for thinking at the edge of the Pacific Ocean. "Its function may be for science," wrote the *Los Angeles Times* in 2016, "but Kahn's structures feel more like a temple to nature."[5] Another architectural publication wrote that "Kahn's scheme for the Institute is spatially orches-trated in a similar way to a monastery: a secluded intellectual community."[6] These connections by Kahn and Salk to nature and monasticism are not incidental. Nor are they—as we may be inclined to suspect—an example of California's noted tolerance for airy bullshit about the power of the environment.

These connections reflect, rather, a commitment to a new idea: that the kind of building you are in has a serious bearing on the kind of thinking you can do, that the very structure and content of your thoughts, the functions of your brain, are profoundly mediated by the physical environment—natural or built—that you happen to find yourself in. In 1992, speaking at an awards ceremony held by the American Institute of Architects, Salk said that his and Kahn's shared intention was "to influence in a posi-tive way the conditions and circumstances of the environment for those working within the institute so that they, in turn, might then influence each other in the work they produced and in so doing, extend their influence beyond through the products of their collaboration."[7] In another speech the same year, attended by President George H. W. Bush, Salk referenced the "turbulent times" they were all living in—this was less than a year after the end of the first Gulf War—and argued for "a new way of seeing and a new way of thinking both about nature and the human side of nature."[8] Science, he said, can be understood only in its relationship to art. He had founded his institute because he had realized that "all of the problems of man will not be solved in the laboratory." Indeed, the laboratory style of thought might *itself* become a problem. Humans have become "pathogens against our planet and pathogens against each other," Salk said. And this tension between human as pathogen and human as cure is what his institute, in its physical form, attempts to resolve. The "timeless" quality of Louis Kahn's design "offers inspiration, hope and promise, as we experience both its beauty and the truths that are emerging from it." This is a design for science that is *not* about the organized production of knowledge, in other words. Rather, it is a design that tries to create the physical, and thereby the psychological, conditions for particular kinds of knowledge: human, mindful, curative, alive to the limits of science itself.

In 2002, following a meeting in San Diego of the American Institute of Architects, a group of architects and scientists from the nearby Salk Institute founded the Academy of Neuroscience for Architecture (ANFA). Its mission, says the academy, is to "promote and advance knowledge that links neuroscience research to a growing understanding of human responses to the built environment."[9] Through workshops, conferences and lecture series,

ANFA is interested in things like how light and sound can be used in health-care settings, how visual perception of space works, and how people respond emotionally to different spaces.[10] The fundamental idea here—and ANFA is just one node in a much larger international scene—is that the work of designing buildings is, at least in part, the work of figuring out how buildings can best meet the psychological and neurobiological needs of the people who inhabit them.

The idea that the mind works differently in different places is extraordinary powerful. It also feels kind of intuitively right. After all, you wouldn't try to file your tax return from a laptop on a bench in the city center. You'd seek out a quiet space with a comfortable chair and enough space to work, somewhere with not much noise, perhaps with walls painted a soothing shade. And you'd do this not simply because it's a nicer place to do the job, but because you have some sense that you'll do the job less well, or maybe won't be able to do it at all, if the physical surroundings are not properly attuned to it. Salk takes this claim a bit further. He doesn't just advance the general idea that a person can reason (or love or despair) *better* in places that are more suited to this kind of mental activity. He proposes the more specific idea that particular physical environments have particular psychological effects—that these can be worked out, analyzed, manipulated, and made use of with the right know-how. It's the idea that spaces can and should be designed for mental activity—and even if this isn't what medieval monks thought they were doing, it's what they were doing nonetheless.

But two more insidious ideas are implied here. One is so obvious and so ingrained in us that we might simply miss it. This is the idea that the spaces that are good for thinking, and also good for mentally resting, are *not* spaces that have the characteristics of urban environments. They are not noisy, bright, smelly, hurried, stimulating, or filled with other people. In fact, we might say, even without the melodramatic divide between Pittsburgh on the one hand and an Italian mountain monastery on the other, that the city is the opposite of everything that Salk took for granted about the kind of physical environment that is psychologically optimal for human beings. Second is the idea that it's not simply your cognitive abilities or your mental activity that's affected—it's not only your ability to do stuff—but the actual deep functioning of your mind and brain. In other words, there are physical environments that can, over time, hurt your brain or mind. The built environment, purely by virtue of its physical qualities, could even induce some of the deeply negative, and sometimes fatal, experiences that today we group under the term "mental illness."

Today, a lot of antiurban thinking derives from this notion— that the city is a space that produces mental illness, not only because of its hectic or worrisome social life but because of its actual physical structure. We have moved from a banal claim (that you can do your best scientific thinking in a nice monastic cave) to a harder argument: that the urban environment damages your mind. To counter this effect, it is suggested, we need to radically remake the city into something more psychologically restorative. We need to make it into something quieter, calmer, greener. We need to remake it such that, in truth, it no longer much looks or feels like a city at all.

———

In 2011, in the city of Mannheim, Germany, a group of scientists gave some research volunteers a score based on whether they were living in a city, a town, or a rural area.[11] They put the same people in a brain scanner and gave them a stress task (they had to perform some mental arithmetic while receiving negative feedback from the scientists). What the researchers found was striking: the higher the population of the place where a participant lived, the more likely they were to have increased activity in a brain area called the amygdala while under stress. The amygdala, they pointed out, is associated with a sense of environmental threat and is often involved in anxiety and depression. But they also found something else: if you factored how many years a person had lived in an urban environment up to the age of fifteen, a whole different brain region came into the picture—the perigenual anterior cingulate cortex (pACC), a major part of the limbic system, involved in dealing with chronic social stress. What this means, the researchers suggested, is that you process stress differently if you grow up or live in a city. Growing up in an urban environment, they concluded, has a negative effect on how you deal with stress, which is clearly and quite specifically visible in the brain.

What might cause this, though? *Why* does growing up in a city affect the brain in this way? In Chapter 1, I mentioned a 2019 study by a group of researchers in Aarhus, Denmark, that tried to answer this question.[12] Denmark has a lot of what are euphemistically called "population-based registers," though in reality what this refers to is a huge, and somewhat creepy, state data-gathering exercise that tracks Danes across a range of life events from birth to death, logging their addresses, employment, and so on along the way. This is problematic in various ways, of course, but it's good news for Danish scientists, who can access an amazing dataset on the whole country. The team in Aarhus were able to use these registers to build their own dataset of more than ninety thousand people who were born in Denmark between 1985 and 2003, who were living in the country at age ten, and for whom they were able to access data on mental health, social class, and where they lived (as I said, creepy). Then they did something really clever; they gave everyone a score based on the amount of vegetation near their house when they were kids, which they were able to calculate using old satellite images. Plotting this "vegetation index" against the medical data, they showed that the more green stuff you had near your house as a kid, the less likely you were to be diagnosed with a mental illness in adulthood. They were even able to demonstrate a dose-response relationship: in other words, as the amount of green space went up, the level of apparent protection against mental illness went up in line with it. Not having green space near your house when you're growing up, the authors concluded, is a major risk factor for developing mental illness; in places like cities, where there's less vegetation, there is a specific and urgent need to increase the amount of urban nature in order to reduce rates of mental illness.

Okay, but then another question: what is green space actually doing that's so protective? *This* question was addressed in 2015 by a team of psychologists in Stanford who sent volunteers out for a walk in and around Palo Alto, the very small "urban" area that surrounds Stanford University.[13] Before they went out, the lead scientist, Bratman, gave the volunteers a "resting-state" brain scan—this is an approach to scanning the brain where, unusually, the person being scanned is given no particular task to do, so the scientist can see how different regions interact with one another when the person is "at rest."[14] The team also gave the volunteers a questionnaire to see how prone they were to "rumination." This term means a kind of pervasive, inward-looking concern with why you feel the way you feel, usually with why you feel *bad* a lot of the time. It's a complicated concept—the word "ruminate," meaning to think or overthink, comes from the Latin *ruminatio*, which means (literally) chewing the cud. We call cows ruminants because they chew, swallow, throw up in their own mouths, and then chew it over some more. If you've ever experienced depression, you can probably see the analogy pretty clearly—and in fact, rumination is a style of thought often said to be heavily implicated in depression.

The researchers sent half the volunteers out on a walk around an elevated green path on the Stanford campus—one that regularly features deer and squirrels, from which you can see nearby Mountain View and, in the distance, San Francisco Bay. The other half were sent on a looping walk down El Camino Real, the busiest street in downtown Palo Alto—this, the researchers noted, was noisy from three lanes of car traffic and lined mostly with one- or two-story commercial units. When the two groups came back from their walks, the team did another brain scan and then administered the rumination questionnaire again. The nature group showed less rumination than before they had gone out on their walk—they weren't obsessively turning things over in their minds as much—whereas the urban group showed no change. Rumination has been linked with a brain region called the subgenual prefrontal cortex—a part of the brain often associated with mood and emotional problems. And, just as with the rumination score, the people who had been on the nature walk showed less activity in this brain region than those who had spent time in Palo Alto. We know, the researchers argued, that urbanization is associated with mental illness, and we know that being in contact with nature—or the lack of this contact—has something to do with it. But we don't know *how* this relationship works. Maybe, they suggested, just maybe, rumination is the key. Natural landscapes provide a kind of positive *distraction* that helps people ruminate less. It helps them think less. It helps them let things go.

Well, maybe. But honestly, it's hard to see what a place like Palo Alto or Aarhus tells us about "urban experience" in, say, Dakar or Manila. The idea that the built environment can be imagined to work more or less the same everywhere, is experienced the same way everywhere, seems to miss the complications of culture and history. So, too, does the idea that "vegetation" is an obvious or universal category. Rather than there being some kind of unmediated passage point between, say, a random tree and your literal brain function, there is surely an *awful* lot of filtering going on based on your background, your social class, what literature you've read, what country you grew up in, and what you had for breakfast that day. The city might be a physical space—but it's also a social environment. And this is where things get messy. To understand what's going on here, we need to move to a different level of explanation—we need to look at the history of how neuroscientists have come to think about this problem. And to understand *that*, we need to take a crash course in how rats find their way around mazes.

———

The history of how we have come to understand the modern mind and its relationship to space is, in significant part, the historian Paul Dudchenko once pointed out, a history of how rats learned to find their way around mazes.[15] In 1900 and 1901, a psychologist called Willard Small at Clark University in Worcester, Massachusetts, published two papers under the title "An Experimental Study of the Mental Processes of the Rat."[16] The hard thing about trying to make general psychological observations on rats, Small noted, was that, on the one hand, you wanted to give the animal as much space for free expression of its own desires as possible. On the other hand, you needed to control the conditions sufficiently to compare the actions of one rat to another. Small's solution to this dilemma was to build a maze—or actually several mazes. A maze, he reasoned, was close enough to the rat's preferred environment of underground tunnels; it had enough options, and enough potential for error, for the rat to have to make some decisions and learn to find its own way around. Most importantly, the maze was a space that could be observed, top-down, from a kind of godlike position, as the unfortunate rat's movements were surveilled and recorded by Small and his assistants. He even modeled his maze on the rectangular maze at Hampton Court Place in London—constructing a dense network of blind alleys and cul-de-sacs to be navigated by the (hungry) rats as they tried to make their way to the edible prize at the center.

Small's interest was in animal intelligence and learning. He didn't care about space at all, really. And yet the maze, an ingenious device for doing psychology with rats, almost accidentally established spatial navigation, and the relationship between thinking and the physical environment, at the center of experimental psychology in a way that the discipline has never been subsequently able to shake off.

Put some food in the center of a maze, said the psychologist Edward C. Tolman in a now canonical paper in 1948, and put a hungry rat at the entrance: the rat's going to make a lot of errors, but eventually it's going to find the food.[17] Keep doing this at twenty-four-hour intervals with the same hungry rat, and over time it will make fewer and fewer errors and find the food more quickly. There are two ways to explain this phenomenon. One is a stimulus-response explanation that imagines the rat as a kind of small, furry telephone switchboard, with the sensory system receiving a set of inputs from the external world and the animal's muscles receiving a corresponding set of outputs. In this view, in response to specific stimuli (going down a blind alley, maybe, or getting a strong smell of cheese), the inputs and outputs become better aligned over time, and the signal comes through with more clarity. But Tolman offered an alternative explanation: what if rats weren't like a switchboard at all but instead were like a bunch of people bent over a map, trying to make sense of it? Sure, the rat is clearly receiving sensory information as it works its way around the maze. But what if, instead of these forming a series of individual learned actions at each decision point, the rat's doing something more ambitious? What if it's using all this sensory information to build, inside its head, a *map* of the space—what if the rat is holding together, mentally, some kind of general representation, image, or understanding of what that physical environment is like and how one might move around it?

The rat, in Tolman's view, is not a stimulus-response machine; it is instead looking for the best signals with which to build its map. He described one set of experiments carried out by another psychologist, who created a maze where, in order to get to the food, the rat has to make a series of choices with many different kinds of options (the correct doors might be light or dark, they might be on the left or on the right, and so on). If these options are randomized, then the situation for the rat is impossible. In this case, says Tolman, the rat *hypothesizes*—it first tries all the right-hand doors, or all the light gray ones, or whatever it is. It does not blindly try options but rather attempts to get some kind of systematic hold on the space. In one of his experiments, Tolman trained his rats to follow a single path to a food source that was across a bridge and at a right angle to where the rat began. Having taught them the path, Tolman then changed the setup so that, at a certain point, what had been a simple turn now radiated into a series of ten possible turns. In the majority of cases, the rats chose the path that corresponded most closely to where the food had been the first time around. In other words, the rats were *not following stimuli*; they were navigating to a specific, mapped-out point in space where they expected to find food; they had a sense of the food not as simply being at the end of a tunnel but as located somewhere in an abstract space. The rats were making maps, Tolman famously argued—*cognitive maps* of space. And they were building these maps—as well as storing them—in their brains.

Tolman, one of the major psychological experimenters of the twentieth century, then gets a bit weird. Cognitive maps come in two types, he says. They might be like narrow strips, where an animal has mapped Point A to Point B. Sometimes, though, the rats have a more comprehensive map of the wider space so that when things get moved around, they can adapt more quickly. Rats make bad maps, Tolman says—strip maps that go only from A to B—when their brains are damaged. But sometimes they also work in strips because there are just too many motivations or frustrations in the setup. Consider, says Tolman, a middle-aged woman whose husband has just died; imagine, indeed, a woman who has "regressed (much to the regret of her growing daughters) into dressing in too youthful a fashion and in competing for their beaux." The excess of frustration—he presumably meant sexual frustration—at the husband's death leads to a regression to the much narrower, strip-like map of her situation. Or consider, he says, the "poor Southern whites, who take it out on the negroes [*sic*]." This is also, says Tolman, an example of a "narrowing of the cognitive map"—an inability, produced by an excess of frustration, to grasp the wider territory, to abstractly grasp the complex interrelations between things, as opposed to a simple focus on A and B. But just look at what motivates the rats to be better mappers and better thinkers, he says. Take away excesses of frustration and motivation—feed everyone enough, keep everyone warm—and people will be able to live (here Tolman slips into Freud's language) in line with the reality principle and not the pleasure principle. In the right circumstances, in other words, people are able to understand the complexities of how the world holds together; their internal maps, their frames for making sense of things, become thick, rich, open. We must, Tolman says, "supply our children and ourselves (as the kindly experimenter would his rats) to the optimal conditions of moderate motivation and of an absence of unnecessary frustrations, whenever we put them and ourselves before that great God-given maze which is our human world." Rather like the map in the story by Borges, which expands and expands until it grows bigger than the territory it purports to show, Tolman's cognitive map also ceases to simply be a representation and becomes, instead, a world-making device in its own right. We have, he says, almost a moral duty to train our brains to make better maps—and thereby better worlds.

It's worth remembering that with World War II just ended and the Cold War just beginning, there was a certain liberal idea that postwar psychology should be a *moral* science, one that would contribute to a global movement of American-led peace and reconciliation by showing how man's wilder urges could be tamed. But in this careful (and scientifically unjustified) turning of the map into something of a metaphor, Tolman treated spatial navigation—human beings' cognitive relationship with space, or our capacity to make our way through our environment in a more or less satisfying and nonfrustrating way—as a royal road to human psychology more generally. From now on, environmental navigation would no longer be a rodent-laden backwater in experimental psychology. It would become the basis for an entirely new structure of psychological thought.

By 1970—a little more than twenty years after Tolman's work—the London-based neuroscientist John O'Keefe had been doing single-unit recording experiments on the brains of rats for some time. In single-unit recording, a microelectrode is used to record electrical activity in a single neuron. O'Keefe had developed his own head-mounted microdrive for rats, a system that is attached to the animal's head and through which neurons can be isolated, and their electrical activity recorded, as the animal moves around more or less freely. During a kind of experimental slip-up, O'Keefe started recording cells in the hippocampus and immediately noticed a correlation between the strength of the hippocampal activity and the animal's motor behavior. This was odd. It was widely accepted at this point that the hippocampus had to do with memory. In a now very famous short paper, O'Keefe and his collaborator Jonathan Dostrovsky described what they did next.[18] They anesthetized a bunch of rats, attached microdrives to their heads, drilled holes in their skulls, and passed a series of electrodes into their brains to see what the neurons were doing. Some of these neurons, they realized, responded when the rat was on a particular part of the platform and facing in a particular direction. One of them fired only when the animal was being restrained and faced in a particular direction; another responded to a moving visual stimulus, but again *only* when the rat was on a particular corner of the platform.

The experimenters tried moving the platform around, turning various bits of nearby machinery on and off, adding and removing a curtain around the platform, and so on. None of these did much except the removal of the curtain, at which point the animal behaved as if the environment had totally changed. What they had perhaps found here, O'Keefe and Dostrovsky suggested, was a "spatial reference map" in the hippocampus of the rat. There might be cells, in other words, that fire when you're facing in a particular direction. The hippocampus, in this interpretation, is actually wired to help you find your way through space. O'Keefe referred to these cells as "place cells" and argued that the hippocampus must be the home of the cognitive mapping system that Tolman had proposed a quarter of a century previously. In a book a few years later, he and Lynn Nagel argued that "the hippocampus is the core of a neural memory system providing an *objective* spatial framework within which the items and events of an organism's experience are located and interrelated" (my emphasis).[19] In other words, this framework doesn't simply locate objects relative to an organism's own position but maps an absolute, objective space, independent of the things in it. In the decades that followed, the branch of neuroscience today known as "spatial cognition" grew into an enormous area of research.[20]

Jonas Salk's vague intuition about why some places are better to think in than others, Stanford psychologists sending some students for a walk down a congested street in Palo Alto, John O'Keefe clutching a rat with a hole in its head on a platform in London in 1969—these may seem to be disparate events. But to understand so many of the taken-for-granted ideas in our own time, we need to engage in what the philosopher Michel Foucault called "the history of the present." To understand how buildings and brains might respond to one another, to grasp how the brain has become understood as an organ deeply affected by the space it happens to be in—and what it can see in that space and what direction it is facing within it—we need to follow the trail backward until what *right now* strikes us as obvious, clear, and true seems, once again, weird, disjointed, and new.

"Hugo," I said to the neuroscientist Hugo Spiers, "tell me about London taxi drivers having unusual brains." We were in Hugo's surprisingly poky office in central London, from where he leads the Spatial Cognition Group at University College London (UCL), setting forth on the path established by figures like O'Keefe. We were talking about work by another UCL neuroscientist, Eleanor Maguire, and her collaborators, which has shown that London black-cab drivers, who have to show that they can navigate the city's multilayered tangle from memory, have on average bigger hippocampi than regular people.[21]

"What I think was really important in that study," said Hugo, "is that when Eleanor Maguire, who had the idea, went and did it, she'd read about the fact that certain birds, the ones that store nuts, have a bigger equivalent of the same brain area than the ones that don't store nuts. So there was a kind of story there that this bit of the brain was specialized. But more importantly, squirrels changed the size of the hippocampus with seasons. So in winter, it's bigger—they need to remember where the nuts are—and then it shrinks in summer, when they don't. So there's a real sense in which, if that's true, then when a human has to learn and remember fifty-eight thousand streets [as London black-cab drivers do], surely that should have an effect on your brain."

I asked Hugo, based on what we know about how people navigate and spatially locate themselves in urban areas, what in his view a good city would look like.

"Well, one option," he said, "would be to create an entire grid like Manhattan, and then people just go, 'I'm on First Street. I want to go to Fifty-Sixth Street.' You just go there, but the problem with that sort of thing is the sense of place gets kind of a little bit reduced...you know? Manhattan has got this wonderful uniqueness to it, but in places where it is highly grid-like, there is a kind of monotony to it."

I silently agreed; New York has always struck me as weirdly dull for a city its size.

"It doesn't feel particularly positive for cities that are built on a literal grid," Hugo continued, "and designing like that isn't something you'd want to do. You need a break from the grid to help people get a sense of space, and the way I would help developers do that is by looking at data on the cities that have the best outcomes. Somewhere like Lisbon might be good."

Later, he said, "If you're trying to think about how you're designing a city, the question is, is this just a generic city, or is it going to be a very corporate business-oriented city, or is it going to be a garden city? One thing we know now that you'd certainly want is green space. So London actually does quite well on this. There is a lot of green space here that makes London livable. But there are cities in the world where it's not so good."

We talked a lot about this and about how "green space" might be a more diffuse category than people want to imagine. You can add a wood to an area, Hugo agreed, and some people will love it. You'll see all sorts of benefits from access to green space. But if something like, say, knife crime goes up in that area, then that could quickly override any positive effect. And if there's no one paid to watch or maintain the wood, it will quickly become an unwelcome or unpleasant space. The simple presence of a wood, in itself, doesn't provide anything.

"There are so many variables," he said, "that you could easily give up and say, what's the damn point in looking at the environment and people's psychology?' And I think some people certainly *did* think like that. The field [of environmental psychology] didn't get funding. It was an area of psychology that really dropped away because it wasn't fundable."

We talked about social factors and how the various cities each of us knew well felt very different and distinctive in ways that were not always easy to figure out. "Most neuroscientists don't get into these kinds of things.... It's hard to get funding for that."

I remember at the time being very struck by this—by the contrast between, on the one hand, what were clearly brilliant, even ingenious experimental designs for thinking about how humans experience urban environments at the neurobiological level. And nonetheless, in spite of these incredibly smart, thoughtful people applying themselves to the complexity of it all, that sense that still, *there were so many variables.* That the city, when you really thought about it from a scientific perspective, was just variables upon variables—variables all the way down. How could we ever truly hope to understand, except in the crudest way, the relationship between our minds and our physical environments? How could we even begin to make sense of urban culture and feeling—those often intangible, even inexpressible qualities that are at the heart of any serious psychic connection between a person and a place?

A little while later, I was back in London for a conference on healthy urban design, which was being held at the Royal College of Physicians. Unexpectedly, for the home of a centuries-old institution housed in Regent's Park, among some of London's most stereotypically grand and "traditional" terraces, the Royal College of Physicians is based in a very beautiful modernist concrete building. Designed by Denys Lasdun, perhaps British architecture's most important modernist, the building is composed of a series of large concrete rectangles, increasing in size and overhanging one another as they extend upward—like "an inverted pale ziggurat," as one journalist put it—held up by sometimes alarmingly thin, unadorned square concrete pillars.[22]

I walked through the enormous atrium and up the beautiful wooden staircase that dominates the interior of the building, straight into a talk by Jeremy Myerson, an academic and designer who specializes in inclusive design, especially how design can meet the health needs of older people. City dwellers, Myerson was saying, tend to enjoy a health advantage over others—but this is not evenly distributed.[23] In my notebook, I carefully wrote words like RESILIENCE and FAIRNESS. The city, said the next speaker, the physician Howard Frumkin, is a prototypical urban habitat—I wrote down URBANIZATION—produced by the extraction of fossil fuels and population growth. But today, he went on, cities are increasingly challenging for human health. We need to prepare, Frumkin said, for flooding, heat waves, and water shortages; we need to think seriously about migration and the need to evacuate cities in the future. We need to think about physical activity but also about *happiness*. Here I sat up a bit. What if cities were designed for happiness? Howard Frumkin asked. There is converging evidence, he went on, that promoting happiness means promoting health. And poverty is bad for happiness; in fact, there is a clear connection between happiness, social capital, poverty, and health that could and should be integrated into urban design. Physical activity and nature contact, he said, are major factors affecting health and happiness in the city. BEHAVIORAL ECONOMICS went into my notebook, and SYSTEMS THINKING.

I was taken with the notion that happiness, an emotional state, might be the key to urban health—that it might be the true goal of good urban design. Could this straightforward desire for happiness, the capacity of our built environment to simply make us feel good, be at the heart of the relationship between mental health and the city? The idea that cities are bad for mental health is not new. In the first era of widespread asylum building—at the cusp of the eighteenth and nineteenth centuries—it was noted that a disproportionate number of asylum inmates were urban dwellers and that indeed, activities like farming, walking in the countryside, what we would today call "nature contact," offered these patients potent curative resources. In 1939, two Chicago sociologists, Robert Faris and Warren Dunham, argued that if you think of the city as an ecological space—like a duck pond, say, or the soil beneath a tree—then you can see how different kinds of mental illness map onto its different zones; different forms of schizophrenia, for example, are visible in parts of the "disorganized" city center where men live alone, where they drink, and so on.[24] These two ideas—first, that the city is an ecology and second, that the ecological study of the city is a critical starting point for studying the growth of mental illness in urban areas—would become enormously influential across a wide range of academic disciplines. Today, the relationship between mental illness and city life is a vexed, unresolved question.[25] But the counteridea I was encountering here—that if bad urban design makes people ill, then good design, surely, must have the opposite effect—was new. Newer still was the scientific exploration of what, precisely, that good design might look like. These questions are, of course, similar to the questions asked by people like Ebenezer Howard and William Lever in the previous chapter—and indeed, people in this world sometimes build on the work of those figures quite self-consciously. But the explicit focus on mental health, and especially on happiness, was nonetheless different. I had been reading a book by the Canadian urban thinker and writer Charles Montgomery, who argues that happiness has been the guiding problem of urban thought at least since Socrates dominated the Athenian agora.[26] Happiness and urban form go together, says Montgomery, whether in the public baths of ancient Rome or the private pleasure gardens of eighteenth-century London. Today, though, he goes on, the most important thing we know about how happiness interacts with urban design is to what extent the city connects people—or keeps them apart. "Even though the modern cosmopolitan city makes it easier than ever for individuals to retreat from neighbours and strangers," he writes, citing neuroscientific studies and studies of the hormone oxytocin, "the greatest of human satisfactions lie in working and playing cooperatively with the people." And the city is our most important machine for accomplishing this.

By now it was nearly lunchtime, and bucking the trend as I do, in seeking cooperation or even conversation with others at these kinds of events, I went out to the park to eat my lunch alone. From nowhere, a fox approached me like a dog, clearly looking for some of my sandwich.

"Okay," I said, tearing off a bit, "you can have some—but I'm not counting this either as nature contact *or* mutual cooperation."

Back inside, a slightly wearisome parade of policy wonks, property developers, and messianic architects was underway. There was a lot of talk about human connection, positive behavior, and nudging. I went to a session on workplace health, sponsored by a manufacturer of office furniture, where we were encouraged to get our colleagues involved in their own well-being story; there was general concern about the health effects of loneliness, and in truth, I had begun to feel somewhat lonely myself. HEALTHY PLACEMAKING, I wrote in my notebook, and PARTNERSHIP WORKING—though I didn't really know what this meant. At one point, someone said, "Sitting is the new smoking." Many people talked admiringly about Copenhagen, which I found weird because I had been to Copenhagen several times and thought it just about the most miserable and isolating place I had been in my entire life.

Finally, a medical doctor called Jacob King came on to talk about urban space and mental health, and in particular the need for design interventions that could be measured, clinically, in terms of their mental health outcomes. He talked about recent clinical trials on nature-based psychotherapy that suggested that the more natural an environment, the more attention is restored, and the more stress is reduced. King caveated this by saying that it might not translate everywhere; maybe what we call green space is not good for everyone or wanted in all places—perceptions matter. This question of perception and difference was nagging at me.

The last speaker I saw was a landscape architect called Bridget Snaith, who talked about racism in parks and park design. She pointed out that when we talk about "green space," we often mean "white space." In fact, she said, there's a lot of cultural difference in landscape preference; not everyone has the same fantasy of rolling hills. This was surely true, I thought—I had long believed that the idea that we all have the same low-key fascist desire for some kind of beaux arts City Beautiful was deeply strange. There is a real absence of ethnic minority representation in urban parks discourse, Snaith went on—as well as a weird Eurocentric idea that nature is a particular kind of thing and that loving it is a universal affect.

I'll return to this idea—that green urbanism, whatever else it is, is also sometimes a deliberate strategy of exclusion. But Snaith was pointing to something that had been troubling me for some time, that what I saw as a weirdly antiurban tendency in urban design—the sense that the city is a place of threat and stress and illness that needs to be controlled or repaired—was only partially about the physical environment of the city. Never mentioned explicitly, but, it seemed to me, sometimes in the background nonetheless, were the very diverse kinds of *people* you find in cities—people, that is, who don't always fit a white, heteronormative, suburban ideal of trust and civic virtue.

During my research for this book, I spent a lot of time attending workshops and conferences that are broadly about how the physical environment affects mental health. At some point during every one of these events, usually quite early on, someone—often a civil servant or a policy person—would talk very earnestly about the work of Roger Ulrich. In 1979, Ulrich wrote a paper pointing out that a general assumption we have, that nature is psychologically good for us, was basically untested—everyone was just taking Frederick Law Olmsted's word for it. So Ulrich set out to test it himself.[27] In fine psychological tradition, he took a bunch of students from his own department who had just taken an exam—he took this, perhaps optimistically, as a sign that they would be stressed or alert—then delivered an anxiety test and showed the students some images he'd had made. Half the students were shown images of green, natural, vegetative landscapes, while the other half were shown images featuring only urban scenes. The students were asked to rate how much they liked each image; then Ulrich administered the anxiety test again and asked the students what kind of place they'd grown up in. If you know the genre, there's not going to be much surprise about how this turns out, but remember that Ulrich was then swimming in fairly untested waters. After looking at the images, the urban group reported worsening scores across a range of psychological states, such as sadness, fear and aggression, and attentiveness. In other words, they were angrier and more frightened after looking at images of cities than they had been before. For the nature group, Ulrich found the entirely opposite pattern: these people felt more affectionate and carefree; they reported both their breathing and heart rate going down. "In contrast to the nature scenes," Ulrich concluded, "the urban views tended to work against emotional well-being."

At the end of his paper, Ulrich speculated on some of the possible lessons. Planners, he said, might want to think about adding greenery to urban spaces. But also, he said, maybe people in charge of places where lots of people are *already* pretty stressed—hospitals, for example—should think about how much contact with nature they provide. "Does a pre-operative hospital patient," he asked, "experience less anxiety if his window overlooks a park rather than, say, a motorway or vegetationless parking lot?" Ulrich's subsequent attempt to answer that last question produced perhaps the most influential environmental psychology paper ever published. In this second paper, he described how he collected the medical records of surgical patients who had been assigned to rooms on two different floors in a hospital in Pennsylvania over a ten-year period. On these floors, as it happened, patients were randomly assigned to rooms that had one of two views. From some of the rooms, you could see a nice clump of deciduous trees out the window; from the others, all you got was a bare brick wall.

Ulrich took the records of all the patients who had had gall-bladder surgery *and* been assigned to a room on one of these floors. He then looked at how long each patient had been in the hospital, how much pain relief they had asked for, whether they had asked for tranquilizers for anxiety, and whatever else the nurses wrote down about them. The results were astounding. Patients who could see trees spent fewer days in the hospital, received fewer notes such as "upset and crying" on their charts, asked much less frequently for potent pain drugs, and had fewer postsurgical complications. In the decades that followed, Ulrich developed a large and hugely influential body of research on the relationship between looking at representations of natural, mostly *vegetal* objects and human well-being, especially in relation to health outcomes. His investigations range from research on hospital gardens, to people's passive experiences of plants, to the relationship between interior design and well-being, to the effects of putting up landscape posters in your office for reducing anger, to the benefits of a hospital garden for people visiting relatives in the ICU.[28]

And yet every time I hear someone reverently cite this work, two things immediately strike me—and they seem relevant more generally to how we think about the relationship between space and the mind. One is about time, and the other is about nature. First, *time*. The 1970s and 1980s, in North America, is an era that has come to be associated with so-called urban decay. Whether we take this as a real thing or just a kind of collective moral panic, it's certainly the case that a prominent cultural trope at the time of Ulrich's research was that the city was a dystopian place, a center of danger, crime, and decay, an older form of human habitat that was by then in steep and likely terminal decline.[29] The 1970s was the decade of New York City's seemingly endless "fiscal crisis," with rubbish piling up in the streets and whole city blocks becoming derelict. It was the era of *Taxi Driver* and *Death Wish*. I'm not arguing that Ulrich or any other researcher is promoting or interested in these kinds of ideas about the city. My point is that, nonetheless, this is the unavoidable cultural context in which these scientific ideas are emerging—this is the precise moment, as the urban historian Otto Saumarez Smith put it, when "modernist orthodoxies in approaches to cities began to unravel."[30]

What was at stake here was a larger crisis in a certain vision of twentieth-century urban planning that had been applied—often in quite an unthinking and arrogant way, it's true—to a great many cities in the three decades since World War II. It was the moment when Jane Jacobs's antimodernist 1961 tract, *The Death and Life of Great American Cities*,[31] was becoming ubiquitous among urban intellectuals, when Robert Caro's *The Power Broker*—an unflattering biography of Robert Moses, the New York City urban planner and great adversary of Jacobs—won the Pulitzer Prize.[32] In other words, it was the moment when the utopian assumptions of twentieth-century architecture and urban planning, at least as these were applied to any kind of collective endeavor, started to sink—quite palpably—into the ground.

This isn't to say that all that was happening here was cultural. It's important to note that these findings about nature scenes and well-being do seem to hold up over time, even though that era of imagined decline, in most Euro-American cities at least, is long since ended, and indeed reversed. But I do think it's worth noting that the highly influential literature on how images of urban landscapes make people afraid, sad, stressed, or whatever comes from an era in which the slow death of the city and a kind of generalized, even *libidinal* interest in the submission of entire urban districts to crime, prostitution, etc. were a major part of everyday popular culture. Certainly such an idea of the city likely prevailed in the places where these studies were being carried out and among the populations being studied (i.e., psychology undergraduates), the majority of whom likely transferred directly from their suburban homes to some self-regarding nowheresville of a college town—Amherst, let's say—without pausing much along the way to question any of their own assumptions about life or the physical spaces that both produce and contain it.

Second, *nature*. It is "a clear cut finding in this research," Roger Ulrich wrote in a 1997 contribution to a volume on "biophilia," that there is "a strong tendency for diverse, European, North American and Asian groups, to prefer natural landscapes over urban or built views, especially when the latter lack natural content such as vegetation and water."[33] The term "biophilia" is often associated with Edward O. Wilson, who published a deeply silly book under that title in 1984.[34] The term describes the idea that human beings have an evolved need to be around natural, living things, like plants and animals, and that if this need is not fulfilled, they will quickly become quite ill. As the philosopher Lauren Greyson puts it, biophilia, or at least this version of the concept, "resembles, in suspicious ways, the theories of disenchantment that trace nearly every conceivable ill plaguing the individual and society to the nomad's fall from grace and the rise of civilization."[35] This evolutionary account of humankind's deep need for nature has been widely influential within scientific studies of the relationship between psychology and the environment. It has given weight, for example, to concepts like "attention restoration theory," which suggests that gazing into nature improves concentration.[36] The latter term is widely used within the world of landscape architecture and in studies of the relationship between mental health and place, though meta-analyses of its effects are not exactly overwhelming.[37]

All of this rests either way on some clear-cut notion of what nature actually is. Rachel and Stephen Kaplan are clear in their landmark 1989 text on attention restoration theory that they intend the term "nature" pretty broadly and inclusively. And yet some studies, Roger Ulrich pointed out in his 1997 paper, suggest that this positive effect of natural scenes deteriorates when artificial elements are introduced: "Electrical transmission towers and power lines, large advertising signs or billboards, and prominent concrete or asphalt road surfaces" have a "strongly detrimental effect" on the preference for rustic landscapes. This is where things get tricky. A scene doesn't become unnatural, surely, just because JCDecaux starts advertising cars in the corner of it. Research in environmental psychology consistently shows a preference for vegetation and water, certainly. But much vegetation, of course, is where it is, and looks how it looks, due to quite brutal and highly industrial human manipulation of the soil. Forests grow and regrow in line with the agricultural and economic needs of humans in the vicinity. Water often moves in the direction that humans have made it move. The beautiful rolling landscapes of the English countryside, so called, are actually the product of industrial-scale and human-driven deforestation; your average Cotswold hillside, where wealthy Londoners pay a fortune to go and commune with nature, is, alas, as brute and scarred a scene as any factory floor.

So people can perfectly well have a preference for green fields and rows of vegetation—each to their own in such matters is my policy—but they cannot so easily claim, I think, that what they are preferring here is *nature*. I don't deny that Ulrich and his many collaborators, and the many (many) people working on attention restoration theory, are measuring something useful. I also want to avoid the boring fallacy of imagining that anything shown to be not quite 100 percent natural must, therefore, be social all the way down. But I *do* want to poke, throughout this book, at the idea that what people find restful in vegetative scenery is the presence or suggestion of nature. I want to dig a bit more into the idea that the city unsettles because it is an unnatural place and not, perhaps, because collectively, we have spent some decades telling young and mostly white college students and their parents that the city is, somehow, a dangerous place, a dying place, and, sotto voce, perhaps, also, increasingly, a too diverse place.

This was all becoming kind of heavy, so I decided to go see Dr. Eleanor Ratcliffe, an environmental psychologist who I'd got to know a bit in the early stages of doing research for this book. We had once gone on the same urban nature walk around some of the more industrial parts of east London, and at one point, I looked back and saw Ellie, quite alone and entirely unselfconsciously, hugging a tree. This, I thought, in a sometimes dull world of statistics and outcomes, is my kind of psychologist. Ellie does research on how green environments can be "restorative" for people—in other words, how they can help people recover when superstressed or overwhelmed. In contrast to some of the experimental work that uses dodgy mobile brain devices, her way of thinking about these topics has always struck me as especially nuanced and alive to complexity.

It's definitely the case, she told me, "that a lot of the environments that are quite stressful, that tax us mentally, have a lot of distractions in them. So an example I often give in my lectures is being at Waterloo Train Station in London. There are so *many* stimuli going on, there are tannoys, and people, and you're trying to find out what time a train is leaving and where the ticket machine is. So there's this hectic auditory and spatial information that's overloading you. Whereas very often restorative environments, like nature, have rather little going on, or what's going on is doing so in quite a slow, measured way. Maybe the leaves are moving or there's a pattern of light on water or birds singing. But these stimuli, these properties in the environment, are not too demanding. And that gives people an opportunity to rest mentally."

We talked a bit about urban versus rural environments and what it might mean not just to compare the two but to compare, say, an urban scene and a hillside that were both considered beautiful. The thing is, though, said Ellie, it's not really *nature* that matters. "Nature has certain positive properties," she went on, "that in some circumstances can help people recover cognitively. Nature isn't cognitively demanding. And very often, the kind of nature that people go to is calming, so it's not threatening—it's very beautiful and it's quiet, so all of these things are conducive to relaxation and stress recovery."

But, she pointed out, there's also a cultural element, as "people associate nature with feeling good." She said, "We're told so much that, 'Oh, you know, go outside'; it's almost like the fetishization of nature, in my opinion. I'm not trying to say that nature isn't good for people, but I think perhaps the claim that there's something magical or special about nature might be a bit overblown. It's just another type of environment. It just so happens that it's a lot more calming."

What was she saying, I asked—that it's more of a cultural thing that we find green spaces calming?

"It's not that the effect isn't real," she said, "but we have all learned that, you know, nature is good for you and makes you feel calm, so *of course* when you go into nature, yes, you really do feel calm."

Then she said, "No one just sits and is exposed to an environment. I mean, I'm sitting in my flat at the moment, and one of the reasons I decided to rent this flat is that it has a really long garden, which reminds me of my childhood garden. So when I saw this garden, I wasn't just being 'exposed' to it; I had these memories of other gardens that I'd known, and I felt good about it because I was thinking about these past memories. And I believe that there is this role of people constructing their experience of what might be a restorative environment using their expectations, their memories, and their past experiences."

This example really struck me. To be a bit simplistic about it, the question I had been turning over in my mind for some time was whether the supposed calming effect of nature—which *I* had never felt, at least—was real. Maybe it was a simple prejudice, but I just wasn't at all convinced that the simple presence of grass and trees could truly have what sounds like, in all truth, a quasi-religious, even transcendental effect on nearby humans. My suspicions were at least partly because I found the most common explanation for why this would be—which is that humans evolved in the African savanna and are naturally driven to seek out environments that somehow reproduce this early experience—kind of laughable, a child's fairy story for weak-minded evolutionary psychologists who believe in "biophilia." But speaking to Ellie reminded me that this was the wrong way to think about it. The issue isn't whether the effect is real—if enough people say they feel the effect, it's real, and that's the end of it. The issue is whether the effect is caused by some *inherent* quality of natural materials, some physical property of trees and grass that just makes people feel good, or if instead it's caused by a cultural expectation. The physical places that we find relaxing turn out to be exactly the physical places that we've been told, for our entire lives, *should* relax us.

In the same way, the spaces that *don't* relax us, that we often find stressful, and that can even sometimes stress us so much that we become ill are also spaces that our culture has long held up as threatening and scary. Of course it's true that cities really are cognitively demanding in some way—they really are often noisy and filled with distracting stuff. But it's also true that we experience these spaces after a lifetime spent being bombarded by what the historian William Cronon calls "the symbolic conventions of the dark city"—we are primed for that stress because we are surrounded by simple-minded cultural narratives about the terrible things that might befall us in urban space.[38] This is a scientific problem—how can you control for such cultural priming when you design an experiment?—but it's a political and a moral problem, too. At a certain point, rather than simply planting green things everywhere, we might need to confront the prejudices and fantasies—racist fantasies, certainly, but also fantasies of class, a disgust at having to encounter visibly unwell or unhoused people, and just plain old free-floating xenophobia and nativism—that have rendered the city such an object of fascinated horror. Maybe it's not "the city" that's making us ill after all. Maybe instead of trying to fix "the city," we could try to fix ourselves and the weird, often quite racist, antiurban public culture that we've allowed to flourish, unchecked, since the last few decades of the twentieth century. In particular, we might learn to think a bit more critically about that great symbol of antiurbanism, whose presence now marks all kinds of strange hopes and desires for better city-making. I am talking, of course, about the urban tree.

CHAPTER 4

The Conquered City

In the autumn of 2020, as the UK emerged from public health restrictions that had seen most shops closed for some time, Westminster City Council—the authority responsible for London's retail-led West End—figured it needed to do something. It wanted to entice people back to the shops and shout out that the city was open again. What the West End needed, the council decided, was a bold new visitor attraction at the less used, slightly grimier end of Oxford Street, near the Marble Arch. So it hired a Dutch architecture firm, MVRDV, which had recently built a giant stairway in the firm's home city, Rotterdam. For London, MVRDV came up with a "hollowed out mountain," a temporary green structure that would loom over Oxford Street's crappy chain stores and restaurants, and "demonstrate the need to add nature to cities."[1] There would be plants, soil, sedum, and forty-five trees across the top of the new structure. Inside, there was to be a "dancing light show that simulates the interconnected root structure of a birch tree forest." The idea was that people would pay to walk up this temporary urban hill, take in the view, and then come back down through the forest experience in the structure's interior. The Mound, said MVRDV—this was the structure's unhappy name—would "encourage Londoners to rethink the area and question why they allowed a former green spot became [sic] surrounded by traffic."[2]

In February 2021, the project was announced to the public, with an artist's impression showing a small grassy hill near the actual Marble Arch. Designed by the Regency architect John Nash in 1827, once the triumphal entrance to Buckingham Palace, today just another sad imperial relic on a traffic island. The Mound tried to somewhat rectify this indignity by connecting the arch to nearby Hyde Park. It would create a "grassy knoll," said the London Evening Standard approvingly, "with mature trees and a walkway to a viewing gallery."[3] In July, the Mound opened to visitors; almost immediately, a Twitter user called Dan Barker[4] posted a long, detailed thread of his visit, for which he had paid £6.50. Barker described the Mound as like being in "the inside of a 25m enormous scaffold, dotted with a few trees." There was an "emptyish storage area," he said, as well as "rubble" and "random cables scattered about." His Twitter thread, carefully dotted with photos of what really did look like a forlorn building site, went viral. Other damning photos of a weirdly brown and treeless fake hillock quickly appeared on social media. Within days, Westminster City Council offered refunds to anyone who had paid to visit the Mound and announced that the attraction would be free until it got up to scratch.[5] In August, with the Mound still not complete, it was revealed that the reported cost of £2 million had risen to £6 million. The deputy leader of the council resigned.[6] By September, the *Guardian* was reporting that the Mound was "drawing crowds keen to see how bad it is."[7] One news outlet called it "London's worst ever tourist attraction" and "a literal mound of dirt."[8]

Finally, in January 2022, bowing to the inevitable, Westminster City Council announced the Mound's hasty closure. An internal report described the episode as "devastating."[9] On its own website, MVRDV said that the Mound "had been left to rot" in the middle of Oxford Street. "As a practice," they said, "we have rarely seen such a loveless execution of our designs." In a final indignity, the art magazine *Frieze* published an "interview" with the Mound by the writer Huw Lemmey, who depicted his subject as crying self-pityingly into a tissue. "I thought I could have meant something," Lemmey ventriloquized the Mound. "Originally, I was supposed to consume the Marble Arch, smothering a symbol of petty human triumphalism. Nature is Healing, you see."[10]

"Nature is healing" was indeed a phrase that had become popular with a certain kind of environmentally minded commentator during the COVID-19 pandemic. It captured an idea that with urban centers temporarily abandoned, the natural, nonhuman world might take the opportunity to "heal" itself—thus implicitly healing us humans, too, physically and morally. Social media was flooded with fake images of dolphins and swans reclaiming the canals of Venice as humans were corralled indoors. At best, this idea represented a kind of naive environmentalism and formed a neat vehicle for the low-budget moral goods (city bad, nature good) in which a lot of popular environmental thinking trades. At worst, it revived the idea most famously associated with the Georgian-era economist Thomas Malthus: that for an overpopulated human world to achieve its natural equilibrium, a lot of people will simply have to die—that, indeed, it might be better if they would get on with their dying sooner rather than later. This is, perhaps, a lot to burden the poor Marble Arch Mound with. But the monument was, quite explicitly, in its own terms, an imposition of "nature" on the city. It was an attempt to somehow fix urban space by turning at least part of one iconic commercial street into a forest. Its decrepitude was, in this sense, oddly instructive; in its physical and ideological abjection, in literally showing us the crudely scaffolded dirt that undergirds so much "urban nature," the Mound offered an unusually naked, unflattering glimpse of a set of ideas and intuitions—about nature, and trees, and parks, and humans—that have become incredibly powerful in urban planning and architecture.

One of these intuitions is that human society is somehow not well—literally and figuratively. We are overproducing and overconsuming; we are becoming fat, hateful, and immoral. We eat too many snacks, and use too many plastics, and spend too much time online, burning up the ever scarcer resources of our precious earthly home—so goes the familiar lament. But the suggestion is also that we are not well in the sense of physical disease: our bad lifestyle, our distance from traditional modes of production, our up-close jangly mode of urban living, our shopping and our discarding, our ill treatment of chickens and cows, all of it creates illness—not only the so-called lifestyle diseases of modern living, like diabetes, but also infectious diseases, as new viral pathogens get bred and spread in an ever more intensely industrialized, tightly connected world. And finally, this thinking goes, we are not well in the sense of mental distress; all this making and consuming, the buying and the throwing away, far from being a joyful act of willful destruction is actually really *stressful*; the work we have to do to keep it all going is miserable; and the artificial cities we have to live in to contain it are noisy, smelly, and forbidding. We live in "an age of excess," says the Indian writer and scholar Sumana Roy in *How I Became a Tree*, "more food and clothes and houses and things than we needed, an extravagant show of wealth and emotions." The trees, by contrast, have things figured out. "Who has ever seen a tree," Roy says, "and exclaimed, 'Such a jealous tree!' the way we do about children in the playground and adults in the auction hall." Hence, for Roy, the fantasy of transformation: "I wanted that confidence of the tree, the complete rejection of all that made humans feel inferior or superior."[11]

Trees, then, are imagined as an ideal solution to the cultural, psychological, and moral degeneracy of the city. Trees can *heal* modern and urban life—or so it is thought. They can heal in a scientific sense but also in a spiritual one. They can help to resolve our internal anxieties as individual people, but they can also intervene in our collective failures as a society. You can, then, see how one very compelling solution to the multiple urban crises of our times arises: plant more trees. Doing so—if we are to believe a UK government press release celebrating "Tree Week" in 2021—will in one swoop make "our towns and cities safer, healthier and more pleasant places to be, helping boost people's wellbeing as well as contributing towards efforts to tackle climate change."[12] Planting trees would transform the spaces we live in. It would give more room to nature and improve the earth's atmosphere. It would cool cities down and increase biodiversity. People could get out to visit the trees, which would relax them a lot. Spending time tree planting and tree tending would also mean less time buying stuff and watching pornography. And people *like* trees. They're big and charismatic. They're shady. They make humans feel good about themselves. Even as pitiless and desiccated a figure as Donald Trump has been seduced, having announced, in 2020, that the US was going to plant a trillion trees.[13] "Nobody's against trees," Marc Benioff, the internet billionaire behind this scheme, told an audience in Davos, Switzerland. "The tree," he said, is "a bipartisan issue."[14] A year before, the esteemed academic journal *Science* had published a paper showing that there was room on the earth for another "0.9 billion hectares" of tree canopy, which could store 205 gigatonnes of carbon.[15] People went crazy. Companies started buying up farmland in all kinds of random places to plant trees. It got so bad that the lead scientist on the paper had to go on the news to tell people to stop—such fevered tree planting risked actually damaging biodiversity as well as reducing space for farmland.[16]

So this was the context in which Westminster City Council—whose beat, I stress, is the most built-up and commercial part of the largest, busiest city in Europe—wanted to spend £6 million on a hill and put a bunch of trees on top. This, truly, would be an act of collective healing. The Mound, said the *Guardian*'s architecture critic, much like New York's High Line or the oak-topped Torre

Guinigi in Tuscany, was an attempt "to harness the charm and power of the elevated tree."[17] In fact, as Ali Karimi wrote in *Architectural Review*, it was just one of several tree-related public installations in European cities that year. These also included a temporary forest in the courtyard of London's Somerset House and another forest planted in the center of a football stadium—originally built by the far-right leader Jörg Haider—in the unhappy Austrian city of Klagenfurt. The problem, said Karimi, is that in a temporary installation, "the tree is inevitably objectified and performative, able to raise questions but unable to be a tree."[18] This seems to me not quite right, though. Because to be a tree today surely *is*, precisely, to be a performer. The urban tree is *not* an unfortunate natural object placed in an unforgiving new context—like a country rube from some bad nineteenth-century novel, torn from its innocent state and made to dance for pennies in the big city. In fact, the Mound, insofar as it accidentally revealed the urban forest as a kind of construction site, as something built out of rubble, electrical wiring, and metal poles, was perhaps more accurate than it knew. Objectification of the tree is not an unfortunate side effect of these projects. Objectification, as far as trees are concerned, is the whole point.

Because the tree is, as much as it is anything else, a cultural object. It's a human object for telling stories about ourselves and the world we think we're creating. One useful way to think about trees, then, is not to focus so much on their ecology or their environmental role, but instead to work to understand why they're suddenly so visible everywhere—in literature, election campaigns, architecture, visual arts, health, and so on. Maybe this sounds melodramatic, but I've been struck by a kind of *treeification* of wider culture over the last few years, especially in relation to our ideas about the urban environment and more especially *still* in relation to our ongoing desire for collective and individual repair in and through that environment. It's as if, all of a sudden, there is no problem of the built or physical or social environment that might not be solved by a well-planted oak, no personal crisis that cannot be fixed by leaning into a sturdy yew or beech. The problem is that, like all cultural objects, trees are complicated—they tell more than one story. Trees can represent a certain naive idea of healing and connection with nature. But they also stand in for something harder—they can represent a nostalgia for some more primitive age; they can make petty human feelings and hopes secondary to the timeless processes of nature; they can represent a world that is not only "more than human," as my colleagues in the geography department like to say, but also distinctly antihuman, too.

Consider the sheer number of ways that trees are imagined to fix modern life—and, in particular, modern urban life. In 2021, the UK government sought applications to its "Urban Tree Challenge Fund," a £10 million scheme to plant 130,000 new trees in towns and cities across England.[19] In a press release, the government said that the trees would be focused on deprived areas. Someone from Slough Council effused that the fund would allow the council to "focus on upskilling for employment, active lifestyles, citizen science and volunteering." It really seems hard to know what a tree has to do with "upskilling for employment," but then, that's the point: there is nothing a tree can't do. In Wales, the government has planted a tree for every child born in the country since January 1, 2008, and—somewhat randomly and perhaps problematically—since April 2014 has planted another in Uganda as well. The aim of this, the Welsh government says, "is to create publicly accessible woodland, build a stronger connection between children, families and their natural environment and engage with local communities."[20]

It gets worse: in late 2021, an eccentric initiative called "The Queen's Green Canopy" surfaced, which urged people to "plant a tree" to mark Queen Elizabeth II's diamond jubilee; plans were also announced to "identify 70 Ancient Trees to celebrate Her Majesty's 70 years of service." The patron of this strikingly feudal initiative was the queen's eldest son, Prince Charles (as he was then). The campaign partnered with the government Department for Environment, Food and Rural Affairs as well as the Royal Horticultural Society. Its "platinum sponsors" included noted environmental leaders such as McDonald's, Coutts Bank, and Rentokil.

On Sundays, I sometimes go into my local chain bookshop and take surreptitious photographs of the latest nonfiction books about trees—there's *The Wood* by John Lewis-Stempel, *Wildwood* by Roger Deakin, *The Wood for the Trees* by Richard Fortey, *The Hidden Life of Trees* by Peter Wohlleben, and its follow-up, *The Heartbeat of Trees*—neither of which is to be confused with either Colin Tudge's book, *The Secret Life of Trees*, or Thomas Pakenham's *The Company of Trees*. For children, there's *The Tree: An Environmental Fable* by Neal Layton. For lovers of adult fiction, there's Richard

Powers's Pulitzer Prize–winning novel *The Overstory*, a novel about lots of different people whose lives are inextricably bound up with trees ("a big novel that tells us as much about trees as *Moby-Dick* does about whales," says the *Times*—though it's unclear whether this is intended as recommendation or warning).[21] For people who prefer audio, there's the BBC's big-budget podcast ecothriller, *Forest 404*, the story of a treeless future dystopia in which human beings' awareness of their unconscious arboreal nature is triggered by an illicit recording of the Amazon rainforest.

In 2019, Singapore's Changi Airport opened "Jewel," a four-story indoor forest, complete with a waterfall, a hotel, three thousand trees, and early check-in facilities.[22] In the same year, Stefano Boeri, an Italian architect already famous for his Bosco Verticale in Milan—two residential towers lined up and down with more than nine hundred trees—proposed a new "Forest Stadium" to replace the dilapidated San Siro football ground, "in which trees surround the field and the stands and living nature becomes the protagonist of the football experience and a new urban landscape, for all citizens."[23] Still, in 2019, in the middle of a bruising election campaign, keen to distract voters from a growing scandal about his youthful enthusiasm for blackface, Justin Trudeau tweeted, "We'll plant 2 billion trees over the next ten years. That's it. That's the tweet."[24] In 2018, a student campaign began at the University of Sussex to switch the institution's default search engine to Ecosia, a Germany-based internet search organization that donates 80 percent of its profits to reforestation organizations. "You search. We Plant" is its slogan.[25] In November 2021, a green fintech firm called Tred launched a Mastercard debit card made from recycled ocean plastic, which allows the user to "plant trees as you spend."[26] I could keep going.

All of this cultural attention to trees as objects of collective rehabilitation also seems somehow linked to a political and economic period in which the environmental activists Extinction Rebellion staged a surprisingly successful intervention in a range of global cities; in which reassembled fascist organizations are suddenly very interested in their respective nations' natural ecological heritage;[27] and in which Amazon founder Jeff Bezos, an almost too-cartoonish idea of the corporate villain, is retooling his Blue Origin aerospace company to advance a very real scheme to abandon the earth for a wooded simulacrum in outer space.[28]

It's certainly understandable that, as the specter of climate disaster comes ever nearer and the looming obliteration of much that currently exists on this planet becomes less deniable, a certain kind of lament for the tree, a kind of libidinal woody *desire*, might seep into the wider culture. And with this fear, sure, there might come a growing suspicion of industrial and urban life, and the destructive economic logic of capitalist growth, whose major piece of supporting infrastructure is, it's true, *the city*.[29] You could, on this basis, interpret the cultural preeminence of trees as simply a rational response to climate change and the economic model that produces it. And yet the London Mound was, as various commentators have noted, at best an *idea* of a woodland—it was foresting as plaintive artistic gesture rather than tree planting as serious ecological action. Maybe there's an intended pedagogical logic here. One can imagine, perhaps, busy shoppers by the Marble Arch, clutching their Primark and Zara bags, brought up short, suddenly reminded of some other, less consumption-oriented life as Westminster Council's dirty Mound looms at them from the horizon. I don't find this plausible, but I can see how other people might.

But I can't stop wondering whether there isn't also something less obvious, something perhaps more *psychological*, going on in this sudden intense collective attention to trees and green spaces. Maybe it's simply guilt about deforestation and an attempt to expiate our past sins, but I'm inclined to think of it as a kind of transference: how else can you explain the fact that the thing we're wantonly destroying, and destroying to the point of our own ecological crisis, is also somehow imagined as the very source of our cultural and psychic salvation? Something is happening in the woods, and it's not simply healing. "The city is our superego," says the writer Luke Turner in his memoir of cottaging in Epping Forest, "rendered in bricks and mortar, concrete and glass. In the forest the id cavorts under the pollards."[30]

Let's take this metaphor one step further and do what any good therapist would do—let's go back to the beginning of things, to where the trouble with trees first started.

In 1607, an uprising against the practice of enclosure blew up in Northamptonshire and quickly spread to the neighboring counties of Warwickshire and Leicestershire.[31] Initially, a landlord called Thomas Tresham erected a series of fences and borders around what had been common grazing land. A crowd of a thousand people descended on the land, dug up the fences, and camped there in what became the first of a series of uprisings against enclosure across the three counties. Among the leaders of this short movement was one "Captain Pouch" (real name John Reynolds), who claimed to derive supernatural powers from a pouch he kept at his side. Eventually, the uprising was put down in bloody fashion by the local gentry's private army; various leaders of the rebellion were hung, drawn, and quartered, with pieces of their dismembered bodies displayed around nearby towns. When Reynolds himself was executed, his famous pouch was found to contain only a small lump of local cheese.

In the wake of these grim events, an agricultural writer called Arthur Standish, much disturbed by what had taken place, spent some years traveling around the affected areas, speaking to people about what had led to the uprising. In the larger sense, what was going on was the emergence of agricultural capitalism—the gradual move away from a communal if somewhat inefficient feudal "open field system" and the development of land into a more intensive, private factory for the production of animal protein and grain, which could then be sold on the open market. A major additional cause of this disturbance, according to Standish, was the high price of fuel brought on by excessive felling of trees. This in turn was at least partly motivated by the needs of the growing glass and iron industries (both of which, requiring consistently very high temperatures, are extremely wood intensive).[32] In 1613, Standish published his *New Directions of Experience…for the Planting of Timber and Fire-wood*, setting out "some projects for the increasing of Woods, the decay whereof in this Realme is universally complained of."[33] In his book, addressed to the king,

Standish provided an ecological solution to a political crisis: he proposed growing more trees to bring fuel prices down as well as to provide food for the peasantry in the form of fruit.[34]

Enclosure was certainly a kind of political violence, but in making sense of this violence, the historian Joan Thirsk pointed out, Standish called the reader's attention to a different set of environmental objects and practices: to soil, the use of lime, and the proper distance between trees. Maybe, then, our own interest in trees isn't just some recent development. Maybe there are long-forgotten events, buried deep in the political and ecological history of the planet, arguments and visions that can be traced back to specific cultural and scientific projects that connect us, anxiously, to trees and to forests. Maybe, indeed, there really are good and long-standing reasons that we simply find the increasingly treeless city to be an alienating, frightening place.

Certainly, fear of tree scarcity was a perennial issue in many European countries up to the nineteenth century. As early as 1534, the English jurist Sir Anthony Fitzherbert published his *Boke of Husbandrie*,[35] an agricultural text that issued various stern lectures on the proper management of wood in and around the manorial farm—including how to carefully cut wood from trees without killing them or doing them great damage. Centuries later, Karl Marx devoted several newspaper columns to a new German law that overrode common rights to wood gathering and treated the taking of wood as a felony theft.[36] Indeed, Marx's very first example of commodity fetishism in *Capital* was the production of a table from wood "furnished by nature."[37] Perhaps, though, the single most influential arboricultural text from across these centuries is John Evelyn's *Sylva*, a work first delivered to the Royal Society—Evelyn was one of the society's founders—in 1662. As might perhaps be expected from one of his age's foremost diarists, Evelyn's *Sylva* is still strikingly readable today. The text mixes pastoral dreaminess and hard-nosed husbandry as well as serious advice on the growth and management of specific tree varieties. Evelyn provides lines of poetry, moments of whimsy, and frequent literary and philosophical allusions. At one point, he breaks off to consider what wood Christ's cross would have been made from, and, having considered the various sources and claims, concludes that—surely—only English oak would have been able to constrain a dying God.[38]

At the heart of the book, though, is a species-by-species account of the trees of England—in their physical description and taxonomy, their growth and development, the soils they prefer, how best to lop them, whether and how they might be transplanted, and what their timber might be good for. Evelyn, a committed royalist, was writing amid the restoration of the English monarchy in 1660, and he emphasized the need to replant woods and forests that had been destroyed during the civil war. Just as, for Standish, forest depletion marked the social and economic decay of early capitalism, so was tree planting, for Evelyn, the mark of England's revival—specifically, the revival of its king—in the wake of internal conflict. In both cases, amid the political tumult of early modernity, the tree was imagined as a *restorative* objective; its serene and regal branches signify social harmony, monarchy, order.

Indeed, as the literary scholar James C. McKusick points out, though Evelyn had a serious and utilitarian purpose in his concern for the military consequences of so much forest depletion, his project also had an imaginative, perhaps we might say *ideological* bent.[39] What Evelyn was creating was nothing less than a new vision of the woods—in which trees are not only natural objects but political and moral figures too. Evelyn, says McKusick, gave the English "a new way of seeing forests," not only as economic assets but also as aesthetic markers of the nation, as the bearers of an "intrinsic sacred character" that needs to be preserved. Here is the nation, then, made sturdy by its canopy of mighty oaks, and here, too, its grateful subjects, like the small creatures of the forest floor, secure in the shelter of these great and regal plants. Here, finally, it seems to me, is how we should read the tree as a moral tale that offsets the shock and violence of a modern, capitalist, republican, and increasingly *urban* world.

In one sense, then, you could read the Mound, and the Queen's Green Canopy, and Donald Trump's trillion trees, and idiot venture capitalists buying farmland in various rural parts of the globe, and all the rest of it as—okay—stupid but also unremarkable. Nonsense as it is, this is simply the continuation of a centuries-old tradition of lamenting the loss of trees, and in particular lamenting their loss to creeping industrialization, urbanization, and colonization. "Cad a dhéanfaimid feasta gan adhmad?" goes a famous Irish-language lament from the late eighteenth century, as English landlords, with no interest in the ecology of their landholdings, stripped the woods from their ill-gotten estates: "Tá deireadh na gcoillte ar lár." "What will we do now for timber," in Eiléan Ní Chuilleanáin's translation, "with the last of the woods laid low?"[40] Deforestation, we might say, is a kind of anxious underbelly of modernity; the tree is the absent presence through which the costs and ambivalences of "progress" are registered.

This isn't quite right, though. Because something changed in the nineteenth and twentieth centuries. Partly this had to do with the scale of deforestation. In his field-defining 1975 book, *Trees and Woodland in the British Landscape*, the ecologist Oliver Rackham pointed out that while up to 1945 there had been a sustained but gentle increase in tree loss, thereafter things went off a cliff: "The next thirty years," he wrote, "were a time of unprecedented destruction of ancient woodland." In this period alone, in fact, about half of Britain's woodland simply ceased to exist. This was a different order of problem, but also a different *kind* of problem, than that faced by people like Arthur Standish and John Evelyn. For them, anxiety about tree loss was in large part a question of economic and military sustainability: in an early-modern economy heavily reliant on timber for fuel, no longer having access to trees might prove grievous indeed. What haunts *us*, though, are not so much economic but rather geological forces—in particular, human-caused climate change as described by that new epoch to which we have given the lamentable name "the Anthropocene." The relationship between trees and cities, or between forests and industries, once operated in a broad sphere of economic rationality; there were costs and benefits to tree loss, after all. In more recent centuries, as the trees have become scarcer, the cities wider, the economies larger, and the planet warmer, things have taken a more historical, psychological, and even metaphysical turn.

This way of thinking has many roots. But one of the thicker ones leads us back to the American environmentalist and polymath

George Perkins Marsh and his magnum opus, *Man and Nature*, first published in 1864.[41] "There is good reason to believe," Marsh wrote, "that the surface of the habitable earth, in all the climates and regions which have been the abodes of dense and civilized populations, was, with few exceptions, already covered with a forest growth when it first became the home of man." Marsh was not only convinced of the earth's secret history as a forest; he also advanced an account of how we might see a new kind of historical relationship between politics and ecology, between depleted forest environments and urban civilizations long since gone; in his view, the fall of the Roman empire was in good part due to the Romans' destruction of their surrounding woodlands.[42]

Man and Nature was, in its day, an enormously influential account of how humans have impacted the earth, and with what consequences for human society. The story of "man and nature," for Marsh, was in large part a story of deforestation. Working with the evidence he had to hand—the deep presence of forests in ancient writings and "primitive art," the remains of trees in soil—he concluded that extensive tree cover had to be the earth's original and natural state. It was only when early humans started to exhaust the sparse tracts of plain and savanna in their immediate environment that they began to expand into the forested areas and to cut the trees. "The destruction of the woods," said Marsh, "was man's first geographical conquest, his first violation of the harmonies of inanimate nature." The need to create space for agriculture—and the happy coincidence that a burned-down forest provided not only space but also excellent soil for agricultural production—was the first disaster. Later came the lumber trade, sea navigation, and the need for wood for ships; then came population growth and the need to burn more wood to keep more people warm and fed. Cutting down trees, indeed, became a symbol of progress and modernity; in France and other European countries, says Marsh, the forest—originally a space demarcated for the king to hunt—became a site of gleeful destruction in revolutionary times.

Marsh was far from the first person to note the geographic and environmental importance of the forest. Nonetheless, he formalized and systematized that knowledge in a way that made forest ecology a central subject within the new science of geography (the American Geographical Society had been founded a decade earlier, in 1851). More importantly, though, in Marsh's work, we find not only an early version of forest science but also the awakening of a modern forest *ideology*—the sense that the planet was *forest first*; that everything after has been a process of geological and moral diminution; and that, in the end, all of human society might amount to little more than a small and short-lived incursion on the planet of trees. For Marsh and his contemporaries—this was also the era of figures like Thoreau and Emerson—trees, as nature, represented an age of innocence, an era of "semi-primitive" goodness, as the literary critic Leo Marx would later put it.[43] And this historical perspective came laden with a future promise—that in spite of the world we have made for ourselves, we might yet reclaim that innocence through the planting and cultivation of the forest.

This idea relies on a view of nature—awesome, inhuman, increasingly under threat—that had become widespread and mainstream only with the emergence of the Romantic movement at the tail end of the century that preceded Marsh. That movement, as it found itself (quite literally) overrun by the outgrowth and effluvia of the nineteenth century's exploding industrial cities, for the first time created something approaching a shared environmental consciousness. Campaigns and protests sprang up—in the Lake District around Manchester, for example. Quite suddenly, a new moral and aesthetic vision was available—a vision that, as the environmental historian Harriet Ritvo points out, could claim a global human stake in the care and protection of the natural environment.[44] Nature—that wet and leafy stuff outside the city—was not only now identifiable as a kind of a thing, as it was for the Romantics, but was also now a *political* thing. Nature was suddenly something to be argued over, defended, and legislated.

This cultural and political vision was bolstered, finally, by a new kind of biological thinking: as the nineteenth century turned into the twentieth, a range of different disciplines—botany, anatomy, and agricultural science among them—started to come together under a new master term, "ecology." In the work, first, of the German naturalist (and proto-Nazi)[45] Ernst Haeckel and later in the writings of the British zoologist Charles Elton and his contemporaries, a new science of plants' and animals' "physiological responses to the physical properties of [their] surroundings"[46] made it possible to understand humans and their environments as deeply intertwined. The question of whether one should live in the countryside or live in the city had become both a serious and a pressing question. It *mattered*, suddenly—philosophically and scientifically—whether you made your life among trees or among chimney stacks. And it began to matter finally, and more than a century later, to me.

———

"We evolved," said our guide, "for, some say, up to two million years living in the forest. And then for the last three hundred years, we've moved to these urban cities. And then everybody's health deteriorated." It was early in November, and my research assistant, Ruth Sharman, and I were in the middle of a wood near the picturesque village of Tintern in the Wye Valley, South Wales. It was a cold, wet morning, and I don't know about Ruth, but in the moment, I felt, if anything, rather keen on the benefits of urban modernity and its various comforts. I kept this opinion to myself, however. We had come to Wales to meet Tom Court, a forest-bathing guide who operates out of a small farmhouse hidden on a wooded hillside not far from the town of Chepstow. Tom had agreed to take me and Ruth on a meditative, sensory walk through the forest—an experience that included, to our shared alarm, encouragement to walk barefoot along the wet forest floor. As thick leafy mulch squeezed in between our toes, Tom told us that we were actually on an old Roman path through the woods that went on to the ruined ancient city of Trellech and eventually, via a pilgrimage route, to St. David's—once the ancient capital of Wales, now a tiny and forgotten city at the edge of a faraway peninsula, jutting forlornly into the Irish sea. "This sensory connection," Tom said, walking nimbly ahead in his own bare feet, "helps us to trigger our sixth sense: our whole self, our electrical connections, our inner savage, as we call it in Wales. We're trying to activate that animal instinct. We're trying to become more animalistic because we then stop using our thinking brain, where we store all the stress and mental problems." We had walked for some hours through the woods, occasionally stopping to rub ferns or yew leaves between our fingers, breathing deeply from our hands to take in the surprisingly sharp and bright smell of the forest. We stopped to look at blown-over pine trees, bright red arsenic-laden yew berries, small rows of yellow coral mushrooms, and just once—Ruth found this—a tiny germinating acorn, lying wet and silent not far from its presumably hopeful mother.

I had contacted Tom because I wanted to get close to something I had first heard a couple of years previously, when I had seen Dr. Qing Li speak in Athens, which I thought might help me understand the widespread desire to have more trees in urban space—Shinrin-yoku, or forest bathing. These were terms I had started to come across more and more as I moved around events on urban greening, spoke to more planners and architects, and read through research on stressed and anxious urban humans. Forest bathing, though it had initially sounded to me like a sort of benignly new age, if slightly bourgeois practice—to be put in the same box as reflexology or "wild swimming," maybe—actually loomed large in the world of people who were trying, in all seriousness, to make contemporary cities less bad for their inhabitants. And their vision wasn't just of a nice, pretty, crowd-pleasing kind of thing (who doesn't like a nice walk among the trees?). Rather, they said, forest bathing is a major intervention in how we could actually inhabit the city of the future: if economic anxieties about urbanization and tree loss had dominated the early-modern world, and had then been replaced by a more geological and ecological view of the disappearing forest that emerged in the nineteenth, I was interested now in how a distinctively *psychological* relationship to trees, both in and out of cities, might carry this story into the present. There is of course nothing new in the idea that nature soothes the troubled mind—this has been a central claim of the various sciences of mental health since their foundation.[47] And yet there was something novel, I thought, in the more recent and much more general claim that we modern city dwellers could *all* do with a regular dose of forested nature; that indeed, the future of urban living probably meant keeping yourself well and stable by getting out among the trees once a month or so; and that living well in the twenty-first century meant finding your preindustrial and preurban self wandering somewhere deep in the forest.

In practice, forest bathing can take a few different forms, but it usually means being led quite slowly and mindfully by a guide through the forest, not necessarily over very great distances, doing different kinds of sensory or meditative practices as you go. Simply being in the forest has a therapeutic effect, Stefan Batorijs, a leading trainer of forest-bathing guides, told me when I first started investigating it, "because it accesses a part of our innate survival system that is preindustrial and unaffected by the neuroses that afflict modern human beings." Stefan's work draws on a distinctive mix of philosophical, literary, and scientific literatures—he's as happy talking about phenomenology and Goethe as he is about the evolution of the vagus nerve and the moro reflex. There's nothing especially Romantic about forest bathing, he said when I brought this up. "The point is that spending time in the forest triggers access to ancient survival mechanisms, which in turn can help us to make more authentic choices in our lives." I also spoke to a scientist called Kirsten McEwan, who carried out a successful trial of a forest bathing intervention.[48] She told me that, as someone who was convinced of the benefits of nature but who was driven by hard evidence, she was keen to collect physiological data on people undertaking forest bathing (things like heart rate) as opposed to surveys or asking people about their experiences. "There's really good evidence from Japan," she told me, "that just breathing in those chemicals [emitted by trees in the forest] gives us a massive immune boost, which can last for a month." Kirsten's own research has shown a positive relationship between heart-rate variability—a measure of heart health—and spending time in nature.

There was no doubt that walking through the forest with Tom felt *good*. I even got used to the barefoot walking after a while—and it's true, it did alter my sensory experience of my surroundings in quite a profound way. I didn't measure my heart rate or check on my vagus nerve, but it seems like you'd have to really try hard to claim that spending a few hours out walking through a broad-leaved forest, with your usual world of work and family suddenly invisible, silenced, even temporarily suspended, *wasn't* at least a bit restorative.

Forest bathing feels like getting in touch with something ancient—and in one sense, that's true. A certain kind of relationship between some aspects of Japanese culture and trees has been remarked upon by outside visitors ever since those visitors were first allowed into Japan in the mid-nineteenth century.[49] The sensory practices that are often at the heart of forest bathing, including the meditative inward focus on bodily sensation, are indebted to a range of what today many call "mindfulness" practices. These have diverse roots, but at least some are entangled in Buddhist traditions that took root in Japan and neighboring countries around the sixth century AD.[50] And yet, as Tom explained to us, the practice of Shinrin-yoku is also thoroughly modern. "After World War II," he told us as we walked through the damp Wye Valley, "and mass bombings of the agricultural land in Japan, everybody moved to these megacities, ten to twenty million people living in a big urban space. Then the government sat back and watched the cost of keeping people alive rise. There were people dying at their desks from stress. There were people committing suicide on unprecedented levels." It was only in the early 1980s that the Forest Agency of Japan began a program of investigation into what today is known as "forest medicine" and only really since the early 2000s that scientists have been researching the connection in earnest.[51]

As they were taken up in Europe and the United States, these practices slotted comfortably into a range of existing traditions. The literary scholar Samantha Walton points out that a wide set of "naturopath" healing practices have been popular in spas throughout Europe since the 1850s; in the United States, around the same time, various gurus built on the ideas promoted by Transcendentalist writers by offering hearty mountain retreats for—in Walton's words—"nerve-shattered and exhausted intellectuals."[52] This was also of course the age of neurasthenia, that mysterious nervous malady of late-nineteenth-century urban life—a diagnosis, the historian Mark Jackson suggests, that "revealed a profound and widespread ambivalence about modern civilisation."[53] On the one hand, then, forest bathing is a practice that sometimes trades in images of timeless connection to nature, and yet it is roughly the same age as the Nintendo Entertainment System, another deeply influential product of 1980s Japanese urban culture. On the other hand, a practice that gains a lot of cultural currency from a sense of novelty and distinction is at least partly based on nature-based solutions to the stress of industrial life that have been with us for hundreds of years.

"It's exploded," Shirley Gleeson, a forest therapy practitioner and trainer, later told me. "When I became interested in this work originally, fifteen years ago, nobody really knew what I was talking about." I'd actually been keen to speak to Shirley after I saw her give a talk at a conference on forest therapy, where I'd been struck by her superaffirmative energy. (And also because I realized that her accent—like my own—was from Ireland's boggy and unglamorous midlands.) A former social worker, Shirley now runs a successful ecowellness consultancy near Dublin, offering training for forest therapy practitioners and guides, sessions for individuals, and events for spas and hotels. "People used to say to me, 'Oh, you're doing that nature stuff,'" Shirley said. "They didn't really understand it, you know? And I mean, now there's this *huge* explosion: ecotourism, nature-based workplace well-being, mental health interventions, green prescriptions.... It's everywhere."

"What changed?" I asked.

"There's more research," said Shirley. "I think the pandemic has been major in terms of really bringing people's awareness to the importance of nature and their local places. I think the health professionals are becoming more open to it. The health systems are under pressure. They need new, innovative ways of working. There's the whole social prescribing movement." She drew a distinction between forest *bathing*, as a kind of ecotourism activity lasting a few hours, and forest *therapy*, as a more rigorous mindfulness-based intervention, usually going on over some weeks with a trained practitioner and aimed at helping people living with chronic mental health conditions. "The more stress that somebody's under," Shirley said, "the likelier they are to develop mental health problems or have a relapse.... A lot of people that have experienced trauma are in fight or flight. So this... *soothing* is vital in terms of kind of reducing that kind of trauma."

This distinction is critical, I think, in terms of how we should think about the burgeoning popularity of forest bathing, not only as a health or well-being practice but also as a kind of commentary on modern urban life. On the one hand, there's the idea of forest *therapy*, as Shirley distinguished it. Here, the claim is essentially that being in the forest, and especially being in the forest in a mindful, structured, guided way, has a measurable effect on people's stress levels—which has a positive effect on a whole range of chronic mental health conditions, among other things. This claim is well placed to meet a growing interest in what's called "green social prescribing" among clinicians and health policy people. Green social prescribing is the idea that a physician could direct a patient to a trained link person, who in turn might send them to something that might be good for them, like a community gardening project or a forest walking group.[54] In this sense, there are good reasons to clearly position forest *therapy* as a (this is my own word, not Shirley's) "mainstream," or conventional, health practice that can be aligned with existing health systems, such as the National Health Service (NHS) in the UK or insurance-based systems in the US and other countries. There's nothing wrong with any of that, of course—and indeed, there is increasingly good evidence to support it.[55]

But the story doesn't end here. Because within the forest bathing community, there is also, I think, another, more philosophical and perhaps more (again, this is my own term) *political* set of ideas about the relationship between humans and the environment, and where this has gone askew, that may align less well with conventional medicine, and indeed with conventional society. Near the end of our walk with Tom, Ruth asked what he understood by "nature connection," a term she had kept stumbling upon while writing her master's thesis on urban foraging. "It's not about connecting with nature for me," said Tom, after a thoughtful pause. "It's about realizing that we *are* nature. But we're disconnected from that notion. We think, as humans, we're the most knowledgeable and advanced species, potentially in the universe. But the reality is we're part of this ecosystem, and at the moment, we're not living in this ecosystem. We're living outside it. And at the same time, we're destroying it."

He thought some more for a minute. "Nature connection is this term that gets bandied about," he said eventually. "It's like people just want to go and touch that world. It's still them versus us. But *this* is where we've evolved. This is our natural habitat. This is where our health is the best. It's not that going to the forest makes your immune system stronger. It's that leaving the forest makes your immune system weaker. This is where we *should* be—we should be out here, foraging berries, and David Attenborough should go"—Tom adopted a plummy English voice—"'look at the humans in their natural habitat.'"

Ruth and I laughed, but he went on quite seriously, "We *are* nature. And that's why we need to 'connect' with it. But we actually feel like our natural habitat is watching *I'm a Celebrity* in a concrete house full of electrical wiring. That's not our natural habitat. Sure, I think you can connect with nature in an urban environment. Will it have the same benefits as coming to a deep ancient forest? No. But it's better than walking the concrete streets."

I really enjoyed walking with Tom. And even I, a committed forest skeptic, found that although I wasn't *soothed*, exactly, it nonetheless became clear to me—I could feel it under my skin—that something experientially distinctive *is* happening, and starts happening quite quickly, when the sound of the modern world fades behind you and there's nothing around except steep gray pillars of birch and pine, a layer of dying leaves on the now vanished ground, and the daylight, such as it is, flickering in and out as if the sun is playing a cruel game with a small child. As a resolutely urban animal, and despite sincere efforts otherwise, I find the forest to be a deeply sinister, even frightening space. And yet I can nonetheless acknowledge an attraction, even a kind of *compulsion*, buried deep at the heart of my own fear. If the forest is not always good, it *is* always different.

"We've become so numb and so soft," Stefan Batorijs, the founder of Nature and Therapy UK, said to me while walking through some woods in the Dartington Estate, South Devon. "We've lost touch with the raw animal faculties that we have within us. We're encouraged to suppress those parts of ourselves in order to fit in socially. But when we go into wilderness areas, it brings us back into touch with something that's primal and eternal within us. It allows us to access all of the accumulated wisdom that precedes a lot of that conditioning that we're subjected to now." Stefan's is not an atavistic attraction—though he reads widely in philosophy, he is clear that his sense of an ancient self is part of our genetic inheritance that we need to rediscover. "People like flowers," he said to me during an email exchange after we met, "because their ancient selves knew that flowers meant fruit. Not being able to detect vegetation in urban areas causes the body to assume drought conditions and respond accordingly. Spending time in the forest triggers access to these ancient survival mechanisms."

Whether or not you agree with this view—I don't, but I find it interesting—it's making an argument that is more complicated, I think, than the straightforward empirical view that being in the forest reduces your stress levels, and this is good for your mental health, and so on. What I think is at stake here, rather, is a serious philosophical critique of urban modernity as such. As Samantha Walton points out, neither the nature cure itself nor the wider cultural diagnosis that gives the cure its energy—the idea that we are made mad and bad by being out of ecological step with the natural world—is new. The Romantics, the Transcendentalists, the first outdoor explorers and park bathers: none of these were into nature simply because the evidence showed that it was good for our health.[56] Or maybe it would be better to say that for them, the moral domain of human health was much wider than it is for us because they had a sense that nature could make good on humanity—that wilderness experience could repair a moral edifice much bruised by industrial civilization and urban life. Green social prescribing might not see itself as continuous with these movements, but it is clear that these histories are still very much present. Even in our resolutely empirical age, where the rhetoric of "what works" governs clinical decision-making, this much deeper sense that the forest corrects a larger historical disaster is not very far below the surface.

In his memoir *Nature Cure*, the celebrated British nature writer Richard Mabey once described an encounter with a young swift in the attic of a house he was occupying with friends.[57] The fledgling had fallen from its nest and lay with its new wings stretched out, unable to take off or move. "We could see," said Mabey, "the price it paid for being so exquisitely adapted to a life that would be spent almost entirely in the air." The image stayed with Mabey as he began his own sideways tumble into a deep depression, pitched from a life to which his body was no less minutely attuned: "I had become," he said, "the incomprehensible creature adrift in some substantial medium, out of kilter with the rest of creation." Mabey interpreted this as a collective rather than an individual problem. "Maybe," he wrote, "that is the way our whole species is moving… we're becoming unearthly." He described how neither pharmaceuticals nor talk therapy nor even a stay in the hospital could get at what was ailing him—until eventually, in a very bad state, he was sent to the countryside to stay with friends.

Once there, he moved into a house that seemed as if it were hewn directly from the forest: there was an oak door, an oak desk, and oak windows from which, in the distance, he could see the oak woods. Over time, within the "woody intricacy" of this new habitat, Mabey began to heal. He is much too acute a thinker, of course, to imagine that simply being surrounded by wood can resolve such a deep malaise—but he is clear that he at least partly attributes his illness to a distance from nature and his recovery to a process of (this is, to say the least, a striking metaphor) "nature entering me." Mabey does not see this as a problem peculiar to him; rather, he reads his own depression as just one story within a wider, *collective* denial of nature. In the same move, we can read his reshaping of his own life as a more ecologically attuned creature in a new kind of vegetal habitus as an example of how we will all have to learn to live in the future.

Richard Mabey is a famous nature writer for a reason: with great subtlety, he draws together the two different but intertwined ideas that animate this vision of a planet of trees: on the one hand, the world of mental health, of depression and anxiety, of diagnoses and clinicians and therapies and pills. And on the other hand, an older and maybe stranger *geological* story of how the planet has changed, how we have changed it, and how, in the changing, our attunement to our physical surroundings has slipped—until we found ourselves in cities filled with concrete houses, laced with electrical wiring, watching bad TV and eating worse food. This is unquestionably a powerful story of individual and collective redemption, and sure, sometimes it ends up with a benighted municipal bureaucrat putting a tree on a traffic island like that's going to solve anything. But still, its cultural force remains undiminished. The dream of the tree is as powerful as ever.

There are three major sources of human unhappiness, wrote Sigmund Freud in *Civilization and Its Discontents*.[58] There are our own bodies, which sicken, wither, and cause us pain. There's the world around us, which can burn down our homes, release a new virus into the human population, or wash a tsunami onto the shore with thirty minutes' notice. And then there are other people—that endless, shifting constellation of our collective achievements and inventions that we call society. Why does this last one, asked Freud, strike so many people as the *true* source of their unhappiness? How has it come to pass that for so many of us, "what we call our civilization is largely responsible for our misery...that we would be much happier if we gave it up and returned to primitive conditions?" The answer, he says, is that civilization replaced individual power with collective power. Just as, in our psychological development as individuals, we gain mechanisms to overcome our base instincts, so in our *collective* process of civilization, we develop social tools to block those dark urges—like violence or incest—still lurking within us, and whose unleashing might still, if we are honest about it, make us *truly* happy.

Maybe this goes too far. But just as we have Eros, says Freud, the desire to make life, so, too, we have its opposite—we have an instinct for death, a drive toward aggression and destruction. Civilization grips this instinct and holds it down "like a garrison in a conquered city." In this process, a person is made to feel bad not only about things they have done or might do but also about things *they will never do.* The external constraint becomes internalized, and the sense of guilt is born. "The price we pay for our advance in civilization," said Freud, "is a loss of happiness through the heightening of the sense of guilt." Freud, by this time one of Europe's most famous and controversial Jewish intellectuals, was writing in

Vienna between the wars and revising his text as the Nazis were becoming a major force in Germany. It is surely no surprise, as the Freud scholar Matt Ffytche points out, that he had come to see humans as "ultimately predatory, and only slightly evolved from an underlying animal condition."[59] Freud's lifelong belief in scientific progress, says Ffytche, is here quite absent. Misery, aggression, and death, at the end point of European modernity, were what preoccupied Freud in his last decade of his life. "Men have gained control over the forces of nature," he says finally, "to such an extent that with their help they would have no difficulty in exterminating one another to the last man. They know this, and hence comes a large part of their current unrest, their unhappiness, and their mood of anxiety."

What are we actually talking about when we talk about nature, and its suppression, and how human happiness is affected by the shifts between these two poles? It is convention by now, in a book like this, to say that perhaps there is truly no "forest" and no "city," no external "nature" that is clearly distinct from human "culture." Rather, there is an endless world of hybridity and mixture, where the green field is in reality a kind of factory; where the barren car park, if you look closely enough, is teeming with whole planets of vegetation and microbiota. In the pine forest, Tom showed us how nineteenth-century speculators had planted the trees at a slant to the sun so that they would grow quickly and tall, all the better for speedy cultivating and chopping. But it turned out that pine was structurally problematic, and so the thin, slanted pines stay where they are. A forest, yes, but also a factory in ruins. I take all of this very seriously. But I want to take seriously too the idea that nature and wilderness are real things. I am willing to entertain the conceit that they exist outside the city, which indeed is hostile to them. I want to say that it really *has* been the work of urban modernity to cast them off, indeed to do violence to them, and not only symbolically or ideologically but as real things in the world. I think I agree with the forest bathers that nature is real, and distinctive, and modernity is hostile to it. But I want to ask, at the same time, whether we are quite so certain that, here, modernity isn't right.

If nature is restorative, what exactly is it restoring? When we go to the woods as a kind of escape, what are we actually trying to escape from? This idea that the woods are where you go for rest and relaxation—I actually have a growing suspicion not only that it might be wrong but that it might even be the inverse of the truth. Forests, to our ancestors, says the author Sara Maitland, "were dangerous and generous, domestic and wild, beautiful and terrible."[60] After all, this is the terrain, she points out, of that strange, morally ambiguous form, the fairy tale, a form in which you are just as likely to be boiled and eaten in a stranger's house as you are to make it home safely: "Coming to terms with the forest," Maitland says, "surviving its terrors, utilizing its gifts, and gaining its help is the way to 'happy ever after.'"

What if it's the *city*, then—that milquetoast territory of fine-grained human regulation and fey politesse, that carefully balanced choreography of desires thwarted and excesses tamed—what if it's the *city* that represents peace and calm? And what if it's the forest—the ungoverned place at the edge of civilization, the place that refuses the artifice and restraint of urban modernity—that is truly the space of tumult, excess, and anxiety? Maybe this only reflects my own lack of faith in my fellow humans, but I am nervous about letting go of civilization's constraints; I would find nothing either restful or enlivening about that loosening. I remember too well that feeling of the cold sun flickering in and out of the branches as if it were playing a game with me—as if in the end, I was just another creature on the forest floor, just another frightened animal out there, quite alone, on the fringes of an indifferent and uncaring planet of trees.

CHAPTER 5

Save Me

In 2011, following an unprecedented decade of drought, the authorities in Melbourne, Australia, commissioned a survey on the state of their city's trees. The results were even worse than expected. Melbourne's tree cover, which the city relies on to keep itself shady and cool, as well as to reduce pollution and manage stormwater, was in a truly desperate state: without intervention, half of the city's trees would be dead within twenty years.

This would be bad news anywhere. But it was devastating for Melbourne, a city whose implicit self-image as a genteel outpost of European colonialism is very much bound up with its rich, extensive tree cover, as well as its more general botanical excesses.[1] This was, understandably, a topic of significant public concern. So the city organized some workshops to involve locals in solving it—using printed maps of the city's urban forest that, perhaps inevitably, people really wanted to take home.[2] To help, Yvonne Lynch, a city government employee, came up with the idea of making a "digital urban forest." For some weeks, Lynch and her team worked with a local digital designer to make a publicly available online map that showed, at a click, every tree in the city—each individually marked, categorized into species, and given an identification number and a health status. You can still look at the map today: tree number 1063779 is a sadly dying plane tree in Bourke Street; tree number 1041057 is a surprisingly heathy young eucalyptus on Rebecca Walk.

The idea was that citizens would use the map to identify trees that looked unhealthy or that had maintenance problems, and then click a link to email municipal authorities about it. That link, though, didn't say, *"Send an email about this tree."* It said, *"Email this tree."*

And that slight shift in imperative turned out to be crucial. For the drought-ridden citizens of Melbourne, suddenly confronted with the digital manifestation of their own dying landscape, the invitation to directly email a tree was an opportunity for arboreal encounter that proved impossible to resist. People began to email the trees. But they didn't so much write with bureaucratic maintenance concerns; instead, they started to get in touch with a much wider set of their own tree-related thoughts and desires.

"Dear Algerian Oak," wrote one user to tree number 1032705, *"Thank you for giving us oxygen. Thank you for being so pretty. I don't know where I'd be without you to extract my carbon dioxide. (I would probably be in heaven.) Stay strong, stand tall amongst the crowd. You are the gift that keeps on giving."*[3]

"*Dear Green Leaf Elm,*" went another, to tree number 1026655, "*I hope you like living at St. Mary's. Most of the time I like it too. I have exams coming up and I should be busy studying. You do not have exams because you are a tree. I don't think that there is much more to talk about as we don't have a lot in common, you being a tree and such. But I'm glad we're in this together.*"[4]

I first heard about these emails during a conference on green roofing infrastructure in one of the vast and deeply weird "coworking" buildings that now occupy the former Olympic site at Stratford in east London. These are basically like aircraft hangars, only kind of pointless apps are made in them instead of planes. As a worker whizzed past me on his electric scooter, en route to buy his coffee from a van that said it was staffed by unhoused people, I remember thinking that here was maybe a contrivance of work and economy that all the green roofs in the world wouldn't make sustainable.

At the time, I had been thinking a lot about how trees might not be innocent bystanders on city streets—how they might play a more direct, instrumental role in how cities are governed and imagined as very particular kinds of modern places. You can see, from this perspective, how saving Melbourne's urban forest might be a big deal for the people in charge: lose the trees and you lose your claim to good, modern, *scientific* management of urban space. But in a wider sense, an urban forest can be a powerful symbol of how the city has claimed and even tamed nature. The city's trees are a potent, living representation of how, in the process of urbanization, we took unruly nature and we organized it. We made it submit to the city's strict grid lines, its rational and hierarchical ordering of buildings, its immovable commuting and delivery schedules. Saving Melbourne's urban forest really matters, then, because if we're no longer able to manage the trees, a big part of what a city *is*, or what it sometimes *claims to be*—a well-ordered space of rational human industry on an otherwise unpredictable planet—is suddenly, quite radically, in question.

When I actually spoke to Yvonne Lynch a few months later, she described how, for months, she would come into her office in Melbourne and begin her day by reading the emails people had sent to the trees. "The stories were so poignant that you would just not forget them," she said. "Some of them brought me to tears." She told me about receiving emails from all over the world—someone emailing a particular tree to say that its presence had protected them from self-harm during a dark period; or a mother writing to a tree that had given her strength when her baby twins were dangerously ill to say that today, her favorite thing to do was to drive silently past this same tree with her mercifully healthy children sleeping in the back seat. "An emotional tapestry of the city has been revealed," Lynch said, talking about the tree emails. "I have been privileged and honoured to be the recipient, on behalf of those trees, of some of those deep thoughts and emotions."

In the previous chapter, I talked about trees in cities and about people in cities trying to get out of cities to see trees as part of a wider turn away from urban modernity. I said that the tree in this sense plays a symbolic and ideological role—it represents a growing anxiety about how our mode of life (physical, economic, even moral) sometimes feels like it's coming apart at the seams. In this chapter, I want to hold on to that idea and extend it into thinking about the concept of an "urban forest" more specifically. After all, if you consider how many trees are actually in it, the city might be something like a forest—or at least, by cultivating its trees and planting more, the city could strive to *become* a forest. I think this idea is weird. But still it might be useful, I thought when I planned out the chapter, because it would take me away from making somewhat sweeping claims about culture and direct me toward the more hard-nosed and serious business of city management. I was poised to write a chapter in the spirit of the philosopher Michel Foucault about how seeing the city as a forest was a way of seeing it as a potentially unruly and wild place that could—if we are careful to use the right tools and don't spare the axe—be brought under rational and bureaucratic control. Control the plants, and you control the people.

But my interview with Yvonne Lynch was an early clue that these terms were too reductive. This is partly because the complex and multifaceted people who work in mayoral offices and city councils around the world simply resist this kind of easy analysis. But this conversation was also an early sign of something else: as I would come to realize, the attachments that people in cities make to trees can't be reduced to a bureaucratic ruse. Trees do something for people in cities—they have psychological importance for urban residents. And, as I was to learn, they have political importance, too.

When I first started attending events about healthy cities, green cities, future cities, and so on, a term I often heard was "ecosystem services." I wrote it in my research journal several times in all caps.

I didn't really know what it meant, and I guessed it was something pretty gross—but still, there was a kind of bureaucratic poetry to the conjunction that attracted me in spite of myself. What could it mean to reimagine a city's river or a bank of street trees somewhere or an urban park that soaked up excess rain as a *service*—like a railway or an electricity pylon or a food-delivery app? What strange magic allowed the grid lines of a local government employee's spreadsheet to redefine various scrappy bits of nature as urban infrastructure, with no less dignity than the most finely engineered bridge?

The notion of "ecosystem services" comes, perhaps predictably, from that most accidentally poetic of the management sciences: economics. The idea is that there are natural ecosystems in cities, and these ecosystems do things for the people who live there. Most of these things are loosely related to health and well-being or to the improvement of the urban atmosphere. Trees, for example, cool people down and make them less stressed. Vegetation filters the air. The soft leafy surfaces of plants help to reduce noise levels. You can drink water from a lake, if you have one, and after that, when the water comes back out of you again, you can treat the sewage in a wetland.[5] According to the geographers Catherine Phillips and Jennifer Atchison, "trees in particular are increasingly valued as contributing to solutions for contemporary urban challenges including climate change, urban heating, air quality, and disconnection with nature."[6] And all this can be quantified, too—even turned into a cash benefit. We know, for example, that excess noise is bad for mental health. If you can figure out, say, how much a square meter of leaf cover reduces the overall noise level in your city, then you can figure out how much the total leaf cover of the city is saving you in hours of clinician time or in pharmaceutical prescriptions or whatever it is.[7]

This is of course what environmental economics does, i.e., putting an unexpected and maybe idiosyncratic monetary value on something whose value is not obviously monetary. The same trick operates in the closely related term "natural capital," where, for example, all the "nature" within a given territory is not only given a nominal monetary value but also even categorized as a kind of *capital*, which is to say as an economic asset (and of course, like all assets, might be cut up, privatized, or sold off). In the UK, for example, the Treasury's "Green Book"—its technical advice on how to apply cost-benefit analysis to a policy proposal—encourages a natural capital approach to decision-making. Natural capital, it says, is a store containing "certain stocks of the elements of nature" that delivers benefits to society through ecosystem services.[8] Ecosystem services, in other words, are benefits that we can acquire through our stock of natural capital. This stuff is catnip to council bureaucrats and local politicians who manage city budgets.[9] The dominant ideology among city managers—whatever their political views—is that good city management is rational, *scientific* city management. And whatever else you might say about it, the ecosystem services framework at least has the air of science, reason, and control about it. "Look," it says, "not even the merest leaf, not the most miserable shrub, is outside our purview." And while it's true that, like most concepts that come from mainstream economics, ecosystem services and natural capital are broadly evil, they're also used by people who are generally trying to do good. If you want to justify the existence of a park, after all, or if you're trying to save a small woodland from the developer's axe, then demonstrating the economic value of that woodland as a vital ecosystem service, part of the city's well-being infrastructure, sounds a lot more convincing to developers, council scrutiny committees, and secretaries of state than wanting to save a woodland because, I don't know, kids play in it or dogs piss in it or whatever the actual reality of the situation is.

But, in cities, concepts like ecosystem services and natural capital are doing something else, too. The practice of urban greening, says the sociologist Hillary Angelo, isn't really about ecology. It isn't so much about providing shade or lowering temperature. Rather, it's about creating what she called "social imaginaries"— or "cultural understanding of the moral order of a social world."[10] These kinds of shared understandings, our sense of what the social world is like and *should* be like, have very real effects, according to Angelo. They shape and structure the worlds we make for ourselves; they give rise to rules and laws; they govern our sense of what's good and guide our actions in trying to reach it.

One such shared understanding, it seems to me, which was very powerful at least until quite recently, is the city that, for good or ill, can be thought of as a kind of human boot print on the surface of an otherwise hostile planet. In an unpredictable and scary global environment, the city can feel like a space of reassuringly human order, calculation, and modernity—a predictable, regulated, and managed sphere of economic and cultural activity. The city, in this account, is essentially a technology for making the natural environment manageable, or at least for making us *think* the environment is manageable. That's what "ecosystem services" does. It takes, say, a little stream, or even a giant lake, and *manages* it—it turns it into just another piece of rationalized infrastructure within the city's ever-growing boundaries.

This managerial logic extends quickly to humans. Urban tree management in the nineteenth century, says the environmental historian Sonja Dümpelmann, as it pruned the unruly and the unexpected and deployed new techniques for creating order out of potential chaos, was in the vanguard of the "Taylorization" of the American city.[11] The urban tree, an object of strictly rational calculation, creates an image of the city as a space under firmly scientific management, with design subsumed to the demands of productivity and efficiency.

This is surely correct—but what happened in Melbourne reminds us that it isn't the whole story, or maybe that this story isn't as powerful as it once was. Something else, some much weirder psychic connection between people and trees, is pushing its way through the dull sheen of this managerial logic—like an unruly root or branch cracking the top of a well-ordered sidewalk.

In Paris a few years ago, the mayor, Anne Hidalgo, announced plans to create a new "urban forest" by planting trees and gardens around four of the city's most famous landmarks. Paris not only aims to be carbon neutral by 2050 but also has a stranger and more ambitious goal, which is to make 50 percent of the city's surface vegetative by the same date.[12] Hidalgo, the *New York Times* reported, "has positioned herself prominently among the mayors of the world's premier capitals as an advocate for what she bills as a new, and necessary, kind of urban landscape."[13] The people in charge of Madrid, not to be outdone, are planning to build a "green wall" around the city, with seventy-five kilometers of forest and half a million new trees.[14] In New York City, an environmental nonprofit called the Nature Conservancy made a first-of-its-kind assessment of the city's tree cover across public and private land, treating the city's seven million trees as a single forest system. This new "urban forest," it argued, "should be treated as a whole system of critical natural infrastructure to sustain New York City for decades to come."[15]

None of this is new, exactly. As Sonja Dümpelmann again points out, tree planting has been central to urbanization in Europe and North America since at least the nineteenth century. In an earlier era of rapid urbanization, trees were a way of creating identities and forming boundaries, both physical and ideological. In Berlin before World War II, Dümpelmann notes, "many conservatives believed that urbanization threatened the superior Germanic race, which was considered to have evolved in the wooded areas of the temperate zone now deforested and threatened by desertification. Tree planting was therefore perceived as salvation." Washington, DC, she goes on, used tree planting, and its self-proclaimed status as the "city of trees," as a way to position itself among—and ultimately supersede—the European imperial capitals such as Paris and Berlin, each famous for its carefully tended trees, parks, and gardens.

Urban trees have always been political, but their politics is not straightforward. Initiatives like Brooklyn's Neighborhood Tree Planting Corps in the early 1970s, says Dümpelmann, in which mostly African American residents self-organized to plant trees in their heavily stigmatized Bedford-Stuyvesant neighborhood, became an act of defiant community building and an important story of the civil rights movement in New York City. On the one hand, this represents a bottom-up desire to make a claim on space, and indeed the status of full humanity in that space, through an organized aesthetic and environmental action. On the other—as Dümpelmann notes—there is a long-standing top-down interest in deploying urban nature as a "civilizing device for citizens deemed unruly; the well-meaning desire to spread green space more evenly between urban space is also legible as an anxiety about those people not (yet) made subject to nature's civilizing influence." When a neighborhood organizes itself to plant some trees, we might read this as an empowering act of taking ownership of some space. But we might also see it as a claim about who is deemed worthy enough to share in the goods of urban civilization. When we plant a tree, we do so partly for our individual pleasure, I am sure. But we do it, too, to make a claim about what kind of person we are—virtuous, decent, and worthy of respect; someone who cares about their environment; someone who is in and *of* nature; and also someone, like all natural beings, who is willing to submit to a well-ordered, functional hierarchy.

These tricky relationships between nature, governance, and design are perhaps nowhere more visible than in the City Beautiful movement, the more or less fascist school of urban design that radiated outward from Pierre Charles L'Enfant's 1791 plan for Washington, DC, and Baron Haussmann's remaking of Paris in the 1850s and 1860s. The City Beautiful movement emphasized aesthetics in urban form, with a certain kind of monumental classicism at its center, working within a hazy assumption that the good city, in terms of governance, virtue, power, civic feeling, etc., is not only encapsulated but *produced* by these qualities.

What distinguished the City Beautiful, however, was not simply a foregrounding of aesthetic effect, but a calculated disinterest in anything else. City Beautiful designers, says the writer and town planner Peter Hall, accepted no brief for the social life of the city; they had no interest in things like urban justice or equality, and even such pragmatic concerns such as commerce and health came some distance behind the column's fascist thrill (the ultimate City Beautiful, Hall points out, would have been Albert Speer's design for Nazi Berlin).[16] And yet, as the geographer Nikolas Heynen argues, in North America the City Beautiful is the reason that so many urban trees still exist today.[17] At the height of North American urbanization, Heynen notes, there was an attempt to import a kind of nineteenth-century European nature ideology, an idea of rugged, dominant man as both in and astride nature, and then to reproduce that ideology within a new colonial context—one in which control of territory, of nature, of other humans was very centrally and explicitly at stake. It's worth remembering that many of today's most beloved City Beautiful remnants were often acts of violent displacement, as in the case of the 1857 destruction of Seneca Village in New York, a settlement of free Black landowners that was razed to enable the building of Central Park.[18]

So there's nothing especially new about the *political* functions of urban trees. As a coherent *scientific* object, however, the "urban forest" is much more recent. Some accounts credit it to the Toronto-based forestry researcher Erik Jorgensen in the 1960s. As Dutch elm disease, an infectious tree-killing fungus, reached that city, Jorgensen and his colleagues realized that tackling it meant not only coming up with new scientific tools and resources but also, says the historian Joanna Dean, "a new way of thinking about city trees" entirely. The "urban forest," which for the first time referred to a city's trees as a single unified organism, was Jorgensen's solution.[19]

Around the same time, the Connecticut Agricultural Experiment Station, a public site for agricultural research that has been in place since the late nineteenth century, held a conference on what it called "the suburban forest."[20] In his introductory address, the organizer, Paul T. Wagonner, located his interest in the subject in a moment of mid-twentieth-century abundance and moral generosity. "Today," said Wagonner, "with oil to warm us and power our mechanical muscles, with bins bulging with plenty to feed us, with electricity to light our way, we can and will restore trees to the land." The suburban forest, he said, is made up of that skein of greenery that suburbanites in places like postwar Connecticut saw knit between their homes. It's the patch of tended lawn around the power plant, the verge on the turnpike, the abandoned farm where a row of neat new bungalows comes to an end. Wagonner, like Jorgensen, wanted to aggregate this messy tangle into a new scientific object that could be properly utilized and studied—the (sub)urban forest. Indeed, as soon as it had a coherent object to look at, the nascent field of urban forestry began to branch out and specialize, including, for example, work on the flora of bombed-out German cities.[21]

The first US National Urban Forestry Conference took place in 1979, and scientific journals and handbooks followed. Older publications renamed themselves to fit in with the new zeitgeist. By the 1970s, the study of the urban forest had developed into a major scientific field.[22]

Today's city mayors and urban planners, then, when they talk about growing or protecting the urban forest, are extending some very specific histories from the late nineteenth and twentieth centuries—histories that are in one sense not really about trees at all, but rather about the everyday politics of urban space and a long-standing desire to produce the city as a safe, efficient territory where unruly objects and bodies are kept firmly under control.

And yet, underneath all of this attention to urban forests, there is also a sense of anxiety, I think—an anxiety about the process of urbanization itself and about the planet that it has wrapped itself around. This is an anxiety about the moral and ecological consequences of human progress and the emergence of the modern industrial world. But it's also an anxiety about whether that world is quite as secure as we thought. It's an anxiety about whether all those things we call "nature" are truly as manageable, or as governable, as modern humans have allowed themselves to imagine. This anxiety, too, has a history. To understand it, we need to stay in the middle decades of the twentieth century and turn to a series of then growing concerns over territory, ecology, and urbanization.

On June 16, 1955, seventy researchers from around the world arrived at a lecture room at Princeton University, where they would remain for the next five days. These scholars were all experts in human habitats and how these had changed over time. They had been brought to Princeton by the Wenner-Gren Foundation (an independent organization that supports anthropological research) and by four core organizers: William L. Thomas, then an assistant director at Wenner-Gren; Carl O. Sauer, a prominent geographer and landscape theorist, well known as an opponent of environmental determinism; Marston Bates, a zoologist from Michigan who was working on "human ecology" under the auspices of the Rockefeller Foundation; and Lewis Mumford, a sociologist, historian, and by then very famous writer on cities. Mumford had just published *The Transformation of Man*, a sweeping study of epochal change and the development of what people could still unblushingly call "civilization." The meeting was an attempt to think, on a grand and global scale, about transformations in human ecology and what these meant for the future of the planet. But it was also marked by the emergence of a newer anxiety, one focused on the state of the natural environment and on the growing evidence of its degradation, marked by a distinctively Cold War sense of the now very real possibility of planet-level disaster.[23]

The meeting was called Man's Role in Changing the Face of the Earth; its stated aim was to explore "what has been, and is, happening to the earth's surface as a result of man's having been on it for a long time, increasing in numbers and skills unevenly, at different places and times."[24] Fifty-three papers were presented and two volumes published, running to well over one thousand pages. The meeting found that "man" had originated more than a million years ago, had largely stayed put in central Africa and southeast Asia for his first 950,000 years—and then, rather suddenly, had spread across the globe. Along the way, humans learned to plant crops, make use of animals, burn things (mainly forests), and build cities. The planet's once-natural habitat was, in the process, radically transformed, a development that accelerated rapidly during the industrial revolution: "Man...changed the surface features," one reviewer of this exhaustive text observed, "the soils, the water, the cover of vegetation, the supply of resources, and even to a certain extent the climate." Recognition of this development, the reviewer went on, now gave human geography a certain kind of moral force—a mission to figure out how to damage less, perhaps even to repair some of the damage already done.[25]

And nowhere more so than in relation to trees. If one thing distinguished man's history on the earth, argued Sir Clifford Darby, the Welsh historical geographer and one of the meeting's most celebrated attendees, it was his attempt to subdue the woodland: "The attack, begun in prehistoric times, has continued for innumerable centuries, and, little by little, as population has grown, the wood has given way."[26] Wood was everywhere in antiquity, Darby pointed out, physically and morally. It was simply *there*, the stuff of everyday life and culture. Homer compared a stricken soldier to a fallen oak and said that the sound of battle was like nothing so much as "the din of woodcutters." Pollen analysis, Darby went on, shows just how much of Europe was originally wooded. In England, certain metropolitan place names encode the history of medieval wood cutting: settlements south of London, for example, often have names (ending with suffixes like "ham") that don't indicate woods. These were the sites of early Anglo-Saxon settlement, where the trees fell first. Places to the *north* of the city, however, more commonly feature endings like "hurst" or "weld," indicating the belated presence of woodlands. Here, Darby suggested, the trees survived much longer. Only in the coniferous belt of the far north, where the soil is less fertile and the system of agriculture meant that woods were partially replenished over time, did anything much survive beyond the early-modern period.

And yet the history of deforestation, Lewis Mumford reminded Darby, is also the history of the city. The natural history of urban life, Mumford argued, begins with ceremonies performed in caves; then comes the cultivation of hard grains and food storage; populations grow, and so do their settlements.[27] With more people comes the elaboration of administration and trade; life becomes larger and more complex. The city grows outward—its overlapping layers of defensive wall marking its age, said Mumford, like the rings of a tree. But something changes. What distinguishes the city from the village is not size or complexity. It is, rather, "a tendency to loosen the bonds that connect its inhabitants with nature, and to transform, eliminate, or replace its earth-bound aspects, covering the natural site with an artificial environment that enhances the dominance of man and encourages an illusion of complete independence from nature." In Mumford's view, the city becomes an *emancipation* from nature. But this was still something of an illusion: the truth was that the city at this stage in history was still largely dependent on the surrounding countryside for its survival. Until, suddenly, it wasn't. With the arrival of the industrial age, Mumford wrote, natural limits on growth, such as water supply, or walls needed for defense, fell away or were superseded. Exponential population growth took place. Now entire districts were urbanized. Urban areas began to reach out to each other like tendrils across the countryside. The city became *counterorganic*. Conurbations appeared, and any land left in between, unwanted by the city, became desert. "The city," Mumford concluded, "by its incontinent and uncontrolled growth, not merely sterilized the land it immediately needs but vastly increased the total area of sterilization far beyond its boundaries." The city surrounds the country like an amoeba surrounds its food—quietly breaking it down, absorbing it, and finally taking it in.

This idea—that the city is a kind of *anti*nature—is pervasive, whether people are celebrating that fact, lamenting it, making use of it, or trying to fix it. It unites well-meaning mayors, desperately trying to tend their own depleted urban forests, and less well-meaning officials and economists, sweating local ecosystem services to improve the city's bottom line.

It's a popular idea—I just don't know if it's true. I'm writing this at my kitchen table in Bristol, a medium-sized ex-industrial British city, almost three-quarters of a century after Lewis Mumford's rather dire diagnosis. When I look immediately to my left, out into our small yard—even the real estate agent who sold us the house didn't dare call it a garden—I can see two decent-sized trees, an untamed wall of hedge, and several overgrown planters, bought and left by my mother after we moved in and not touched once by us since. On the table in front of me, there is a strange little plant in a pot, really more of a leaf, that my wife found in the street and took home, and in the next room is an overgrown and neglected *Monstera deliciosa* that we were given as a wedding present and now can't bring ourselves to throw out. On the street outside, the walls of our small front garden are lined on both sides by weeds—through laziness on our side and I think a vague gesture at "rewilding" on the part of the local council on the other. Ten minutes' walk down the road is a large park, which, like much of the city, is topographically strange and features a long slope of trees as you walk in, dotted with thoughtfully placed benches, much loved both by parents of toddlers and teenagers drinking cider. Of course, this is in some way the story of living in a bourgeois neighborhood, where the bountiful presence of trees is at least partly a class signifier. There's an old Marxist debate about whether this kind of commodified nature—what Marx calls "second nature," like my poor lifestyle signifier *Monstera* in its fancy little pot—even counts as nature at all. But I want to leave that to one side. The truth is that urban spaces are festooned with vegetation, wanted and unwanted, useful and annoying, pretty and ugly. Once you start looking, there's green stuff everywhere in cities—and much of it not obviously under any kind of authority or control.

With this in mind, and directly in opposition to their midcentury ancestors, many geographers today argue that the city should be seen as an "urban ecology."[28] The idea that the city is a uniquely *human* space, these geographers point out, that it excludes nature, even to the extent that things like trees have to somehow be *brought back in*—well, this has always been a bit of a fantasy. And usually, as in Mumford's natural history, a negative fantasy at that: people imagine a sprawling dystopia of clean, man-made, high-tech futurity. But that simply doesn't exist. Even in the most hypermodern urban spaces, mold creeps down the walls; rain pools in small divots and becomes a home for algae; birds drop seeds and acorns; insects somehow always find a way inside. "Beneath the street the beach," went the famous Situationist slogan of Paris 1968—but "beneath the street the dirt" is the more salient reality. And in your average badly maintained British or North American city, not even very far beneath.

The city, say Matthew Gandy and Sandra Jasper, two writers working in this tradition, whatever science fiction images we have of it, has never lacked vegetation: the very earliest cities often prominently featured gardens and planting as expressions of imperial and territorial power. And people in cities have always set aside space for the cultivation of plants—whether for food, medicine, or simply the pleasure of being among them.[29] But also, Gandy and Jasper point out, plants have always simply grown, unplanned—often little regarded—in urban space. This is especially the case around sites of ruin or destruction—like the 420 different species of plant that the Victorian botanist Richard Deakin counted growing on the walls of the Colosseum, then a neglected and rather wild place, in the 1850s.[30]

The city, then, has always been a botanical place—whether we are talking (this is Gandy and Jasper's typology) about remnant plants (which were basically there before humans transformed the landscape and are still there now), constructed plants (which have been specially selected and planted in particular urban spaces for whatever effect), or adaptive plants (which weren't there before the city but have arrived now, albeit without deliberate human intervention or cultivation, and have found the city a congenial enough place to stay).

What's important about this perspective is that it isn't centrally about "greening" urban space, "rewilding" the city, or whatever. To want to "rewild" the city, after all, is to start from the position that "the city" and "wildness" are two different kinds of things; that "man" and "the environment" stand in some kind of formal opposition to one another; that urbanization, indeed, can largely be defined as a site of struggle between them. This is the central assumption that the Princeton conference started with. The idea found its way into growing fields of research, like geography and ecology which never much questioned it. But it's also an assumption driving much of the world of "ecosystem services" and "nature-based solutions" and "urban forestry" today—a weird, almost *psychic* separation between nature and the city that underpins a good deal of the obsession with trees, and other green things, that we see in so much contemporary urban thinking.

I realized, while reading Gandy and Jasper's paper, that in trying to understand the role of trees in urban space, I had been looking in the wrong place—or at least, I had been looking in a very limited kind of place. I had spent my time at conferences for planners and urban policy makers, reading pronouncements by ambitious city mayors, reading texts about the history of forestry and urban landscaping, and so on. Maybe, instead, I needed to speak to some people who had *always* thought that cities were natural spaces as much as anything else; people who, a bit like the emailers in Melbourne, had a deep connection to the urban tree landscape and a vision of how trees might really be at the center of a good city, in a way that wasn't at all about control or utility; people for whom the unruly, wayward, sometimes politically awkward aspects of city trees were not only entirely okay—but were maybe even the whole reason for cherishing them in the first place.

"Here's one," said Christine. We all stopped and looked. "This is a tree," I said.

"This tree," said Christine, standing protectively against the trunk, "was condemned for having caused damage to the pavement that was impossible to fix." I looked down. The pavement looked totally fine. "As you can see," Christine said pointedly.

It was spring 2022. I had come to Sheffield, in northern England, to meet some of the people involved in the city's extraordinary tree protests, which had ended only a few years earlier. In 2012, Sheffield City Council signed an enormous contract with a private company, Amey PLC, to manage and renew highways in the city—including Sheffield's highway trees. A survey suggested that around a thousand trees were in such bad shape that they'd need to be felled. Notices started to appear on trees, and quite quickly, neighborhood groups sprang up to oppose the program. These eventually coalesced into the Sheffield Tree Action Groups (STAG). Letters were written and petitions delivered, to no avail. By the end of 2015, more than three thousand trees were gone.[31] Then things got heated.

"This stuff around trees damaging pavements," I said to Christine, "did people ever really find it credible?" Secretly I was thinking about wheeling a pram around some of the pavement near my home in Bristol, where tree roots really did sometimes make it impossible to pass. "It became clear," said Mark, who along with

Christine was the cochair of STAG, "that they were using excuses to fell the trees. All the experts we spoke to said, 'This isn't a reason to fell a tree.'" Christine joined in: "None of the arguments stacked up," she said, suddenly very passionately, "because this is a £2.2 billion contract where they have money to do various things, and it was obvious that a lot of the trees were just being felled because they had chosen to fell half the street trees. It was a policy decision to do it. Then when people protested, they started saying, 'Oh, they're damaging the pavement, disabled people can't negotiate the street.' Not that they'd been able to for the last twenty years anyway because of the state of pavements everywhere."

"Let's take a picture," I said and pointed my phone at the roots.

During a campaign to protect the trees on one particular road, several people were arrested. The council got court injunctions to stop people from entering zones near trees. Protesters began jumping the barriers or finding other ways to circumvent the rules.[32] Threatening legal notices were sent out; private security staff were brought in with an instruction to use "reasonable force" to get the protesters away from the trees. And then quite suddenly, in January 2018, with more than five thousand trees gone, citing health and safety concerns, the council "paused" the program. During the pause, which was not initially meant to be long term, the council finally changed tack and entered into mediation with protesters. There was a joint statement on a new approach, an apology from one of the leading councilors, and eventually an entirely new partnership and new approach to managing the street trees—which included outside expert groups as well as STAG. In 2023, a damning independent report said that the council seemed, during the period of dispute, motivated largely by a desire to simply get its own way. It said that the council had used disproportionate measures, including asking the police to be tougher with protesters, as well as pursuing people through the courts: "Some of the things the Council did were, in the view of the Inquiry, unacceptable," the report summary dryly noted. "Some of the ideas it flirted with, but did not pursue, were worse."[33]

I had met Mark Brown and Christine King on Rivelin Valley Road in Sheffield's northern suburbs, the site of some of the most contentious tree protests in the city. Honestly, it wasn't the loveliest place I had ever been and certainly didn't match the image in my head of a leafy area threatened by finger-jabbing council bureaucrats. When I got off the tram, right at the end of the line, a big sign advertised, "Real pet grub." That was the vibe. Rivelin Valley Road itself struck me as a rather boring tree-lined road. "It's apparently one of the longest avenues of lime trees in Britain," said Mark, "so it's quite an iconic thing. And the council wants to fell quite a lot of the trees." We were joined by Siobhan O'Malley, a resident who had also been involved in the protests. I liked all three immediately. They struck me as extremely nice, thoughtful, and—for want of a better word—absolutely regular people. They were passionate and knowledgeable, but reasonable and pragmatic too. They seemed exactly like the kind of people you'd *want* involved in local politics in your city.

We walked up Rivelin Valley Road, where, thanks to the campaign, most of the trees had been saved. It was quiet, and we were right by a nature reserve with a small stream running through. Really, it no longer felt as if we were in the city. "It started off as thirty-five trees that they were going to fell," said Christine, "but the council took some of them off and it went down to twenty-one; I think they've taken twelve."

"In isolation," Mark chimed in, "'removing twenty-seven trees out of hundreds along this road,' you might say...."

Yeah, I said. I was kind of thinking that didn't sound so bad. "But when it was tied into the citywide campaign," he went on, "where thousands were being taken down in a very short time, it was the same objection. We started protesting all the trees, really, because the council just doubled down."

The plan to cut the trees did seem crazy. As we walked up the road, Christine pointed out individual trees that had been saved. Some of them had little hand-drawn love hearts pinned on. "I think initially," said Mark, "I became vaguely aware of the campaign, and I just thought, 'Oh, well, the council know what they're doing, it's just residents worried about their house prices.'" I was glad he'd said that because the thought was in the back of my mind, too. "And then they did this Rustlings Road raid," Mark went on, "where they arrested some pensioners, and I thought, 'This is really not right,' and I looked into it a bit more, and the more I looked into it, the more I thought, 'There's some real bad stuff going on here,' and I wanted to get involved." He paused. "This thing about house prices didn't ring true for me. I could never afford a house. I can only afford to rent one. But one of the first things I remembered about Sheffield [when I moved there first] was walking through some of the suburbs, through these lovely avenues of big trees, and I thought, 'These are for everybody.'"

We went into the nature reserve and walked by the small brook. There was the faint sound of cars on the road, and it started to rain a little. "At the time," said Siobhan, "I was having a work-related issue, and I was out a lot because staying indoors is no good for you mentally, and I love nature. I'm a forager; that's what I do now: I teach foraging instruction about wildlife, biodiversity, and habitat. At the time, I was doing it for myself, my son, and my mental health, just to get outdoors, see nature, see the wild birds, and to know it's all going on around you. It's so helpful when…almost the meaningless stresses of society sometimes get too much. It becomes a confused jumble, whereas nature is a beautiful, meaningful thing that we can all access. It's what supports us, it's all around us, it cradles us in times of need."

We talked about how frightening the campaign to save the trees had been and how heavy-handed the official response. Campaigners would receive local intelligence on where felling crews were going to turn up and then race to get there first, to get close enough to the tree so that it couldn't be pulled down safely. This often meant physical confrontation with private security guards. But more sinister, Mark said, was the wider threat of legal action, huge court costs, and criminalization. Christine said that she and another protester had been dragged out of one protest by their arms and dumped face-first onto the ground in front of a police officer, who denied seeing anything. "I had to sleep on the right side for a couple of months," she said. "I think I bruised the bone." I started to realize, as we talked, that the campaign was about the trees, but it was about other things, too—trust in public officials, some sense of fairness and decency, but also just personal experiences of the city. "There was this one tree," said Christine, "the Independent Tree Panel said it was worthy of special consideration because it was such a fine tree, but they didn't care, they felled it, and it's the psychological violence of that that really sticks with you. It makes you angrier."

There is something about trees, I thought as we were talking, that seems absolutely central to a lot of people's ideas of what a good city—a good society—is like. And so when the trees came down, an awful lot of other things came down with them. "Trees are a world unto themselves, aren't they?" said Siobhan a bit wistfully. "Every tree is a world, and for a lot of street trees, that is somebody's world. One of the trees that got chopped down, this little girl used to go past and pet this tree and had a name for it, and it's gone now. It was a massive tree that the crows and the rooks and the pigeons... there must have been ten or fifteen species that would roost in this tree every night, and we would see them in the morning when we'd do our little vigil when they were coming to take it away, and you'd see this little world of all the different species chattering to life, and insects and lichens and flowers, the things that trees support, you can't replace that; no baby tree is going to replace that."

We went to a café. I was still trying to wrap my head around how things had gotten so out of hand. "There was a certain amount of aggression that never turned into violence," said Mark. "We always made a point of passively protesting, and one or two people got pushed around when they brought out the security guards; I got pushed to the ground a couple of times, but the point was always to be passive and not fight back because, well, for one thing, it's not in my nature, but also you lose the argument because they'll say, 'Oh, look at these violent protesters.'"

We got to talking about some of the reactions from local residents—not all of them positive.

"One of the protesters had a hosepipe turned on her," said Christine.

"That *is* unpleasant," I said.

"People who didn't like trees were pretty aggressive," she went on.

"Very loud about it, yeah," said Siobhan.

"And they'd say," Christine said, "'Don't get me wrong, I love trees, but that one's got to go.'"

"Yeah," said Siobhan. "'I just don't want them outside my house' was what my neighbors would say."

Christine sipped her tea, and we all paused. "You could get the wrong impression, though," said Mark, "if you just listened to the loud people because quite often, when things had settled down, we'd get someone coming out of the house next door, saying, 'I'm really grateful for you being here. I don't feel brave enough to stand up to my neighbor, but you're able to come and do that.'"

"From what I saw," said Siobhan, "for every one angry person screaming their head off, there were three people sat in a house, going, 'Thank God somebody's said something.'"

"There was somebody who would walk past and whisper, 'Thank you,'" Christine said. "Even though there was nobody in earshot, she still didn't feel brave enough to say it out loud."

"Because if anyone was looking out their window," said Siobhan, "and saw them talking to you, that was it, their neighbors would be..." She trailed off.

"Yeah, there was a bit of friction between neighbors," Mark said.

"My neighbor still likes to give me digs about how much she hates the trees outside," said Siobhan, "every so often, if I happen to mention them."

"Why does she hate the trees?" I asked.

"Because they make the moss fall onto a brickwork in her yard and make the birds poo in her garden. The leaves have to be swept up, and the petals from the beautiful cherry tree next to her house make everything sticky. I think that's the extent of her issues with it."

"There's this obsession with neat and tidy that's quite prevalent these days," Mark said.

"They're the sort of people who bleach their yards," Siobhan added.

"Yeah," Mark replied, "people who can't control the world, but they control their garden. They pick up every last leaf and nature doesn't fit into that."

"We've lost our connection to nature somehow," Christine said, "but that's the thing about street trees; street trees bring nature into the city, and they bring seasons into the city. If you think of a street, it'll get hotter and it'll get colder, but a tree gives you the seasons."

It was becoming late now, and I was getting ready to wind things up. "There's definitely a psychogeography," said Mark, "where certain streets, we go back there, and it will trigger extreme emotions because it was such a powerful thing that happened there."

"It must really change your relationship with the city," I said.

"I still haven't driven down the Chatsworth Road," he replied. "It's a beautiful line of lime trees, nowhere near where I live, but they took them all."

There was a pause.

"Three years of felling, lies, insulting people," said Christine, looking down at the table. "Three years of creating division in the community. I'm furiously angry about that." She talked about some war memorial trees that had been threatened. A very elderly man, she said, would sit on the council steps to protest about it. Christine at the time was involved in confidential negotiations between the council and the protesters. She knew the council intended to scale back, but she wasn't allowed to say anything. "I wasn't allowed to say, 'Go home, mate, you don't need to be here, you've won,' and it got leaked by somebody because it was obvious what the council was going to do; they were going to wait until Armistice Day, they were going to walk past this bloke in his mid-eighties and go, 'Aren't we brilliant, we've saved these trees.'"

Christine paused for some time. We were all silent.

"It was all about PR," she said. "There was nothing about individual people or how people felt." She was talking to herself now, I thought, more than to us.

"Because the council has never acknowledged the damage they did, they've never given us an apology, they just said, 'Move on, we're not felling now, so everything's different, forget it now.' If we could do that, there'd be no PTSD [post-traumatic stress disorder]. There'd be no counseling. But there's a massive well of pain and anger. You think you're all right. And then it just comes out."

I was on a tram back to the train station, trying to make sense of this conversation and looking at the map on my phone, anxious as usual to make sure I got off at the right stop, when the name of a building on the map, right by the station, leaped out at me: Béton House. Béton, I thought, surely had to be a reference to *béton brut*—or raw concrete, the material that gives "brutalism" its unfortunate name. What modernist marvel could this be? The tram stopped, and, taking a chance, I turned right, away from the station. I climbed up a steep set of landscaped steps, past a group of bored-looking workmen and a small clump of teenagers getting weakly high, until I reached the top of a hill. The city of Sheffield was spread out in front of me, into the west and south, and fading into the Peak District in the distance. "I'll bet you say you love Sheffield city center," my friend Eva had said to me over dinner the previous night, "just to be contrary." And it was true, I did. But from up here, you didn't have to try hard to find the city beautiful. And then suddenly, I saw that right behind me was a set of huge postwar housing blocks. I knew exactly where I was: I was at the Park Hill estate.

Park Hill was built in the late 1950s to replace a notorious area of back-to-back Sheffield housing, itself hastily established to provide homes for workers who had come in from the surrounding countryside to find work in the city's developing heavy industries. It was part of a piecemeal nationwide project of "slum" clearance, which had been taken up with renewed energy after World War II. For this sprawling site, two Architectural Association graduates, Jack Lynn and Ivor Smith, under the direction of city architect John Lewis Womersley, were selected to design a complex of interlacing concrete blocks linked by walkways—the famous "streets in the sky"—all of it quite directly quoting Le Corbusier's then recently completed *cité radieuse* at Marseilles. Built across a sloping hill, the flats were designed to maintain a steady horizontal facing out into the city, with thirteen stories at the longest end and four at the shortest.[34] The project was, said one commentator, "testament to an era when young British architects were revolutionizing the field of residential architecture with radical housing programs."[35] The buildings were wrapped by wide outdoor decks, big enough to get a milk float around; at the estate's high point, there were one hundred flats, four pubs, schools, shops, doctors' surgeries.[36] The space around the buildings was largely pedestrianized, "with the ground between the buildings laid out as a park space threaded with a system of footpaths including several small play areas."[37]

Park Hill's story was more or less the story of all ambitious urban social housing in England in this period—a grand project in the 1960s, quickly followed by a kind of studied neglect and managed decline as successive Conservative governments began to redirect the state away from any responsibility to provide housing, selling off what they could and carefully neglecting what they couldn't.[38] Park Hill was also badly affected by the collapse of heavy manufacturing in Sheffield, and especially the steel industry; many residents lost their jobs. The estate quickly got a reputation for deprivation, crime, and social problems. One of the blocks was demolished by the council, and it seemed as if the rest would quickly follow. Park Hill's "status has changed gradually," wrote the architecture critic Owen Hatherley, "from a source of intense municipal socialist pride to dilapidated sink estate."[39]

But then something surprising happened: in 1998, Park Hill

was given a grade II listing, a formal classification marking a building of special interest that should be preserved if at all possible. Now there was no way the remaining blocks could be demolished.

In 2004, the development company Urban Splash was contracted by Sheffield City Council to redevelop the site. Urban Splash had made its name in warehouse developments in Manchester and Liverpool in the 1990s and had since become a go-to company for eye-catching "regeneration" projects throughout England. At Park Hill, it added color panels to what had been brick infill and built a big new open gateway to the estates. It shortened the decks and landscaped the grounds. The flats themselves were enlarged, made open plan and "modern." About six hundred flats were to be sold on the open market, their council tenants having largely moved on, with just two hundred available for "social rent."[40] The writer of a book on modernist estates interviewed two of the new residents, both university lecturers: "We are both big fans of modernist architecture," one explained. "It is incredibly convenient for work, and it gives us an opportunity to live in a different way—our other house is a 1903 terrace house."[41] In some of the undeveloped low-rise blocks, a small hub of original tenants still remained.

All of this is objectively sort of terrible. It represents the collapse of a certain kind of urban utopianism, which had been borne along by ambitious, resolutely modern design, and its replacement by a cheesy gentrification project for middle-class professionals. It means the removal of another large swathe of public housing and the reimagination of modernist design from at least *trying* to be—even if it always was kind of an elitist project—a democratic, even a socialist practice and its transformation, instead, into a kind of lame lifestyle signifier for people with good salaries but unsatisfying lives who probably use terms like "midcentury" and buy Ercol chairs on eBay.

But it's also very beautiful, as capitalism's excesses so often are. I actually gasped when I turned a corner and was confronted by the blocks. This might be, I thought, something close to what it would have been like to see these blocks for the first time—even if they then must really have looked futuristic, whereas now they code as a familiar piece of hipster nostalgia. But still. The blocks have been washed back to a kind of pink hue, and the colored panels really work. The whole thing has the weird feeling of a kind of municipal Legoland—but in a good sense. I took some pictures of one of the blocks framed by a tree whose branches were bent almost as if to grandly present the wonder behind it, and sent one to my friend Rod. "I see," he wrote back, "so trees are good when they're in front of modernist buildings." This was a familiar tease from my friends, who were convinced that I was writing a book about how trees are bad. But I wasn't, I would insist. I was writing a book about how trees are *complicated*. And it was true; sometimes I did think that people who went on a lot about trees in cities, or about the state of the urban forest, were really talking about how much they didn't like a place like Park Hill; a place that still had that twentieth-century human confidence that Lewis Mumford was starting to become nervous about all the way back in 1955; a place that would gladly cut the hill into a straight line and load it with spacious new homes, and doctors' surgeries, and playgrounds, and pubs for thousands and thousands of people who could otherwise never have afforded any of it. But that thesis was incomplete, I realized. I was thinking about Christine then, and the man on the council steps, and all the other tree protesters, and what they had been through in defense of their own idea of a tree-lined urban utopia. Here, I thought, was quite another vision of forested urban modernity, one that I could, perhaps, finally get behind.

Around the buildings, Urban Splash had erected panels etched with people's memories of the place in its pregentrification phase, memories that were powerful enough to still be moving, even if you thought there was something kind of grotesque about someone's literal memory being materialized as a memorial to—even a kind of recuperation of—its own evisceration. "We were not guinea pigs in our eyes," said one. "It wasn't brutalist, it was new and clean and exciting. There were playgrounds and grass to play on yet the city was only a short bus ride or a gentle stroll away." The words were in gold etched onto a free standing blank slate slab. It looked like a tombstone. I took out my phone to check the time. Ten minutes to the train back to Bristol. I looked back over the city one last time. Then I went back down the hill, got on my train, and went home.

CHAPTER 6

The Twentieth Century
Did Not Take Place

In July 2019, *Time* magazine reported that Barcelona's most famous church, the Sagrada Familia, had announced a completion date—more than 130 years after its construction had begun. "Thanks to an influx of funding," the magazine noted, "some striking innovations and a lot of old-fashioned craftsmanship, the famously unfinished church is now on schedule to be completed in 2026, the 100th anniversary of the death of its architect, Antoni Gaudí."[1] The euphoria was short-lived. Just two years later, reporting on still ongoing attempts to put a giant twelve-point star on top of one of the cathedral's main towers, the *Guardian* informed readers that due to COVID-19 delays, the latest completion date had been shelved—with no new one announced.[2] People were up in arms. Questions were being asked about what exactly was being done with all the income from visitors, while locals protested about a plan to fix a huge stairway to the main entrance, which would involve knocking down three city blocks. It wasn't even clear, people said, that the stairs had anything to do with Gaudí's original plans.

I've always felt a strange sense of attachment to the Sagrada Familia. It was, I think, the first properly famous building I ever visited—part of a brief stop-off on an unusually adventurous school tour in the mid-1990s. I wish I could say that its weird, bulging spires and polychrome-forest interior were imprinted on my small provincial mind, thereby seeding an abiding fascination with nineteenth- and twentieth-century architecture. But the truth is that my only memories of that trip are that it was too hot, that we spent most of our time on a bus, and that we discovered the exotic continental pastime of Rollerblading. I have no idea what any of us made of arguably the most famous piece of ecclesiastical architecture in Europe.

Still, we would have been a good audience for it. Just a few years earlier, most of us had undergone the Catholic coming-of-age sacrament, confirmation,[3] in a rather less famous modern building—the Church of Christ the King in Turners Cross, a small working-class suburb just south of the city center in Cork, Ireland. Christ the King is an exceptionally strange religious building to find in Cork, or anywhere else in Ireland really, where church design tends to be as grimly unimaginative as the practice it encloses. Christ the King, though, is different. It's built entirely from concrete—the first such church in Ireland—and composed of a series of thin, rectangular concrete pillars that move up and out from a central hexagon, and then around the sides of the building, before meeting at the front and forming an almost incidental spire. This gives the church a strikingly narrow, high, and rectangular front elevation—dominated, even more unexpectedly, by a nineteen-foot-high modernist statue of Christ, radiating serenely between a set of concrete zigzag reliefs.

The Church of Christ the King was designed by a Chicago architect, Barry Byrne, who was commissioned by the bishop of Cork after he had read an article about Byrne—written by Lewis Mumford of all people—in the lay Catholic magazine *Commonweal*. "Here is an architect," Mumford enthused, "who has reconciled tradition and innovation; here is an artist who expresses the continuity of the church with its own past, without attempting to stereotype its present activities."[4] Byrne had been trained by Frank Lloyd Wright and was associated with Wright's "prairie school" of architecture—but he got his major break by taking over the practice of Walter Burley Griffin when Griffin won the commission to do the master plan for the new garden city of Canberra, Australia, in 1913.[5] This all makes for a very beautiful, very strange, and very incongruous architectural inheritance in a Cork suburb—and one lying completely at the other end of the scale from Gaudí's weird, bulbous construction. If Turners Cross has the clean hexagonal shape of a modern steamship, the Sagrada Familia is more like a wreck dredged from the bottom of the ocean— swollen with water and time, cankerous with shells and buboes, a thick brown mess of blobs, trunks, spires, turrets.

Barry Byrne is recognizably a twentieth-century modernist. But Gaudí is much harder to pin down. On the one hand, the methods he used to design the Sagrada Familia—famously, he hung a model of the church on weighted strings, upside down, and let gravity arrange the spires into their final form[6]—are often taken as a forerunner of the "parametric" or "form-finding" approach championed by many of today's self-consciously avant-garde computational architects.[7] Forget human design, says this school of thought—let the earth's physical parameters, like gravity, or the flow of water, or the way that bubbles form, decide how a design plays out. At the same time, Gaudí's relationship to Gothic style could easily place him among those who today understand themselves as "traditionalists" in matters of architecture and design. Indeed, for all its oddities, the thick-turreted Sagrada Familia is recognizably a piece of nineteenth-century Gothic revival, an attempt to establish its author's own speculative continuity with centuries of European church building.

How did Gaudí produce this strange simultaneity between the old and the new, such that the church even seems to stand outside of time and history altogether? The answer, I think, has to do with his work's relationship to *nature*. The spires of the Sagrada Familia, after all, swell and gather like living things; they look encrusted and aged; indeed, the experience of the interior of the church is often compared to the experience of being in a forest, with the ceiling propped up by a thick phalanx of columns "shaped like tree trunks."[8] Gaudí, says the Mexican architect Javier Senosian, "took nature—'the work of the supreme architect' as he called it—as his model and archetype."[9]

Christ the King in Turner's Cross, the church that I more or less grew up around, is an unambiguously twentieth-century modernist construction. With its use of new materials, its straight lines, and its open spaces, with its explicit break from its surroundings and its hint at a broader social transformation in the offing, the church occupies a very specific and defined period in architectural history. The Sagrada Familia, however, is very different. Here is a church that began its life in the nineteenth century—and is, somehow, still under construction in the twenty-first. It's almost as if it missed the twentieth century altogether, straddling the periods directly before and after modernism without ever touching down in that remarkable, debased, and often very violent period.

This contrast is worth paying attention to, I think. When I began doing the research for this book, when I started reading and talking to people who were interested in the relationship between architecture, cities, and nature, who were interested in neuroscience and human-scale planning and the benefits of trees, I was struck by how often they linked what they were doing with work that preceded the twentieth century. Often, it seemed, not only were contemporary ideas about cities, buildings, and nature at odds with the "modern" or "modernist" architecture of the twentieth century but people concerned with these issues were even looking back beyond that period altogether, almost as if it had never happened, rather as one might awkwardly glance over the shoulder of an unwanted guest at a party. And this seemed to be something that united people who otherwise, in terms of their architectural notions, looked like they had nothing much to do with one another at all. I found it to be the case for conservative "traditionalists," who enthused about conventionally beautiful Georgian squares in otherwise dank English provinces, but it also held for future-oriented experimentalists, the kind of people who talk in suspiciously vague terms about genetics and code and who get commissioned to design swishy museums in sad, postindustrial cities.

For Gaudí, the use of natural forms seems to make the Sagrada Familia both very contemporary, a building truly of the twenty-first century, and very old, a building that stretches back into the middle ages. In the same way, for contemporary architects working with nature, whether they are traditionalists trying to re-create beautiful and naturally soothing olde-time squares, or parametricists (I'll come back to this word) reimagining design as if it were a kind of biological or geological blueprint, it's almost as if modernism—with its synthetic materials, its hard right angles, its human-centeredness, its willingness to stamp its mark very explicitly on the environment—*never happened*. It's almost as if there is a desire on the part of people who are very invested in nature and biology, and how the two might relate to architecture and design today, to simply act as if the twentieth century never happened in the first place.

So I was interested—and concerned. Here, after all, are groups of people who otherwise have nothing to do with one another, who indeed are often very opposed to one another but who share one huge, dominant, and, to me, very troubling idea. On the one hand, there are self-consciously avant-garde people using new computational methods, advancing strange ideas about buildings and genetics, deeply concerned about ecology and the environment, and often attached to the most prestigious architectural academies. On the other hand, there is a large contingent of rather fogeyish people, working in often regional architectural practices, committed to reproducing forms that have traditionally and somewhat conservatively been imagined as beautiful, restful, and well ordered for many centuries.

But the idea that unites these two groups, whether they love classical porticos or computer-coded curves, and also the idea that disturbs me, is the idea that the human being, whatever else it is, is a natural and biological creature first of all; that the great mistake of the century that ended a few decades ago—and is now very firmly ended—was that we tried to build a new world from scratch; that the *real* disaster in modern planning and design, the foolish notion that we're still paying for, was that we allowed ourselves to imagine that we could actually transcend our pitiful, wretched, earthly, and irretrievably *natural* state.

Downing College, Cambridge, is probably the most grimly traditional and backward-looking part of the UK's most grimly traditional and backward-looking city. The main bit is conceived as a kind of eighteenth-century arcadia, with grand but still rather self-effacing low-rise classical facades gathered around an unmoving, dead-looking lawn. There are some embarrassed-looking trees, and here and there, you can find students sitting on benches, or at the foot of a column, like well-placed statues in some mad aristocrat's idea of Georgian picturesque. In May 2022, I was there, nonetheless, trying to find the college's much newer convention center, built in the 1980s thanks to a gift from a prominent graduate, the multimillionaire low-calorie diet guru Dr. Alan Howard—but even this had been designed by the architect, Quinlan Terry, to blend into the dull, landscapey classicism that marked the rest of the scene. Here, it seemed, was Cambridge in miniature: on the surface, an ersatz re-creation of classical antiquity: timeless, traditional, sedately unmoving. And yet hiding in plain sight was the only thing making this limp charade even half possible in the twenty-first century, i.e., the city's real existence as an eager catalyst and shiny death node of high-tech bioscience and venture capitalism.

I was there for an event on architecture and health hosted by Cambridge's Centre for the Study of Classical Architecture as part of a wider attempt to understand how buildings affect human biology and psychology. Put simply, classical, or sometimes "traditional," architecture is an approach to architecture that's a bit backward-looking, self-consciously rooted in history, not favored at all by architecture's academic establishment, kind of right wing—but in a low-key way—and very much not cool. It isn't a unified or coherent movement ("traditional" cottages in, say, Shropshire are not the least bit classical, for instance).[10] But it nonetheless captures a general way of thinking about architecture that harks unashamedly back to ancient Greece and Rome, often also to the fantasied neatness of Georgian England's urban squares, and sometimes also to an interest in a kind of crafty, bustling idea of the medieval European city. It typically emphasizes some combination of civic grandeur and pride, but also modesty and knowing one's place; an attention to neatness, order, and symmetry, but also to allowing space for something quirky and individual; an interest in decorative elements, but from a fairly defined list; and a concern with building to a "human scale," or at least in a way that is recognizably *for* human beings, their everyday lives, and what is imagined to be their natural conviviality. It splits the history of architecture in two, with the advent of the twentieth century as the breaking point at which these long-standing ancient principles were abandoned and a radical and terrible rupture took place.[11]

What's crucial is that this way of thinking about architecture doesn't see itself as a historical style or a preference like any other—in the way that we might say, I don't know, "I like the Parthenon, you love the Guggenheim, tomayto-tomahto." Instead, traditional and classical architecture see themselves as part of a timeless tradition celebrating all that is eternally beautiful and good in built form. This means that people in these traditions sometimes see our relationship to architecture, and the buildings we tend to like, not as a product of taste or culture, or a random outcome of the historical period or place you happened to be born in, but rather as something governed by timeless, and indeed biological, principles of how buildings and humans naturally go together. You can like the Guggenheim if you want to; good for you. Just be aware that you're wrong, immoral, and maybe even a bit sick. Though there is nothing inherently right wing about all of this, classical and traditional architecture are often associated with the political right—indeed sometimes with the far right, who have lately made "modern architecture" a symbol of all they find wrong and degenerate about the contemporary world. Not for nothing did Donald Trump, in a parting shot of characteristically impotent spite, issue an order mandating that all new federal buildings must follow "classical and traditional architecture" styles.[12]

As I arrived at Downing College, though, quite in contrast to Trump's bumptious inanity, I found tweed, bonhomie, and genteel pastries on the lawn before the small assembly was redirected into Quinlan Terry's rather grand auditorium to think about how classical architecture and health might go together. Modern "hospital cities," the event handout declared, "are seen as dystopian worlds full of frightening technicality." This seemed weird to me as I settled into my seat in a corner of the room. I was no fan of the typical concrete hospital campus, but "frightening" seemed a bit much. "How we shape the interior and exterior environments of buildings that provide healthcare," the handout continued, "are questions of high currency." This is "not just about how we manage health, but... how we manage public policy and improve society itself."

The star attraction was John Simpson, a well-known classical architect who had recently worked on the Defence and National Rehabilitation Centre, expanding a facility for injured servicemen and -women into a center for the wider population. Due to "increasing neurological evidence of the benefits of traditional architecture to wellbeing," the center's website notes, "Stanford Hall, a grade II listed country house in the heart of Leicestershire was chosen for the project."[13] The idea had come from Gerald Grosvenor, the sixth duke of Westminster, who convinced the then UK defense secretary to back the project. The refurbished hall was formally handed over by the duke's son, Hugh Grosvenor—then a twenty-six-year-old aristocrat with about £10 billion to his name following the death of his father—as a gift to the nation in 2018.[14] I was still struggling to make sense of this distinctly British mélange of aristocracy, wealth, violence, health, and classicism as Simpson flashed up images of eighteenth-century hospitals. Look, call this a postcolonial chip on the shoulder all you like—but it seemed to me that the object being stapled together in this weird matrix of aesthetics and healing was not the injured serviceman or -woman. It was, in fact, the United Kingdom itself, a nation that, underneath its picturesque charms, remains thoroughly in hock to its financialized aristocratic class—an exhausted intellectual and aesthetic production whose misplaced sense of global import is (barely) held together by the shattered bodies of mostly working-class soldiers. Here, I thought, maybe a bit self-righteously, was what a dystopian world full of frightening technicality sounded like to me—*not* a 1960s hospital stuck on the edge of some provincial town.

Anyway, I hadn't come to hear John Simpson, but rather an architect called Donald Ruggles, whose book *Beauty, Neuroscience & Architecture* I had recently been engrossed in while trying to make sense of what exactly being in touch with nature might mean for architectural style.[15] What we call beauty, Ruggles argues in his book, is something like an evolved neurological capacity for recognizing visual patterns that are more likely to produce pleasure than pain. When we see a pattern we like, the ancient, emotional part of the brain triggers an endorphin release that the more recent *thinking* bit of the brain registers as a feeling of pleasure. When we say of a building or a work of art, then, that "it's beautiful," what we're really doing is giving voice to this sense of chemical pleasure. Some natural patterns, such as fractals, produce these effects. But Donald Ruggles's particular interest is a pattern that he calls the "nine square"—an intersection of two vertical lines and two horizontal lines to form nine boxes (like a tic-tac-toe board), which Ruggles argues is the visual basis of most of humankind's most famous structures, from the Parthenon to the US Capitol. The nine square, says Ruggles, in any event is "one of the root patterns provided by nature." It is recognized by tiny infants in human faces and is the basis of parental bonding.

In his Cambridge talk, Ruggles described how, as organisms, we need beauty to achieve homeostasis (a term for good biological regulation). We have a drive to seek out "beauty-pleasure events," moments when we see beautiful things and experience pleasure as a result. Such beautiful things, he said, are nonthreatening, coherent, and recognizable; beauty is what a baby sees in its mother's face—and so, I guess, when we look at a beautiful building and take pleasure in it, we are really gazing on the face of a kind of giant collective mother figure. But the critical thing is that beauty is not some aesthetic frippery; it's a natural thing, an evolutionary need. In its absence—for example, when confronted by contemporary architecture that does *not* use these kinds of patterns and is therefore ugly—we become stressed, even unwell. And this is why classical architecture matters: it literally makes us feel well. Architects, Ruggles said as his talk closed, are the new leaders of the health and well-being movement.

This is a claim made by lots of people who are interested in traditional approaches to architecture and design, or at least in an architecture that operates at a more recognizably "human" scale than the grand and ambitious visions of the twentieth century. To put it perhaps too simply, traditional architecture is good because it is good for us; it aligns with human nature. Modern architecture is bad because it denies and excludes the forms we naturally yearn for and that we actually need to be surrounded by in order to stay well and happy. When I later spoke to Nicholas Boys Smith, founder of the urban design social enterprise Create Streets,[16] who had also been at the event in Cambridge, he told me that his own ideas about the built environment were underpinned by a set of first principles and primary questions: "Where are people happy? Where do people like to be? What do people want to be in? And what's good for people?" It seems hard to object to this. But words like "happy" and "good," for all their gentle appearance, can be forceful. On its website, Create Streets says that it's trying to support "beautiful, sustainable places" that are "correlated with good wellbeing and public health outcomes."[17] It's not that people can't enjoy good well-being in tower blocks, Nicholas Boys Smith said to me, just that it might take more work. "The type of home that I think most of us tend to be most happy in," he went on, "are ones in which it's quite quick and easy to retreat into the private realm, but also where one can quite rapidly advance through a portal into the public realm, where we can engage with everything else." If you simply and undogmatically follow the evidence about what spaces are good for people, what they say they find beneficial, then you are likely to head down a particular aesthetic or structural path: "The evidence," he said to me, "supports a fairly traditional approach to urban morphology: block structure with clear private and public space; a clear framework of blocks and plots and streets with greenery interwoven throughout; vertical infrastructure that encloses a square, or a park, or a street."

This is all fair enough, I think. But even allowing that people *do* often say they favor more traditional or "human-scale" developments with natural materials, a gentler relationship to size, some loose feeling of "heritage," "belonging," and so on[18]—even if we accept all of this, we're still not obliged to simply take the public at their word. Indeed, it is wholly possible that insofar as traditional buildings really do make people happy (or at least insofar as people *say* they make them happy, which is not the same thing), this is not because of any built-in biological predisposition. It's not some random preference, outside culture and history, that we have to just accept at face value.[19] We could also argue—at least *I* would argue—that it's a product of the fact that we inhabit a stifling, backward-looking, and rather stupid age in which reactionary ideas about aesthetics and design dominate mainstream conversation, while the politically dodgy claims that "old is good," that "heritage" is valuable, and so on are simply out there, unquestioned, as if distributed through the water system like a moral nutrient. In this sense, "traditional" style might make people happy because they have learned over time—they have been rigorously *taught* over time—to associate that style with what they are told elsewhere are good and positive aspects of society. Alternatively, it might not make people happy at all, but when asked in surveys about architectural preferences or invited to participate in experiments, people know the culturally appropriate response and duly offer it. Either way, we can't simply conclude that people gravitate to traditional styles *naturally* or for no reason. To the extent that people do indeed often seem to favor traditional buildings, this is inseparable from the fact that they have been taught since early childhood to be repelled by anything new and modern, to internalize a dull conservative horror at the more forward-looking, revolutionary, social forms of collective inhabitation that emerged, slowly, painfully, and very partially, over the course of the twentieth century.

There is an intellectual heritage here. And a good deal of it passes through the conservative philosopher Roger Scruton, in particular through his ideas about beauty. The thing about beauty, according to Scruton, is that it's not a subjective matter where one opinion is as good as another—beauty is rather what Scruton called an ultimate value, "as important as truth and goodness."[20] Beauty, Scruton says, is even "a universal need of human beings." Without it, we are in "a spiritual desert." His first book, *The Aesthetics of Architecture*, in which he began a career as one of the world's most influential proponents of traditional building, is very wrong but also undeniably clever and original—as well as hugely influential.[21] In the book, Scruton says that experiencing architecture is not a simple sensation, like being touched. Rather, it involves intellectual work—you have to think and reason when you experience a building. And like any piece of intellectual work, experiencing architecture can be done well or poorly; your experience can be right or wrong. This is different from, say, the experience of looking at a tree, where a tree is a tree is a tree—an instance of what Scruton called *literal* perception. When you are engaged in literal perception, you're taking in basic information. A tree. Fine. Nothing else to say. In an *imaginative* experience, by contrast, you have to choose an interpretation. In this sense, the experience of a building, Scruton says, "admits of argument and proof, can be described as right, wrong, appropriate and misleading," and so on. Scruton separates what he called aesthetic pleasures—which are basically intellectual—from more sensual pleasures, which are immediate and have no real relationship to thought. Getting into a nice hot bath, for Scruton, is a sensual pleasure. You don't have to interpret your bath; it just feels nice on the bum. A truly *aesthetic* pleasure, on the other hand, the kind of pleasure you take in a building, is an intellectual act. Architectural taste, in Scruton's view, is not a spontaneous thing like enjoying your bath; it is an act of *reasoning*.

Scruton saw taste in architecture as objective, but not in the sense that there is a "truly" good architecture that you can simply recognize. He didn't think that Roman columns are just objectively lovely. He meant objective in the sense of a morally correct architecture. A Georgian streetscape, in Scruton's terms, should be preferred by planners not because it is somehow the nicest kind of street but because it is the most *good* kind of street. It's good in the same way that charity and love are good, i.e., eternally, universally, and inarguably. This is, for what it's worth, Scruton's big departure from Immanuel Kant—who argued that aesthetics and morality were not the same thing at all. Aesthetic experience, said Scruton, is about the search for "order and meaning." A building either confirms our humanity or alienates us from it. A Georgian streetscape, for example, reflects "the desire for a common public order." But compare that polite, well-ordered, mannerly Georgian frontage with, say, a public housing estate—"the maddest of all Utopian schemes," said Scruton, "where streets are replaced by empty spaces from which towers arise, towers bearing neither the mark of a communal order, nor any visible record of the individual house, and demonstrating in their every aspect the triumph of that collective individualism from which both community and individual are abolished."

Scruton published *The Aesthetics of Architecture* the same year that Margaret Thatcher became prime minister of the United Kingdom; his work caught a conservative zeitgeist that saw modern housing estates not simply as dysfunctional or ugly but as morally wrong, even bad for people. British social historians remember the decade that followed as one in which the state started a process of almost total disinvestment in the provision of public housing—especially as it was manifested in modernist schemes, the dominant form of social housing since World War II. This all took place through a combination of privatization and quasi-abandonment. Partly, this was simple Conservative ideology: public housing was a reminder that economic forces other than the market might produce attractive places to live, for many people, in surprisingly efficient ways. But it was also carried along by a series of specific arguments. In 1977, David Watkin, a historian, had suggested that architecture should have nothing to with "social policy" and that the mysterious individual genius of the architect was all that mattered.[22] In 1985, the geographer Alice Coleman published *Utopia on Trial*, which drew on the controversial concept of "defensible space" to argue that the very design of tower blocks made them susceptible to crime and social breakdown.[23] But the most important intellectual and political force undoubtedly came from people like Roger Scruton, who argued that kinds of architecture produce kinds of people—that, to put it in plain terms, bad streets and bad buildings make for bad humans, too.

As one contemporary observer astutely pointed out, there is a strange layering of often sophisticated moral philosophy and crude Thatcherism in Scruton's writing.[24] The veneration of traditional architecture may well have been couched in a gentlemanly language of rights, expression, and human nature, but the wrecking ball that came for the tower blocks of the 1950s and 1960s was moved as much by the desire for profit, and a general indifference to human misery, as by any high-flown ideas about humankind's timeless genius. In 2009, Scruton, whose ideas were by now mainstream among right-leaning politicians and intellectuals, made a documentary for the BBC, *Why Beauty Matters*. In the film, which is often unintentionally very funny, he goes on a walk around the center of Reading. The town, he says miserably, represents "the greatest crime against beauty that the world has yet seen, and that is the crime of modern architecture." The camera dwells on shots of admittedly not very lovely office buildings. "Everywhere you turn," Scruton says, "there is ugliness and mutilation....Everything has been vandalized." Poor Reading! Traditional architecture, by contrast, with its ornament and detail, "satisfies our need for harmony." It reminds us that we are not just animals with appetites, that we have "spiritual and moral needs, too." There is a close-up of a leaf and some dreamy choral music. Encounters with such beautiful things, intones Scruton in full-on messianic mode, should be understood as "calling us to the divine."

You might laugh—but I want to take this school of thought seriously here, not least because of how influential it has been. After all, this sense that traditional building satisfies a very real inner desire, the idea that it organizes our built-in natural inclination toward harmony and order, that it resolves the dystopian nightmare of twentieth-century public housing in particular, has clear real-world effects. In 2022, the American Institute of Architects—the main professional body for architects in the United States—threw its weight behind the bipartisan "democracy in design" bill, legislation trying to stop an incoming formal turn from modernism to classicism in the design code for US federal buildings.[25] In the UK in 2021, the then housing minister, Robert Jenrick, unveiled a national planning framework for new housing, asking councils to emphasize "traditional stonework" in the south of England, while in the north, new houses were to be designed in line with that region's "redbrick heritage."[26]

Roger Scruton died in 2020, leaving, whatever you think of him, a remarkably influential legacy. But if you want to follow his influence today, if you're looking for people pursuing research programs that trade in many of the same ideas, you need to set aside talk of the divine, or Kant, or what it could mean to encounter a nice leaf in Reading town center on a Tuesday afternoon. You need to look instead for people who talk about architecture and the brain, and landscape patterns, and the unconscious—and, in particular, about how a person's gaze can now be minutely tracked and measured as it moves across and through a visual scene.

"So this is Villa La Rotonda," said Ann Sussman to me down a Zoom connection from her home in Massachusetts. It was now some months since the Cambridge conference. "It's a really famous building in Italy. George Washington hired an architect in 1800 and built a building like this. That's why we have the same elevation on every $20 bill." We were looking at a shared screen, where I could see a front-on view of a beautiful white cubic structure placed delicately on top of a grassy hill, as if from a child's model. The building was fronted by a classical portico, held up by six slender columns, and on top of the portico was the outline of a dome. This home was designed in the late 1560s by Andrea Palladio, the most famous and successful classical architect of renaissance Italy, in the countryside near the then Republic of Venice. On my screen, though, the image of the building was covered with yellow dots of varying sizes, which were connected by thin lines, like a network diagram. "So this is really fascinating," Ann went on. "This technology is what Honda, BMW, GM, Procter & Gamble use." She was showing me how she uses eye-tracking software—literally, software that tracks where you direct your gaze—to study how people are unconsciously attracted to particular design features. "What the dots are doing," she explained, "is tracking how the research subject's brain, without her awareness, makes her look. You're really seeing your animal brain architecture at work here." The suggestion, in other words, is that your brain knows what you're doing before you yourself do, that to know what really matters aesthetically, we don't need to ask you what you think you like; we just need to track where your brain tells you to look.

As Ann flicked through some more slides, we talked about the use of scientific tools in marketing and web design and the effort that huge companies are putting into figuring out how long it takes you to pay attention to a particular on-screen button. Trying to understand how the subliminal brain works is a major growth area in business schools, with eye tracking just the tip of the iceberg. The idea is that we don't necessarily consciously know what we like or what will capture our attention in a scene. In fact, when we take in a view, our gaze is directed not by what we think we want to look at, but rather by an evolved capacity for identifying danger in the landscape. We're not aware of this. Instead, our evolved brain takes in the scene before we have any idea what's going on. This evolutionary adaptation, it's claimed, is why we have a subliminal attraction to particular sorts of scenes, elevations, and vistas—these are scenes, like overlooks or open savannas, from where danger can clearly be seen (recall here what we said earlier about biophilia and attention restoration theory). This is also why landscapes that don't look much like the places we were living in when our brain evolved this capacity—modern cities, for example—produce so much stress.

Now on our shared screen, we were looking at an image of a flat and—I had to admit it—very uninviting modern building. "Can you see," Ann said, very seriously now, "how dangerous facades like this are for the nervous system? You're going to have more cortisol secretion." She explained how companies like Apple can measure how much people smile when they see something. "And what's amazing," she said, "is you can really see the biological impact of your design intervention because when you smile, that releases oxytocin; that's a hugging hormone." In her book *Cognitive Architecture*, cowritten with Justin B. Hollander, Ann Sussman argues that "the repetitive parallel lines common to most modern built environments stress the brain."[27] Parallel lines are unusual in nature; they don't feel natural to us. And so it requires work—demanding, stressful work—to take them in. Humans "evolved to assess their environment," Sussman and Hollander write, "the natural one, quickly and not the modern industrial or post-industrial one. Pointed shapes, such as barbs, thorns, quills, sharp teeth, were ever-present threats in our evolutionary past.... We evolved for this past environment, and remain designed for it."

This view has some pretty sharp consequences. In one reading, modernist building design—with its straight lines, its sometimes blank facades, its hidden doors, and its lack of decorative features—seems so ill-suited to our evolved brain function that it might even be the outcome of some kind of neurological pathology. This is something Ann Sussman takes very seriously. "Key fathers of modern architecture," she said to me, "were German World War I vets." And they all suffered from PTSD. "When you have PTSD," she went on, "your brain doesn't let you see reality normally or neurotypically." I guess I looked skeptical at this point—and the truth is, I *was*. "I was invited to present at a medical conference in 2019," she said, "and then I asked a psychologist who teaches at Harvard Medical School, and other leading trauma psychologists in New York, to look at my slideshow of modernist architecture. And this is what they said: if you never told me who lived there, I could tell this person had been traumatized. Classic PTSD." Bauhaus founder Walter Gropius, she argued, who served for some years on the Western front, designed buildings that resemble bunkers and trenches because of how the war had damaged his brain. "Gropius," Ann said definitively, "was mentally ill. He'd wake up screaming in the middle of the night." I guess I still looked skeptical. "Look," she said, "Walt Disney decides in 1955 on an empty orange grove to make the most successful tourist destination in the world. He designs Disneyland Main Street, about a mile long, not a modern building on it. Why do you think he did that? Because he had intuition that this is what people wanted. He sent his *Imagineers* all over Europe to look at where people were happiest, and then he replicated that to invent the happiest place on earth. When you go down a modern street, your brain, your body, actually can't regulate your nervous system because it doesn't have the fixations to make you feel safe, because of how we evolved for vigilance. What traditional architecture does is it gets us out of the vigilant state because it gives us the subliminal fixations the brain desires. When you build modern architecture, by contrast, you're building stressful architecture."

I took all this in slowly.

"Traditional architecture," Ann Sussman said with finality, "externally expresses the hidden brain design that most naturally meshes with our nervous system."

In the late 1960s and early 1970s, just as Roger Scruton, fresh from his PhD at Cambridge, was introducing a course on aesthetics at Birkbeck College in London, a widespread panic emerged about the sustainability of human development on planet earth. If the postwar decades had established endless growth as the apparently normal state of economic affairs in Europe and North America, by the late 1960s, drawing on the more critical work of economists like J. K. Galbraith as well as on Rachel Carson's surprise hit, *Silent Spring*, policy makers and think tanks had begun to become skittish about how long all of this producing, consuming, and growing could go on.[28] In 1972, the Club of Rome—a weird, self-appointed group of what today we would call thought leaders—commissioned a report, *The Limits to Growth*, which used a computer model to predict a sharp decline in the earth's population as industrial and ecological capacity was reached. When a series of rolling oil shocks emerged the following year, it seemed as if the capacity of the earth and its resources to endlessly sustain human activity, and human habitats, was suddenly, and quite radically, in question.

In 1969, the Glasgow-born landscape architect Ian McHarg published his landmark book, *Design with Nature*, a work that carried this widespread sense of ecological anxiety into the worlds of architecture and city planning.[29] Like many others, McHarg had come to see urbanization and industrialization as a kind of "self-mutilation," a disaster for the natural world. He lamented the "bondage" of industrial civilization and even described his own home city, Glasgow, as a "smear" on the surrounding countryside. *Design with Nature* was a kind of antiurban polemic, a book about limiting the city and preserving "the bounty of that great cornucopia [the countryside] which is our inheritance." It was a huge and instant success. Over the course of the 1970s, McHarg became an influential figure—"one of the very few landscape architects since Frederick Law Olmsted Sr.," noted Anne Whiston Spirn, herself a famous landscape architect, "who have commanded widespread notice, respect and influence outside the design and planning fields."[30]

McHarg was hardly the first planner or architect to foreground nature. But he was distinctive—and enormously successful—in how he wrapped an emergent sense of midcentury ecological crisis into the fields of planning and architecture. He was not simply arguing, in that familiar hand-wringing sort of way, for a more "sustainable" approach to planning. He had a sharper account of human civilization as, whether we like it or not, ecologically and biologically constrained—and in how the planet might yet remind us (at least some of us) of that constraint. There's something very dodgy here, however. If McHarg's position is at least partly rooted in an understandable concern with preserving the natural environment, it also has the familiar chemical whiff of the jackboot about it. "The real fundamental division in the world," he wrote in a 1971 pamphlet, "is between these people who are not planetary diseases and those who are necrotic pathological tissue walking around pretending to be men."[31] This is, of course, a wholly fascist sentiment. As the historian Peder Anker makes clear, McHarg, who was much inspired by the South African racist and segregationist ecologist John Phillips, was working in a British colonial tradition of landscape design, contrasting the degenerate West with the "harmonious naturalism of the 'Orient.'"[32]

McHarg worked at famous universities; his books were reviewed in mainstream papers; he had the ear of politicians and policy makers. If we wanted to, we could add his US-based interest in ecological design to a UK-based concern with aesthetic philosophy—equally mainstream and influential—and we could use these as the starting point for a genealogy of today's broadly conservative interest in traditional design and planning as a kind of biological necessity. But McHarg wasn't the only person with design training who was becoming anxious about the state of the planet in the 1960s and 1970s. On the opposite coast of the United States, experiments in ecological design and living emerged not from the Ivy League but from a more free-floating early internet culture and what the writer Douglas Murphy calls the "cybernetic ecology" of people like Buckminster Fuller and Stewart Brand.[33] By the 1980s, this mix of ideas and influences would lead to the bizarre Biosphere 2 experiment, in which a group of volunteers attempted to spend a year living sustainably in a sealed greenhouse, an event that was grounded in—in Murphy's words—"an odd mix of space-age nostalgia, environmental utopianism and mass entertainment."

This period also produced spaces like the New Alchemy Institute, a ranch and research center concerned with the production of food and with how to build new communities around agricultural experiments. New Alchemy was founded, wrote the science writer Nicholas Wade in *Science* after he visited in 1975, by "a small group of people who consider that modern American agriculture is a mighty edifice built on sand."[34] The institute—funded by, among others, the Rockefeller Brothers Fund—worked on organic farming methods as well as what its leaders called "bioshelters," greenhouses that were designed to sustain an entire food ecosystem. It's true, wrote Wade, that like many of their contemporaries, the group had an antitechnology, somewhat apocalyptic bent. But it was here, nonetheless, that two of the founders of the New Alchemy, John Todd and Nancy Jack-Todd, set out the first principles of what we today call "biomimicry" or "biomimetic design."[35] And it was from here, finally, that a second, highly consequential tradition emerged for thinking about the nexus of ecology, design, and human life.

Biomimetic design is design that mimics forms or processes from nature, whether this means mimicking the shape of a natural object, such as a leaf or a peanut shell, or reproducing some process or principle, such as how a termite nest regulates heat. Crucially, biomimetic design does this (or is supposed to do this) not for aesthetic reasons but out of a desire to reproduce some good or useful effect of the natural world. It may sound simple, but these principles have traveled a long way from 1970s cyborg-hippie culture to the cutting-edge work of major international design firms today.

The materials scientist Julian Vincent gives the example of the Bundle Towers, a proposed replacement for the World Trade Center designed by Foreign Office Architecture (FOA) in 2002.[36] Skyscrapers have developed over time to handle the challenge of height by using large structural beams at the edges; this means the higher you go, the more structure you need at the edges—and so, as a building goes higher, its interiors shrink, its occupants are farther back from natural light, and so on. Taking a cue from how natural materials like bamboo solve the problem of growing upward, FOA proposed a skyscraper composed of "a bundle of interconnected structural tubes," or a series of thin, undulating rods, bumping into each other as they snaked upward, thereby reducing the need for heavy structural materials at the perimeter. This is a classic biomimetic approach, looking at how a natural process has evolved to solve an environmental challenge—in this case, the need to remain stable while growing upward—and modeling an architectural form to reproduce it.

Just as the roots of this approach are entangled in the early days of Silicon Valley, today much of the world of biomimetic architecture leaks into a related set of "computational" or "generative" approaches to building design. This is partly because a lot of computational power is necessary to do the calculations that make biometric designs thinkable. But it's also because patterns generated in nature are, at least in principle, expressible in numbers: the patterns that appear on the wall of an expanding bubble, for example, as air pushes its wall outward, can be set out mathematically and modeled with an equation.[37] This means you can take some material, a very thin film, for instance, and, using the parameters of your bubble-wall equation, realistically model what will happen to the film when it comes under the same constraint as the bubble (that is, how it would act if there was air expanding within it). You can then use that model as the basis of a design. Suddenly, a whole world opens up in which architects are able to use the strict parameters provided by generative structures found in nature—a bubble expanding, a leaf growing, a river flowing toward the sea—to map out novel three-dimensional forms.

Take the Beijing National Aquatics Centre, built for the 2008 Olympic Games, with its famous soap-bubble exterior. This was designed using a proof from two physicists who had established, for the first time, the science of how bubbles fill space as they expand.[38] As the engineering firm Arup put it (it was part of the design consortium), "the building's form is inspired by the natural formation of soap bubbles. Arup's designers and structural engineers realized that a structure based on this unique geometry would be highly repetitive and buildable, while appearing organic and random."[39]

Of course the term "inspired by" is doing a lot of work here. Ultimately, these designers were perhaps less interested in imitating nature than they were in making a cool and functional building for their client—which is fair enough. But in this sense, "biomimetic" architecture, for all its claims to being innovative and different, is generally still rooted in a very conventional notion of how design works. In the end, no matter how much your building looks like a peanut shell or an ant farm, somewhere a person in an expensive suit is maintaining a spreadsheet that ensures it's offering a reasonable return on investment. For *other* people in this emergent genre, though, such as the architect and theorist Achim Menges, what matters is following biological *principles* and letting the aesthetic and functional chips fall where they may. Consider a brick, he said to me in an interview; a brick at the top of a wall takes only a fraction of the load of one at the base, yet we build the two bricks exactly the same, using up the same resources, as if they all had to be so sturdy. An evolutionary system would probably not be so wasteful—and these kinds of *principles* from nature are what matter, and are worth mimicking (I am paraphrasing Menges here), not a roof that looks like forest canopy, for example,

Imagine if, rather than a blueprint for a building coming from the mind of a human designer, it just sort of *emerged* from a set of inputs—a bit like a flower emerges from the code of a germ cell. There are genetic rules governing what the flower will look like, obviously, but there is also some variety as the emerging flower meets its local, environmental conditions. In what Achim Menges and his collaborators call "morphogenetic computational design," architects use computers to mimic this kind of process in nature. If you think of a finished building as if it were a human, a cat, or a nice oak tree, then think of the morphogenetic architect as someone trying *not* to create the organism, but rather to figure out the genetic code from which the organism sprang.[40] Of course, organisms don't simply emerge in their environment and then sit there unchanged; they respond to the environmental conditions they find themselves in. In the same way, the morpho-ecological approach in architecture works with materials that have an interactive, ongoing relationship with the environment—materials that will change and adapt over time.

This isn't new, exactly. The copper dome on a nice neoclassical building from the nineteenth century is green today because the oxidizing copper, exposed to the elements, produces a patina to protect itself. The people who put that dome on there knew this was going to happen—they were planning on an environmental adaptation. But morpho-ecology goes a step further, even transforming architecture into something biological as such. The goal is not simply to figure out how human planning might be ecologically improved, but rather to imagine how architects and designers could *make natural environments*. This means getting away from the constraints and rules of modernist design—this is where you work; this is where you sleep; this is the space for the factory; this is the space for the home—and producing space where things change over time, where the boundaries aren't clear, where spaces and buildings are "constructed through social operations and the local experience of space-time."[41] Instead of having a material that you can shape or form in particular ways, you let the material find its own form as it actually comes to exist in the world. Rather than being put in place by the master designer, the material now learns to organize itself.

This all quickly becomes supertechnical, superphilosophical, and superweird. We are talking about buildings growing, after all, and about using things like mushrooms and watery scum as building materials—but we're also talking about high-powered computing and extremely futuristic-looking design. In this world of generative architecture, the design historian Christina Cogdell points out, "the lines between computation, architecture and biology begin to blur."[42] One recent academic paper on artificial intelligence in architecture wondered, quite seriously, whether the capacity of neural networks to learn to generate images might mean that machines could even *hallucinate* buildings in the future.[43] This weird oscillation between machine and organism, between the dull mandates of geology and wild sci-fi phantasm, is absolutely characteristic and has aesthetic consequences. As Cogdell again put it, generally "the final products share a common aesthetic, one that entails an interconnected proliferation of component-based forms that morph through different curvatures, resulting in a stylized organic appearance." In other words, what begins in a world of extremely dense philosophy, and hugely sophisticated computing, in some of the world's finest architectural research institutions often ends up as a fancy office building that's a bit curvy or kind of looks like a shell. As with all human endeavors, the gap between desire and reality is sometimes rather large here. But also, in a way, that doesn't matter very much. What matters here is the *desire* for architecture to be something else—not an engineering practice involving materials, space, a certain amount of money, the needs of the clients, and so on, but a biological process in which an object produces and reproduces itself in relationship to a natural environment and according to a set of evolutionary processes that are *themselves* incrementally morphing over time, in a feedback loop with a set of biological and environmental conditions. The usually stated aim is for the architect to be less of a designer, less of an artist, and more of a scientific researcher. That means there's a certain abdication of agency here—even of humanity as such. I couldn't help but wonder, as I read these texts, whether the desire to play with living systems, with life, doesn't betray a different kind of fantasy—whether the true desire here is to be thought not a biologist but, in fact, a minor god.

At the beginning of 2019, I saw an advertisement online for a conference on "living architecture" in Seville. On a whim, I got on a plane and arrived—it was by now mid-March—in the middle of a religious festival, where groups of sinister-looking besuited men paraded life-sized effigies of Christ and the Virgin Mary through the steaming early-evening streets. The next morning, fuzzy with Catholicism and sherry, I took my seat among an audience of mostly local students in the university auditorium's gleaming white plastic chairs to hear some of the leading proponents of a radical new approach to architecture and nature. The goal is not about creating "good architecture," the architect and designer Waltraut

Hoheneder told the conference in a dazzling opening address. "That was twenty years ago." A plant, Hoheneder said, has basically the same problem as a house—managing water and solar energy, creating shade. She talked about the structural use of hydrogels, mycelium, algae, and 3D-printed calcium carbonate; she talked about no longer seeing growth as directional and economic, but rather as cyclical and biological; she talked about how water can transport nutrients and regulate temperature around a space; she talked about building in Antarctica and on the international space station; she talked about artificial life, and why we should think about buildings as partners, and also about fungal webs and the moon. I scribbled frantically, half delirious with heat and manzanilla in the weirdly intense spring weather. "What is the unit of design in nature?" asked the next speaker, the British experimental architect Rachel Armstrong. In Venice, she said, there are two architectures—on the surface, the Venetian Gothic that we all know, and then there is also the scum that reveals itself between high and low tides, forming a kind of "second city," In my notebook, I wrote WETNESS, VITALISM, GROWTH and then, a bit overcome, left to walk under the orange trees, loosely in the direction of the Cathedral Santa Maria de la Sede, the world's largest Gothic cathedral, where I had planned to see (and vaguely curse) the tomb of Christopher Columbus.

On the way, though, I got lost, and more by accident than design, I eventually somehow found my way to Las Setas—the famous "Mushrooms of Seville," an urban renewal project designed by the German architect Jürgen Mayer, which also claims to be the largest wooden structure in the world. Facing much technical complexity, it was finally completed in 2011 amid the familiar public controversies about cost overruns. It now claims to be more popular than the cathedral. There's apparently a market there and a walkway along the top, but it was just so hot that day, and this ersatz wooden mushroom wasn't doing much to help me regulate my body temperature, so I left fairly quickly and sought shelter instead in the dark little nineteenth- and twentieth-century bars, which were much cooler and full of more sherry, cold meat, and these weird little hard crackers that are so salty and moreish and yet really feel like they're going to break your teeth. As I lightly split some more veneers, I was thinking hard about the politics of these experiments and what it might actually mean to reimagine design as a process of nature, and where all of this might lead a person.

In 2008, the year of the Beijing Olympics, the architect and theorist Patrik Schumacher, then a partner in the firm of Zaha Hadid and now its leader following Hadid's death in 2016, proposed the term "parametricism" or "parametric architecture," which he then developed into a kind of oddball social theory. "The key issues that avant-garde architecture and urbanism should be addressing," Schumacher wrote, "can be summarized in the slogan: organizing and articulating the increased complexity of post-Fordist society. The task is to develop an architectural and urban repertoire that is geared up to create complex, polycentric urban and architectural fields which are densely layered and continuously differentiated."[44] Society, in other words, is no longer neatly ordered along the industrial lines of the twentieth century; we no longer have the factory, and then the houses near the factory, and farther on the town center, where you spend your pay from the factory. What we have now is...well, something else. "Interarticulate," Schumacher commanded his readers, "hyberdize [*sic*], morph, deterritorialize, deform, iterate, use splines, nurbs, generative components, script rather than model." This is all pretentious bollocks, obviously, but architectural theorists, for whatever reason, seem to get a kind of ejaculatory pleasure from this kind of thing. Still, Schumacher has a strategic goal that is clear enough: he wants to remake the notion of style, taking it away from being a set of aesthetic preferences, or a question of fashion, and into something more like a program of biological research.[45]

Rather than having building design simply dissolve into a messy pluralism in the wake of modernism's failures—as critics like Charles Jencks argued in the 1990s—parametricism can be a hegemonic new style. What's driving Schumacher is an attempt to reconcile, on the one hand, a vision of society as something deeply complex and intertwined, where the different bits are not obviously separated from another, but *some* kind of order is still working itself out; and, on the other hand, an architectural style that can meet this pattern through its own system of "organized (law-governed) complexity" that works like "natural systems." Society today, we might say, is more like a beehive than a factory, so why are we still designing factories rather than beehives? Or better still, why are we "designing" at all, rather than taking the beehive as a model of how a complex natural system can *itself* generate the physical structure that houses it?

For a few years, parametricism was hot stuff at the self-consciously avant-garde architectural institutions. By 2016, though, Schumacher was desperately working to halt what he saw as its "increasing marginalization" in the profession, which he blamed partly on the 2008 financial crash.[46] His response was "parametr-icism 2.0"—an attempt to move away from manifestos and engage in "serious, relevant, high-performance work." Moving from individual buildings to whole cities, he also called for a "para-metric urbanism" in which unfettered free-market logic would resolve the complexities of urban planning. "The market process," Schumacher wrote, "is an evolutionary one"—like the unfolding of a genetic code, it involves mutation, selection, and reproduc-tion. Buildings or neighborhoods are like new species settling into an ecological niche. Rethinking urban planning from such a perspective reduces disorienting visual chaos in cities, or what Schumacher calls "garbage spill urbanism." The master architect is here in search of order, and he takes order to be natural. There are, needless to say, worrisome antecedents to such views of the city. That same year, in a speech in Berlin of all places, Schumacher suggested privatizing all urban space and eliminating social hous-ing. Protests predictably ensued. "I've been depicted as this kind of villain, as this fascist," he complained to the *Guardian*.[47]

In the end, maybe precisely because he is so limited a thinker, Schumacher is a useful figure for seeing how two apparently very different ways of thinking about the urban environment—one tra-ditional and backward-looking, the other technology-driven and futuristic—are nonetheless united by a single political vision. In his writing, you get a clear distaste for the convivial mess of urban modernity, a pearl-clutching horror at the shonky utopianism that drove so much public design and planning in the middle decades of the twentieth century. This is precisely the same distaste and dislike, of course, that one gets from the clay-fingered scribblings of King Charles. Schumacher and Charles are driven by a shared desire not only for hierarchy, rationality, and order, but for the reproduction of these elements, in the built environment, *as they have been given to us in nature.* Architecture reproduces the social order, and the social order is a product of nature. Nature—poor, benighted, built-over nature—is understood by both as a collection of technological instructions *and* a set of moral indictments. These are just two kinds of antiurbanism, in other words, moved by the same central conceit: that the city is or should be a living thing; that tending it and cultivating it, as one might cultivate a vegetable plot or a pasture, is the royal road to resolving the seemingly endless crises that cathect our increasingly fractious and anxious urban age.

In the end, it's not style that matters for either traditionalism or parametricism; it's ideology. Patrik Schumacher's work—as far from "traditional" as it is possible to get—expresses the belief that we are biological creatures living in ecological space, that our buildings should align with complex, natural, evolutionary processes because this is the form that our society is taking. Order, in this approach, is maintained not through a rigid, top-down hierarchical organization, but through the gradual intertwinement of bottom-up biological codes. For someone like Donald Ruggles, by contrast, traditional architecture expresses the fact that we have evolved to appreciate particular forms, and that if we don't continue to build those forms, which we call "beautiful," then we are actively working against our nature in a way that is likely to make us unwell.

For all that they may affect to disdain one another, what these positions share is an abhorrence of the twentieth century as a period when architecture and biology became disastrously unhooked from one another. The parametric architect looks *forward*, into a radical future of daring and overbearing design; the urban traditionalist looks *back* to what we used to know about columns, facades, and cute little chimney pots. But this is a trivial difference. What holds the two together—what, in the end, largely dominates architectural and urban thinking today—is a singular conviction that the central problem of architecture in the twentieth century is that it left nature too far behind.

Toward the end of the writing of this book, I went back to the Church of Christ the King in Turners Cross for the first time in, I think, several decades. It was a miserable day in early January—the kind of bruisingly dark and wet morning that made me question my decision to leave Bristol, to return to live in Cork, the city where I grew up. Finding myself unexpectedly at a loose end, with Christmas over and a new job yet to start, I decided to cycle back to where I'd truly come from—to the city's unglamorous southern suburbs and their rows of semidetached and terraced postwar houses, but also to that strange gray ziggurat looming over the slate roofs, which still seemed most plausibly explained as a kind of cosmic glitch, an error inserted from an entirely different timeline.

Inside, shaking off the rain and not really sure why I'd come here, I realized that Christ the King—which was completely empty—is actually all triangles. They fold down, like inverted steps, from the ceiling to the aisles, only to then rise up again behind the altar in serrated concrete rows, forming a large triangular screen facing the nave, which is then topped with a small, very plain golden cross. From this pinnacle, the congregation moves back and out in another set of threes, organized into neat, plain rows of wooden benches. Along the back wall, I found subtly decorative panels composed of three different cuts of stone—polished, whitewashed, rough. I noticed, too, for the first time that the stations of the cross that ran up and down the sides of the church—that bane of childhood Good Friday services—were carved directly into the stone and then painted over. On the noticeboard, a reliable lady advertised cleaning services; marriage counseling was offered to worried couples; there were several entreaties to consider becoming a priest.

I sat down heavily. It was hard to believe that when I was a child, this place had stood in for everything that I fantasized—as so many adolescents fantasize—I might one day get away from: provincial conservatism, inward-looking self-satisfaction, the dull reproduction of a reactionary moral system that even its own defenders didn't bother pretending to believe in. Obviously, I didn't get away (no one does). But now, anyway, the church and its universe hit kind of differently. The space was sadder and smaller than I remembered it, of course, as is always the case with one's childhood world but somehow, too, as an enclosure, the church seemed more morally and politically ambiguous, maybe even more hopeful, than I recalled. What world were they trying to bring into being, I wondered, the commissioners, designers, builders, and worshippers at this giant tomb-like monolith in a then desperately poor country, only barely and partially independent, still bearing the scars of civil war? This was a world, certainly, no less than that materialized in the work of Antoni Gaudí, that was also wrestling with time—tied, in one sense, to the reproduction of a particular kind of clerical tradition but also striving to represent the hopes and ambitions of a wider community that, suddenly and perhaps unexpectedly, had become unmoored from its own fate.

Christ the King is an attempt to catechize a certain vision of modernity, industry, and rationality—of new forms of collectivity, even new ways of being and living in space. The church's architect, Barry Byrne, says the historian Vincent L. Michael, wholly embraced the "positivist discourse of twentieth-century modernism" for which "societal ills became solvable design problems."[48] His work in designing churches—Byrne was himself a progressive Catholic—was deeply congruent with the "machine-age rationalism" of figures like Walter Gropius, Le Corbusier, and Ludwig Mies van der Rohe—some of whom Byrne had met on a European trip in 1924, which included a visit to the then thriving Bauhaus. Tradition or precedent in Byrne's work, wrote Lewis Mumford, "is in the nature of the Church's ceremonies and observances, rather than in the crystallization of these elements into some special architectural form in, say, the thirteenth century."[49] For him, the church is not a set of spires and buttresses and gargoyles; it is simply "a sanctuary surrounded by a congregation." Here, for the many faults of the institution it sustains, is a provincial Irish Catholic church reaching out to European modernism and to European urbanism between the wars; it's a building that, in the face of so many temptations otherwise, at least attempts something other than the simple reproduction of traditional form, that refuses the ineluctable working-through of fate, of history, of environmental conditions, of slowly developing human biology.

This message from 1931, the year of the church's construction, seems quite lost today, amid a debate about the city and its form, dominated by a reactionary antiurbanism as it appears in different guises—here, traditional and focused on human nature; there, future-oriented and concerned with ecological preservation. These are ultimately, each in their own way, negative and fatalistic ideologies—one looking to the imagined certainties of the past, the other to a half-desired apocalypse in the coming decades. What each understands as nature or biology, whether it comes in the form of a Doric column or a soap bubble, is, in the end, little more than a miserable politics of inevitability, an attempt to quieten any loose talk of reason, modernity, collectivity, transcendence, or change. And if we are not minded to simply defend words like "reason" and "progress"—which have themselves propelled a great deal of political violence—nonetheless, the Church of Christ the King, a piece of ecclesiastical architecture in provincial Ireland, offers an unexpected reminder that other futures are still imaginable; that it might still be possible to put a glitch in these deathly visions; that something unexpectedly gray and graceful, something clean and sharp and new, might yet cut through a landscape, and a timeline, that we have now been too long given to imagine as unchangeable, eternal, inevitable, *natural*.

ACKNOWLEDGMENTS

I'm grateful first to everyone who took the time to talk to me during the research for this book, not all of whom made it to the page but all of whom were nonetheless critical to helping me make better arguments. Even where there's disagreement, I've tried hard in the text to make sure people's voices and arguments are always represented seriously and with care—I hope this comes across!

Research for this book was funded through an award from the Leverhulme Trust, for which I am extremely grateful. I have written a good deal about William Lever's twentieth-century legacy in these pages. I am glad to see the trust currently foregrounding work on Lever's legacy, and I look forward to seeing how this work develops in the future.

Thanks to Chris Wellbelove, my agent, who was the first person to recognize that there was actually a book here and who then successfully nagged me into writing that book. I met Chris mostly though a scheme run by the UK's Arts and Humanities Research Council and the BBC called New Generation Thinkers—I'm extremely grateful to everyone involved in that scheme, working hard to keep it afloat amid difficult times for humanities research.

I'm grateful to everyone who has had an editorial hand in this book—especially at Faber, Fred Baty and Alex Bowler, and at Basic, TJ Kelleher, Lara Heimert, and Kelly Lenkevich; a great deal of what's on the page here is due to the careful ministrations of Fred and Lara in particular, though they bear no responsibility for the infelicities that remain.

I did the writing for this book in three exceptionally convivial and intellectually rich places: first, the School of Social Sciences at Cardiff University; second, the Wellcome Centre for Cultures and Environments of Health at the University of Exeter; and now, having returned home, the Radical Humanities Laboratory and Department of Sociology and Criminology at University College Cork. There's no space to mention the many, many people at all three places who have helped me to think more sharply and carefully about the arguments I make here. But thank you to all!

Most of all, I am grateful to Neasa, Finbarr, and Mary, with whom I lived in several different cities during the writing of this book. I do honestly sometimes wonder if the resolutely affirmative view of city life in this book comes, in large part, from having always shared urban space with Neasa Terry, the best person I've ever met, and then some time later with the other two, who also have their charms. But there's nothing much to be done about that now.

NOTES

INTRODUCTION

1. For biographical detail here, I rely on Laura Wood Roper, *FLO: A Biography of Frederick Law Olmstead* (Baltimore, MD: Johns Hopkins University Press, 1973).

2. Frederick Law Olmsted, "Preliminary Report upon the Proposed Suburban Village at Riverside, near Chicago," *Olmsted: Writings on Landscape, Culture and Society*, ed. Charles Beveridge (New York: Library of America, 2015).

3. Frederick Law Olmsted, "To Edward Everett Hale," *Olmsted: Writings on Landscape, Culture and Society*, ed. Charles Beveridge (New York: Library of America, 2015).

4. Dorceta E. Taylor, *The Rise of the American Conservation Movement: Power, Privilege and Environmental Protection* (Durham, NC: Duke University Press, 2016).

5. Peter Hall, *Cities of Tomorrow: An Intellectual History of Urban Planning and Design since 1880* (Oxford, UK: Blackwell, 1996).

6. Ebenezer Howard, *Garden Cities of To-morrow* (1898; repr., Cambridge, MA: MIT Press, 1965).

7. Frank Lloyd Wright, *The Living City* (New York: Horizon Press, 1958).

8. See https://twitter.com/BIG_Architects/status/1433023271352651779.

9. See https://cityoftelosa.com/#CityofTelosa.

10. Henry George, *The Writings of Henry George. Progress and Poverty: An Inquiry into the Cause of Industrial Depressions and of Increase of Want with Increase of Wealth: The Remedy* (Doubleday and McClure Company, 1898), https://www.gutenberg.org/cache/epub/55308/pg55308-images.html.

11. Bjarke Ingels, *Yes Is More: An Archicomic on Architectural Evolution* (Cologne, Germany: Taschen, 2009).

12. Telosa, accessed April 19, 2023, cityoftelosa.com.

13. See What Is Neom?, https://www.neom.com/en-us/regions/theline.

14. Tom Ravenscroft, "Saudi Arabia Unveils Plans for Octagonal Floating Port City in Neom," *Dezeen*, December 21, 2022, https://www.dezeen.com/2022/12/21 /oxagon-floating-port-city-neom-saudi-arabia.

15. Ruth Michaelson, "'It's Being Built on Our Blood': The True Cost of Saudi Arabia's $500bn Megacity," *Guardian*, May 4, 2020, https://www.theguardian.com /global-development/2020/may/04/its-being-built-on-our-blood-the-true-cost-of -saudi-arabia-5bn-mega-city-neom.

16. Mohammed Rasool (2022) "Saudi Arabia Sentences 3 Men to Death for Refusing to Vacate NEOM Development Site," *Vice*, October 11, 2022, https://www .vice.com/en/article/5d3kkd/neom-saudi-arabia-howeitat-tribe.

CHAPTER 1: CITY LIFE

1. On this voyage, see "GH," "Bauhaus Aboard!," originally published as part of the Bauhaus 100 series on the Bauhaus Kooperation site, accessed April 18, 2023, https://www.bauhauskooperation.com/kooperation/project-archive/magazine /discover-the-bauhaus/bauhaus-aboard.

2. Eric Mumford, "CIAM and the Communist Bloc, 1928–59," *Journal of Architecture* 14 (2009): 237–254.

3. For biographical detail in this chapter, I draw especially on Nicholas Fox Weber, *Le Corbusier: A Life* (New York: Knopf, 2008).

4. See Brian Ackley, "Le Corbusier's Algerian Fantasy: Blocking the Casbah," *Bidoun* (Winter 2006), https://www.bidoun.org/articles/le-corbusier-s-algerian -fantasy.

5. See Simone Brott, "The Le Corbusier Scandal, or, was Le Corbusier a Fascist?," *Fascism* 6, no. 2 (2017): 196–227.

6. Le Corbusier, *The Athens Charter* (New York: Grossman, 1973).

7. Peder Anker, *From Bauhaus to Ecohouse: A History of Ecological Design* (Baton Rouge: Louisiana State University Press, 2010).

8. Le Corbusier, *The City of Tomorrow* (London: Architectural Press, 1947).

9. Le Corbusier.

10. On Greek modernism, see Yorgos Simeoforidis and Yannis Aesopos, *Landscapes of Modernisation: Greek Architecture, 1960s and 1990s* (Athens: Metapolis Press, 1999).

11. On phytoncides, see Anna Lena Philips, "A Walk in the Woods," *American Scientist* 99, no. 4 (2011): 301.

12. See Qing Li, *Into the Forest: How Trees Can Help You Find Health and Happiness* (New York: Penguin, 2019).

13. Kristine Engemann, Carsten Bøcker Pedersen, Lars Arge, Constantinos Tsirogiannis, Preben Bo Mortensen, and Jens-Christian Svenning, "Residential Green Space in Childhood Is Associated with Lower Risk of Psychiatric Disorders from Adolescence into Adulthood," *PNAS* 116, no. 11 (2019): 5188–5193.

14. MaryCarol R. Hunter, Brenda W. Gillespie, and Sophie Yu-Pu Chen, "Urban Nature Experiences Reduce Stress in the Context of Daily Life Based on Salivary Biomarkers," *Frontiers in Psychology* 10 (2019), https://www.frontiersin.org/articles/10.3389/fpsyg.2019.00722.

15. I'm referring here to work by Roger Ulrich in the first instance and Edward O. Wilson—both of which I consider in a bit more detail in Chapter 3.

16. See Nadia Khomami, "London Garden Bridge Project Collapses in Acrimony after £37m Spent," *Guardian*, August 14, 2017.

17. United Nations Human Settlement Programme, World Cities Report 2022 (United Nations, 2022).

18. See Mark Spence, "Dispossessing the Wilderness: Yosemite Indians and the National Park Ideal, 1864–1930," *Pacific Historical Review* 65, no. 1 (1996): 27–59.

19. Dorceta Taylor, *The Rise of the American Conservation Movement: Power, Privilege and Environmental Protection* (Durham, NC: Duke University Press, 2016).

20. See Thomas Fisher, "Frederick Law Olmsted and the Campaign for Public Health," *Places Journal*, November 2010.

21. See Frederick Law Olmsted, "The Greatest Glory of Nature," *Olmsted: Writings on Landscape, Culture, and Society*, ed. Charles Beveridge (New York: Library of America, 2015).

22. See Richard Grusin, "Reproducing Yosemite: Olmsted, Environmentalism, and the Nature of Aesthetic Agency," *Cultural Studies* 12, no. 3 (1998): 332–359.

23. See Theodore S. Eisenman, "Frederick Law Olmsted, Green Infrastructure, and the Evolving City," *Journal of Planning History* 12, no. 4 (2013): 287–311.

24. Donna Haraway, "Teddy Bear Patriarchy: Taxidermy in the Garden of Eden, New York City, 1908–1936," *Social Text* 11 (1985): 20–64. See also Anna Bramwell, *Ecology in the Twentieth Century: A History* (New Haven, CT: Yale University Press, 1989).

25. On the history of health professionals and urban green space in the UK, see Clare Hickman, "'To Brighten the Aspect of Our Streets and Increase the Health and Enjoyment of Our City': The National Health Society and Urban Green Space

in Late-nineteenth Century London," *Landscape and Urban Planning* 118 (2013): 112–119.

26. Select Committee, Report from the Select Committee on Public Walks, 1833.

27. See Frederick Law Olmsted, "The People's Park at Birkenhead, near Liverpool," *Olmsted: Writings on Landscape, Culture, and Society*, ed. Charles Beveridge (New York: Library of America, 2015).

28. Hickman, "'To Brighten the Aspect of Our Streets."

29. On this history, see Hazel Conway, *People's Parks: The Design and Development of Victorian Parks in Britain* (Cambridge, UK: Cambridge University Press, 1991).

30. Haraway, "Teddy Bear Patriarchy"; Bramwell, *Ecology in the Twentieth Century*.

31. Hickman, "'To Brighten the Aspect of Our Streets."

32. See again the work of Clare Hickman, *Therapeutic Landscapes* (Manchester, UK: Manchester University Press, 2014).

33. See Charles E. Beveridge and Paul Rocheleau, *Frederick Law Olmsted: Designing the American Landscape* (New York: Rizzoli, 1995).

34. Feargus O'Sullivan, "Paris Wants to Grow 'Urban Forests' at Famous Landmarks," *City Lab,* June 19, 2019, https://www.citylab.com/environment/2019/06/paris-trees-famous-landmarks-garden-park-urban-forest-design/591835.

35. Lewis Mumford, *The Culture of Cities* (New York: Harvest/Harcourt, Brace, Jovanovich, 1970).

36. Steven Vogel, *Thinking Like a Mall* (Cambridge, MA: MIT Press, 2016).

37. See Times Editorial Board, "Editorial: If We Want Wildlife to Thrive in L.A., We Have to Share Our Neighborhoods with Them," *Los Angeles Times*, November 7, 2022.

38. Christine Dell'Amore, "Wild Animals Are Adapting to City Life in Surprisingly Savvy Ways," *National Geographic Magazine*, June 7, 2022.

39. William Cronon, *Uncommon Ground: Rethinking the Human Place in Nature* (New York: W. W. Norton, 1995).

40. Tom Ravenscroft, "Vincent Callebaut Proposes a Roof That Generates Energy and Food for Notre-Dame Cathedral," *Dezeen*, May 9, 2019.

CHAPTER 2: THE GARDEN BATHED IN SUNLIGHT

1 Rohan Varma, "Architecture as an Agent of Change: Remembering Charles Correa, "India's Greatest Architect," *ArchDaily*, June 16, 2016, https://www.archdaily.com/789384/architecture-as-agent-of-change-remembering-charles-correa-india.

2. Joseph Rykwert, "Charles Correa Obituary," *Guardian*, June 19, 2015, https://www.theguardian.com/artanddesign/2015/jun/19/charles-correa.

3. "Royal Gold Medal," Royal Institute of British Architects, accessed April 19, 2023, https://www.architecture.com/awards-and-competitions-landing-page /awards/royal-gold-medal.

4. See "A Speech by HRH The Prince of Wales at the 150th Anniversary of the Royal Institute of British Architects (RIBA), Royal Gala Evening at Hampton Court Palace," May 30, 1984.

5. Hugh Pearman, "Prince Rains on 150th Parade," *RIBAJ*, August 13, 2018, https://www.ribaj.com/culture/ribaj-125-archive-september-2018-prince-charles -hampton-court-speech.

6. Pearman.

7. HRH The Prince of Wales, *A Vision of Britain: A Personal View of Architecture* (London: Doubleday, 1989).

8. "History: The Masterplan," Poundbury, accessed April 19, 2023, https://pound bury.co.uk/about/history/.

9. Léon Krier, *Albert Speer: Architecture 1932–1942* (New York: Monacelli, 2016).

10. Owen Hatherley, "King Charles Has Some Very Strange Ideas about How Cities Should Look," *Jacobin*, September 2022, https://jacobin.com/2022/09 /king-charles-architecture-cities-poundbury-krier-conservative.

11. Léon Krier "TRADITION—MODERNITY—MODERNISM: Some Necessary Explanations," *Architectural Design* 57 (1987): 38–43.

12. Here I am drawing on Lawrence Goldman, "The Social Science Association, 1857–1886: A Context for Mid-Victorian Liberalism," *English Historical Review* 398 (1986): 95–134.

13. On urban mortality in the period, see Simon Szreter, "Mortality and Public Health, 1815–1914," in *New Directions in Economic and Social History*, ed. A. Digby, C. Feinstein, and D. Jenkins (London: Palgrave, 1992).

14. Benjamin Ward Richardson, *Hygeia: A City of Health* (1876), https://www .gutenberg.org/cache/epub/12036/pg12036-images.html.

15. James H. Cassedy, "Hygeia: A Mid-Victorian Dream of a City of Health," *Journal of the History of Medicine and Allied Sciences* 17, no. 2 (April 1962): 217–228.

16. On Howard's biography, see Robert Beevers, *The Garden City Utopia* (London: Palgrave, 1988); see also sections on Howard in Peter Hall, *Cities of Tomorrow: An Intellectual History of Urban Planning and Design in the Twentieth Century* (Oxford, UK: Blackwell, 1996).

17. Ebenezer Howard, *Garden Cities of To-Morrow* (Cambridge, MA: MIT Press, 1965).

18. In this section, I am drawing on a brilliant PhD dissertation—see Jeremy David Rowan, "Imagining Corporate Culture: The Industrial Paternalism of William

Hesketh Lever at Port Sunlight, 1888–1925" (PhD diss., Louisiana State University, 2003).

19. Here and elsewhere I draw on David J. Jeremy (1991), "The Enlightened Paternalist in Action: William Hesketh Lever at Port Sunlight Before 1914," *Business History* 33 (1): 58-8.

20. Josephine Tierney, "Report of Scoping Survey of the Lever Brothers' Plantations in the Solomon Islands and the Congo, 1900–1930," 2021, https://royal africansociety.org/wp-content/uploads/2022/05/University-of-Liverpool-Scoping -Report-Lever-Bros-Plantations-in-the-Congo-and-Solomon-Islands-1900-to -1930.pdf.

21. See "History of the Trust," Leverhulme Trust, accessed April 18, 2023, https://www.leverhulme.ac.uk/history-trust#:~:text=The%20Leverhulme%20 Trust%20was%20established,Margarine%20Unie%20to%20form%20Unilever.

22. Amy Sergeant, "Lever, Lifebuoy and Ivory," *Early Popular Visual Culture* 9, no. 1 (2011): 37–55.

23. See Elizabeth Outka, *Consuming Traditions: Modernity, Modernism and the Commodified Authentic* (Oxford, UK: Oxford University Press, 2008).

24. Amanda Rees, "Nineteenth-Century Planned Industrial Communities and the Role of Aesthetics in Spatial Practices: the Visual Ideologies of Pullman and Port Sunlight," *Journal of Cultural Geography* 29, no. 2 (2012): 185–214.

25. As I write this, I wouldn't actually swear to there having been a stream. But the fact that there definitely is one in my mind's eye is at least some kind of data point about the atmosphere of the place.

26. William Lever, "Mr. Lever's Address on Visit of International Housing Conference to Port Sunlight, 9 August 1907," Warwick Digital Collections, 1907, https:// wdc.contentdm.oclc.org/digital/collection/health/id/68/.

27. Jeremy, "The Enlightened Paternalist in Action."

28. See Reuben Loffman and Benoît Henriet, "'We Are Left with Barely Anything': Colonial Rule, Dependency, and the Lever Brothers in the Belgian Congo, 1911–1960," *Journal of Imperial and Commonwealth History* 48, no. 1 (July 2019): 71–100.

29. See Jules Marchal, *Lord Leverhulme's Ghosts: Colonial Exploitation in the Congo* (New York: Verso, 2017).

CHAPTER 3: A RAT IN A MAZE

1. Dora Vargha, "Between East and West: Polio Vaccination across the Iron Curtain in Cold War Hungary," *Bulletin of the History of Medicine* 88, no. 2 (2014): 319–343. Here I also draw on Barry Trevelyan, Matthew Smallman-Raynor, and Andrew D. Cliff, "The Spatial Dynamics of Poliomyelitis in the United States: From

Epidemic Emergence to Vaccine-Induced Retreat, 1910–1971," *Annals of the Association of American Geographers* 95, no. 2 (2005): 269–293.

2. See Christos Lynteris, *Visual Plague: The Emergence of Epidemic Photography* (Cambridge, MA: MIT Press, 2022).

3. For versions of the Salk story, see John Paul Eberhard. "Architecture and Neuroscience: a Double Helix," in *Mind in Architecture: Neuroscience, Embodiment, and the Future of Design*, ed. Sarah Robinson and Juhani Pallasmaa (Cambridge, MA: MIT Press, 2015), and Emily Badger, "Corridors of the Mind: Could Neuroscientists Be the Next Great Architects?," *Pacific Standard*, 2017, https://psmag.com /social-justice/corridors-of-the-mind-49051. Notably, in an exhaustive biography by Charlotte DeCroes Jacobs (*Jonas Salk: A Life* [Oxford, UK: Oxford University Press, 2015), the story appears fleetingly and then only as something mentioned by Salk some years later.

4. On this history, see Dora Vargha, *Polio across the Iron Curtain: Hungary's Cold War with an Epidemic* (Cambridge, UK: Cambridge University Press, 2018).

5. Carolina A. Miranda, "Louis Kahn's Salk Institute, the Building That Guesses Tomorrow, Is Aging—Very, Very Gracefully," *Los Angeles Times*, November 22, 2016, https://www.latimes.com/entertainment/arts/miranda/la-et-cam-salk -institute-louis-kahn-20161107-htmlstory.html?utm_medium=website&utm _source=archdaily.com.

6. Luke Fiederer, "AD Classics: Salk Institute/Louis Kahn," *ArchDaily*, 2017, https://www.archdaily.com/61288/ad-classics-salk-institute-louis-kahn.

7. See "Remarks by Jonas Salk, on the Occasion of the Presentation of the 25th Year Award for the Design of the Salk Institute by Louis I. Kahn at the American Institute of Architects Awards Ceremony," ALA Convention in Boston, MA, June 19, 1992, Salk Papers, Special Collections and Archives, UC San Diego Library, University of California, San Diego (hereafter Salk Papers).

8. See "Remarks by Jonas Salk, in Response to the Salk Institute's receiving the American Institute of Architects' 25-Year Award at the Accent on Architecture Gala Celebration for Excellence in Architecture," Kennedy Center, Washington, DC, January 22, 1992, Salk Papers.

9. "Mission," Academy of Neuroscience for Architecture, https://www.anfarch .org/mission.

10. See Alison Whitelaw, "Introducing ANFA, the Academy of Neuroscience for Architecture," *Intelligent Buildings International* 5 (suppl.) (2013): 1–3.

11. Florian Lederbogen et al., "City Living and Urban Upbringing Affect Neural Social Stress Processing in Humans," *Nature* 474 (2011): 498–501.

12. Kristine Engemann et al., "Residential Green Space in Childhood Is Associated with Lower Risk of Psychiatric Disorders from Adolescence into Adulthood," *PNAS* 116, no. 11 (2019): 5188–5193.

13. Gregory N. Bratman et al., "Nature Experience Reduces Rumination and Subgenual Prefrontal Cortex Activation," *PNAS* 112 (28) (June 29, 2015): 8567–8572.

14. See Felicity Callard and Daniel Margulies, "The Subject at Rest: Novel Conceptualizations of Self and Brain from Cognitive Neuroscience's Study of the 'Resting State,'" *Subjectivity* 4 (2011): 227–257.

15. Paul Dudchenko, *Why People Get Lost: The Psychology and Neuroscience of Spatial Cognition* (Oxford, UK: Oxford University Press, 2010).

16. Willard S. Small, "An Experimental Study of the Mental Processes of the Rat," *American Journal of Psychology* 11, no. 2 (1900): 133–165; Willard S. Small, "An Experimental Study of the Mental Processes of the Rat II," *American Journal of Psychology* 12, no. 2 (1901): 206–239.

17. Edward C. Tolman, "Cognitive Maps in Rats and Men," *Psychological Review* 55, no. 4 (1948): 189–208.

18. John O'Keefe and Jonathan Dostrovsky, "The Hippocampus as a Spatial Map: Preliminary Evidence from Unit Activity in the Freely-moving Rat," *Brain Research* 34, no. 1 (1971): 171–175.

19. John O'Keefe and Lynn Nadel, *The Hippocampus as a Cognitive Map* (Oxford, UK: Oxford University Press, 1978).

20. For a good guide to some of this history, see Rodrigo Mara, "The Cognitive Roots of Space Syntax" (PhD diss., University College London, 2009), https://core.ac.uk/download/pdf/1687777.pdf.

21. Eleanor A. Maguire et al., "Navigation-Related Structural Change in the Hippocampi of Taxi Drivers," *PNAS* 97, no. 8 (2000): 4398–4403.

22. Rowan Moore, "The Royal College of Physicians—Just What the Doctors Ordered," *Observer*, September 7, 2014.

23. In these sections, I draw on my notes of the talks, which capture the content of what was being said but not exact quotations.

24. Robert E. L. Faris and H. Warren Dunham, *Mental Disorders in Urban Areas: an Ecological Study of Schizophrenia and Other Psychoses* (Chicago: University of Chicago Press, 1939).

25. For more on this, and especially for an elaboration of the historical background, see a book I wrote with Nikolas Rose, *The Urban Brain* (Princeton, NJ: Princeton University Press, 2022).

26. Charles Montgomery, *Happy City: Transforming Our Lives Through Urban Design* (New York: Penguin, 2013).

27. Roger S. Ulrich, "Visual Landscapes and Psychological Well-Being," *Landscape Research* 4, no. 1 (1979): 17–23.

28. To cite just one example, see Byoung-Suk Kweon, Roger S. Ulrich, Verrick D.

Walker, and Louis G. Tassinary, "Anger and Stress: The Role of Landscape Posters in an Office Setting," *Environment and Behavior* 40, no. 3 (2008): 355–381.

29. Kevin Baker, "'Welcome to Fear City'—the Inside Story of New York's Civil War, 40 Years On," *Guardian*, May 18, 2015.

30. Otto Saumarez Smith, "The Inner City Crisis and the End of Urban Modernism in 1970s Britain," *Twentieth Century British History* 27, no. 4 (2016): 578–598. He is in fact a member of the same distinguished extended family as the architect George Saumarez Smith, who we met in the previous chapter.

31. Jane Jacobs, *The Death and Life of Great American Cities* (New York: Random House, 1961).

32. Robert Caro, *The Power Broker: Robert Moses and the Fall of New York* (New York: Knopf, 1974).

33. Roger S. Ulrich, "Biophilia, Biophobia and Natural Landscapes," in *The Biophilia Hypothesis*, ed. Edward O. Wilson and Stephen R. Kellert (Washington, DC: Island Press, 1995).

34. Edward O. Wilson, *Biophilia: The Human Bond with Other Species* (Cambridge, MA: Harvard University Press, 1984).

35. Lauren Greyson, *Vital Reenchantments: Biophilia, Gaia, Cosmos and the Affectively Ecological* (New York: Punctum Press, 1984).

36. Rachel Kaplan and Stephen Kaplan, *The Experience of Nature: A Psychological Perspective* (Cambridge, UK: Cambridge University Press, 1989).

37. Heather Ohly et al., "Attention Restoration Theory: A Systematic Review of the Attention Restoration Potential of Exposure to Natural Environments," *Journal of Toxicology and Environmental Health*, Part B, 19, no. 7 (2016): 305–343.

38. William Cronon, *Nature's Metropolis: Chicago and the Great West* (New York: W. W. Norton, 1992).

CHAPTER 4: THE CONQUERED CITY

1. See "Marble Arch Mound," MVRDV, accessed April 18, 2023, https://www.mvrdv.nl/projects/456/marble-arch-hill.

2. "Marble Arch Mound."

3. Jonathan Prynn, "Marble Arch 'Mound' Plan to Lure Visitors back to West End with 25m-High Hill Set to Provide Sweeping Views," *Evening Standard*, February 16, 2021, https://www.standard.co.uk/news/london/marble-arch-mound-oxford-street-westminster-b919890.html.

4. See Dan Barker, Twitter, July 26, 2021, https://twitter.com/danbarker/status/1419787260107558918.

5. See Tom Ravenscroft, "Marble Arch Mound Attraction Reopens and Made 'Free for Everyone to Climb' in August," *Dezeen*, August 4, 2021, https://www.dezeen.com/2021/08/04/marble-arch-mound-mvrdv-free/.

6. Mark Brown, "Marble Arch Mound: Deputy Council Leader Resigns over £6m Cost," *Guardian*, August 13, 2021, https://www.theguardian.com/uk-news/2021/aug/13/marble-arch-mound-deputy-council-leader-resigns-over-cost.

7. Patrick Butler and Mark Brown, "Marble Arch Mound Draws Crowds Keen to See How Bad It Is," *Guardian*, August 23, 2021, https://www.theguardian.com/uk-news/2021/aug/23/not-pretty-marble-arch-mound-draws-crowds-keen-to-see-how-bad-it-is.

8. Jill Starley-Grainger, "A Review of London's Worst-Ever Tourist Attraction and Where to Go Instead," *EuroNews*, August 27, 2021, https://www.euronews.com/travel/2021/09/25/the-mound-is-london-s-worst-ever-tourist-attraction-here-are-the-best-alternatives.

9. City of Westminster Business and Children's Policy and Scrutiny Committee, "Internal Review—Marble Arch Mound Report (Part 1)," October 27, 2021, https://westminster.moderngov.co.uk/documents/s44227/Westminster%20City%20Council%20Internal%20Review%20Report%20Part%201.pdf.

10. Huw Lemmey, "An Exclusive Interview with the Marble Arch Mound," *Frieze*, January 12, 2022, https://www.frieze.com/article/exclusive-interview-marble-arch-mound.

11. Sumana Roy, *How I Became a Tree* (New Haven, CT: Yale University Press, 2021).

12. "Millions of Funding for Projects in England to Plant Hundreds of Thousands of Trees," Gov.uk, November 27, 2021, https://www.gov.uk/government/news/millions-of-funding-for-projects-in-england-to-plant-hundreds-of-thousands-of-trees.

13. Alexandra Kelley, "Is Trump Really Planting a Billion Trees?," *The Hill*, September 30, 2020, https://thehill.com/changing-america/sustainability/environment/518994-is-trump-really-planting-a-billion-trees.

14. Will Feuer, "Salesforce CEO Marc Benioff Says over 300 Companies Have Agreed to Help Plant One Trillion Trees," CNBC, January 23, 2020, https://www.cnbc.com/2020/01/23/salesforce-ceo-marc-benioff-300-companies-to-help-plant-1-trillion-tree.html.

15. Jean-Francois Bastin et al., "The Global Tree Restoration Potential," *Science* 365, no. 6448 (July 2019): 76–79.

16. Steffan Messenger, "Climate Change: Corporate Mass Tree Planting 'damaging' Nature," BBC, November 10, 2021, https://www.bbc.co.uk/news/uk-wales-59220669.

17. Rowan Moore, "Why the Marble Arch Mound Is a Slippery Slope to Nowhere," *Observer*, July 24, 2021, https://www.theguardian.com/artanddesign/2021/jul/24/why-the-marble-arch-mound-is-a-slippery-slope-to-nowhere.

18. Ali Karimi, "Cultivating the Arts: The Tree Out of Context," *Architectural Review*, October 12, 2021, https://www.architectural-review.com/essays/ecology /cultivating-the-arts-the-tree-out-of-context.

19. That's about £77 per tree—which seems expensive.

20. Though, charmingly, the Welsh-language word for children is "plant," which shares a Latin root (*planta*, meaning something like offshoot) with the quite different English word "plant."

21. Jonathan Bate, "Review: The Overstory by Richard Powers—Moby-Dick with Tree-Huggers," *The Times*, March 24, 2018.

22. Katya Kupelian and Abby Narishkin, "Look inside the new $1.3 billion complex at Singapore's Changi Airport, with a 130-foot indoor waterfall," *Business Insider*, April 17, 2019.

23. I am relying here on Google Translate. See "San Siro: Uno Stadio-Bosco per Milano," Stefano Boeri Architetti, November 14, 2022, https://www.stefanoboeri architetti.net/project/san-siro-uno-stadio-bosco-per-milano/. This proposal was not successful, but discussion on it was reignited in 2022 as the winning proposal continued to run into difficulties; see Rob Ridley, 'Forest-Stadium' Vision Set to Be Presented for Stadio Giuseppe Meazza," TheStadiumBusiness, November 4, 2022, https://www.thestadiumbusiness.com/2022/11/04/forest-stadium-vision-set -to-be-presented-for-stadio-giuseppe-meazza/.

24. See https://twitter.com/JustinTrudeau/status/1177613585381543936.

25. Toby Berrett, "Meet 'Sussex on Ecosia,' the Sussex Students Saving the World with a Search Engine," *The Tab*, 2018.

26. See https://tred.earth/tred-card/.

27. Marine Le Pen, leader of the party once known as the Front National, which now openly calls itself an environmental party, described Europe as "the world's leading ecological civilization." See Norimitsu Onishi, "France's Far Right Wants to Be an Environmental Party, Too," *New York Times*, October 17, 2019, https://www .nytimes.com/2019/10/17/world/europe/france-far-right-environment.html.

28. Paris Marx, "Jeff Bezos' 'O'Neill Colony' Dreams Ignore the Plight of Millions Living on Earth Now," NBC News, 2019, https://www.nbcnews.com/think /opinion/jeff-bezos-blue-origin-space-colony-dreams-ignore-plight-millions-ncna 1006026.

29. David Harvey, *The Urban Experience* (Baltimore, MD: Johns Hopkins University Press, 1989).

30. Luke Turner, *Out of the Woods* (London: Weidenfeld and Nicolson, 2019).

31. I am drawing here on the work of the historian Steve Hindle. See in particular his article "Imagining Insurrection in Seventeenth-Century England: Representations of the Midland Rising of 1607," *History Workshop Journal* 66 (2008): 21–61.

32. See Joan Thirsk, "Arthur Standish," *Oxford Dictionary of National Biography*, September 23, 2004, https://www.oxforddnb.com/display/10.1093/ref:odnb/97801 98614128.001.0001/odnb-9780198614128-e-26229;jsessionid=0AB6E38B25BAF 20C6AD8EF4EED6B12A3.

33. Quoted in Thirsk.

34. Arthur Standish, "New Directions of Experience" (Ann Arbor, MI: Text Creation Partnership, 1613), http://name.umdl.umich.edu/B08132.0001.001.

35. Sir Anthony Fitzherbert, *The Boke of Husbandry*, 1531, https://quod.lib .umich.edu/e/eebo/A00884.0001.001/1:4.86?rgn=div2;view=fulltext.

36. Peter Warde, "Fear of Wood Shortage and the Reality of the Woodland in Europe, c. 1450–1850," *History Workshop Journal* 62, no. 1 (2006): 28–57.

37. Karl Marx, *Capital*, Vol. 1 (1867), https://www.marxists.org/archive/marx /works/1867-c1/ch01.htm#S1.

38. John Evelyn, *Sylva, or a Discourse of Forest Trees and the Propagation of Timber*, 1662, https://www.gutenberg.org/files/20778/20778-h/20778-h.htm.

39. See James C McKusick, "John Evelyn: The Forestry of Imagination," *English Faculty Publications* 17 (2013): https://scholarworks.umt.edu/eng_pubs/17.

40. See "Kilcash" in Eiléan Ní Chuilleanáin, *The Girl Who Married the Reindeer* (Oldcastle, Ireland: Gallery Press, 2001). See also Matthew Rowney, "Broken Arbour: 'The Ruined Cottage' and Deforestation," *European Romantic Review* 26, no. 6 (2015): 719–741. I'm grateful to Ger Mullaly for pointing this connection out to me.

41. George Perkins Marsh, *Man and Nature or, Physical Geography as Modified by Human Action*, 1864, https://www.gutenberg.org/files/37957/37957-h/37957-h.htm.

42. See Andrea Wulf, *The Invention of Nature* (New York: Vintage, 2016).

43. See Leo Marx, *The Machine in the Garden: Technology and the Pastoral Ideal in America* (Oxford, UK: Oxford University Press, 1964).

44. Harriet Ritvo, *The Dawn of Green: Manchester, Thirlmere and Modern Environmentalism* (Chicago: University of Chicago Press, 2009).

45. Haeckel not only popularized in Germany a variety of social Darwinism that ascribed different value to different "races" but also was enthusiastic about killing sickly infants and was a founder of the aggressively imperialist and racist Pan-German League. His popular book, *The Riddle of the Universe*, which had sold half a million copies by the time Hitler came to power, was received by an enthusiastic German public as "a scientific religion which established the truth of German romantic nationalism, Aryan superiority, and the true value of the folk" (quoted from George J. Stein, "Biological Science and the Roots of Nazism," *American Scientist* 76, no. 1 [1988]: 50–58).

46. See Paul Warde, Libby Robin, and Sverker Sörlin, *The Environment: A History of the Idea* (Baltimore, MD: Johns Hopkins University Press, 2018).

47. See Clare Hickman, *Therapeutic Landscapes* (Manchester, UK: Manchester University Press, 2013).

48. See Kirsten McEwen et al., "A Pragmatic Controlled Trial of Forest Bathing Compared with Compassionate Mind Training in the UK: Impacts on Self-Reported Wellbeing and Heart Rate Variability," *Sustainability* 13, no. 3 (2021): 1380.

49. Glen Moore and Cassandra Atherton, "Eternal Forests: The Veneration of Old Trees in Japan," *Arnoldia* 77, no. 4 (2020): 24–31.

50. See Robert H. Sharf, "Is Mindfulness Buddhist? (and Why It Matters)," *Transcultural Psychiatry* 52, no. 4 (2015): 470–484.

51. See "Introduction to the Japanese Society of Forest Medicine," Society of Forest Medicine within the Japanese Society for Hygiene, November 29, 2008, http://forest-medicine.com/epage01.html.

52. Samantha Walton, *Everybody Needs Beauty: In Search of the Nature Cure* (London: Bloomsbury, 2021).

53. Mark Jackson, *The Age of Stress: Science and the Search for Stability* (Oxford, UK: Oxford University Press, 2013).

54. At the time of writing, the Department for the Environment, Food and Rural Affairs, supported by the Department of Health and Social Care and the NHS, has funded a large two-year formal evaluation of green social prescribing across seven test sites in the UK. As one psychiatrist put it to me, the best way to think about it might be simply asking a patient, "What's been the role of nature in your life?"—and, if it's been a source of security or comfort, then seeing what's out there to help someone access it.

55. See Vadim Saraev et al., "Valuing the Mental Health Benefits of Woodlands," (Edinburgh: Forest Research, 2021).

56. Walton, *Everybody Needs Beauty*.

57. Richard Mabey, *Nature Cure* (New York: Vintage, 2008).

58. Sigmund Freud, *Civilization and Its Discontents* (New York: Penguin Freud Library, 1991).

59. Matt Ffytche, *Critical Lives: Sigmund Freud* (London: Reaktion Books, 2022).

60. Sara Maitland, *Gossip from the Forest: The Tangled Roots of Our Forests and Fairytales* (London: Granta, 2006).

CHAPTER 5: SAVE ME

1. If you ever want to know about the surprisingly extensive relationship between colonialism and plants, visit the Royal Botanic Gardens in Melbourne, founded in 1846; take in the rolling, lush greens of European and Australian trees; if you're feeling lucky, go into the herbarium and ask them to show you some of

the specimens collected in the 1770s by Joseph Banks—which they still store there. Banks was the botanist who traveled with Captain Cook on Cook's first voyage to Australia, who later became president of the Royal Society in London and helped set up Kew Gardens with George II, and for whose plant-collecting enthusiasm Cook eventually gave the harbor where they had first anchored the name Botany Bay.

2. I'm grateful to Yvonne Lynch for additional help with this background—any outstanding inaccuracies, as well as the wider interpretation, are wholly my own.

3. I am taking these extracts from Adrienne LaFrance, "When You Give a Tree an Email Address," *Atlantic*, July 10, 2015.

4. For a really good academic analysis of these emails and their relationship to urban conviviality, see Elizabeth Straughan, Catherine Phillips, and Jennifer Atchison, "Finding Comfort and Conviviality with Urban Trees," *Cultural Geographies* (2015): https://doi.org/10.1177/14744740221136284.

5. Per Bolund and Sven Hunhammar, "Ecosystem Services in Urban Areas," *Ecological Economics* 29, no. 2 (1999): 293–301.

6. Catherine Philips and Jennifer Atchison, "Seeing the Trees for the (Urban) Forest: More-Than-Human Geographies and Urban Greening," *Australian Geographer* 51 (2020): 155–168.

7. See Vadim Saraev et al., "Valuing the Mental Health Benefits of Woodlands," (Edinburgh: Forest Research, 2021). For a useful summary from a public health perspective, see Danielle Shanahan et al., "Toward Improved Public Health Outcomes from Urban Nature," *American Journal of Public Health* 105 (2015): 470–477.

8. See "Enabling a Natural Capital Approach guidance," Gov.uk, August 4, 2021, https://www.gov.uk/government/publications/enabling-a-natural-capital-approach-enca-guidance/enabling-a-natural-capital-approach-guidance#introduction-to-natural-capital.

9. I say this as a former council bureaucrat.

10. Hillary Angelo, *How Green Became Good: Urbanized Nature and the Making of Cities and Citizens* (Chicago: University of Chicago Press, 2021).

11. "Taylorism" was a quasi-scientific management philosophy popular in the early twentieth century, which tried to make spaces like factories more efficient by doing things like analyzing workflows really closely and cutting out unnecessary actions. Sonja Dümpelmann, *Seeing Trees: A History of Street Trees in New York City and Berlin* (New Haven, CT: Yale University Press, 2019).

12. India Block, "Paris Plans to Go Green by Planting 'Urban Forest' around Architectural Landmarks," *Dezeen*, June 26, 2019.

13. Adam Nossiter, "The Greening of Paris Makes Its Mayor More Than a Few Enemies," *New York Times*, October 5, 2019.

14. Jaime Velázquez, "Madrid Building a Huge Urban Forest in a Bid to Combat Climate Change," *Euronews*, July 19, 2021.

15. Michael L. Treglia, Montserrat Acosta-Morel, Darran Crabtree, Kate Galbo, Tami Lin-Moges, Alaina Van Slooten, and Emily Maxwell, "The State of the Urban Forest in New York City," Nature Conservancy, 2021, https://www.nature.org/content/dam/tnc/nature/en/photos/TheStateoftheNYCUrbanForest.pdf. See also "Future Forest NYC," Nature Conservancy, July 26, 2020, https://www.nature.org/en-us/about-us/where-we-work/united-states/new-york/stories-in-new-york/future-forest-nyc/.

16. Peter Hall, *Cities of Tomorrow: An Intellectual History of Urban Planning and Design in the Twentieth Century* (Oxford, UK: Blackwell, 1996).

17. Nikolas C. Heynen, "The Scalar Production of Injustice within the Urban Forest," *Antipode* 35, no. 5 (2003): 980–998.

18. See Matthew Gandy, *Concrete and Clay: Reworking Nature in New York City* (Cambridge, MA: MIT Press, 2003).

19. See Joanna Dean, "Seeing Trees, Thinking Forests: Urban Forestry at the University of Toronto in the 1960s," in *Method and Meaning in Canadian Environmental History*, ed. Alan MacEachern and William J. Turkel (Toronto, ON: Nelson, 2009). Dean includes the enticing detail that Jorgensen was an associate of the U of T's then star professor, the gnomic media theorist Marshall McLuhan, having been tasked with advising on tree management around the celebrity academic's home. "Urban Forest," Dean points out, a conjunction of seeming opposites, seems very close to some of McLuhan's own coinages, such as "Global Village." In this sense, you might even say that the concept of the urban forest, in spite of its earthy connotations, is actually little more than a side product of Cold War media theory.

20. See Paul E. Wagonner and J. D. Ovington, *Proceedings of the Lockwood Conference on the Suburban Forest and Ecology*, Bulletin 652 (New Haven, CT: Connecticut Agricultural Experimental Station, 1962).

21. Matthew Gandy, *Natura Urbana: Ecological Constellations in Urban Space* (Cambridge, MA: MIT Press, 2022).

22. See Rowan A. Rowntree, "Urban Forest Ecology: Conceptual Points of Departure," *Arboriculture & Urban Forestry* 24, no. 2 (1998): 62–71.

23. See Michael Williams, "Sauer and 'Man's Role in Changing the Face of the Earth,'" *Geographical Review* 77, no. 2 (1987): 218–231.

24. Preston E. James, "Man's Role in Changing the Face of the Earth: A Review," *Economic Geography* 33, no. 3 (1957): 267–274.

25. James.

26. H. C. Darby, "The Clearing of the Woodland in Europe," in *Man's Role in Changing the Face of the Earth*, ed. W. L. Thomas (Chicago: University of Chicago Press, 1956).

27. Lewis Mumford, "The Natural History of Urbanization," in *Man's Role in Changing the Face of the Earth*, ed. W. L. Thomas (Chicago: University of Chicago Press, 1956).

28. For an introduction to this perspective, see Nik Heynen, Maria Kaika, and Erik Swyngedouw, *In the Nature of Cities* (New York: Routledge, 2006).

29. Matthew Gandy and Sandra Jasper, *The Botanical City* (Berlin: Jovis Verlag, 2020).

30. Richard Deakin, *Flora of the Colosseum of Rome* (London: Groombridge & Sons, 1855).

31. See "History," Sheffield Tree Action Groups, accessed April 18, 2023, https://savesheffieldtrees.org.uk/history/.

32. Ellie Violet Bramley, "For the Chop: The Battle to save Sheffield's Trees," *Guardian*, February 25, 2018, https://www.theguardian.com/uk-news/2018/feb/25/for-the-chop-the-battle-to-save-sheffields-trees.

33. Sir Mark Lowcock (KCB) (Independent Chair), "Sheffield Street Trees Inquiry," 2023, https://www.sheffield.gov.uk/sites/default/files/2023-03/sheffield_street_trees_inquiry_report.pdf.

34. See "Sources for the Study of Park Hill and Hyde Park Flats," 2010, https://www.sheffield.gov.uk/sites/default/files/docs/libraries-and-archives/archives-and-local-studies/research/Park_Hill_and_Hyde_Park_Study_Guide_v_1-12.pdf.

35. Bart Bryant-Mole, "AD Classics: Park Hill Estate/Jack Lynn and Ivor Smith, *ArchDaily*, accessed April 18, 2023, https://www.archdaily.com/791939/ad-classics-park-hill-estate-sheffield-jack-lynn-ivor-smith.

36. "Park Hill," BBC, May 25, 2008, https://www.bbc.co.uk/southyorkshire/content/articles/2007/03/07/park_hill_feature.shtml.

37. "Sources for the Study of Park Hill and Hyde Park Flats."

38. See John Boughton, *Municipal Dreams: The Rise and Fall of Council Housing* (New York: Verso, 2018).

39. Owen Hatherley, "Regeneration? What's Happening in Sheffield's Park Hill Is Class Cleansing," *Guardian*, September 28, 2011, https://www.theguardian.com/commentisfree/2011/sep/28/sheffield-park-hill-class-cleansing.

40. Paul Dobraszczyk, "Sheffield's Park Hill: The Tangled Reality of an Extraordinary Brutalist Dream," *Guardian*, August 14, 2015, https://www.theguardian.com/cities/2015/aug/14/park-hill-brutalist-sheffield-estate-controversial-renovation.

41. Stefi Orazi, *Modernist Estates: The Buildings and the People Who Live in Them* (London: Francis Lincoln, 2015).

CHAPTER 6: THE TWENTIETH CENTURY DID NOT TAKE PLACE

1. Lisa Abend, "Inside Barcelona's Unfinished Masterpiece," *Time*, July 8, 2019, https://time.com/sagrada-familia-barcelona/.

2. Stephen Burgen, "Huge Star atop Sagrada Família Rekindles Residents' Complaints," *Guardian*, November 29, 2021, https://www.theguardian.com/world /2021/nov/29/huge-star-atop-sagrada-familia-rekindles-residents-complaints.

3. In which one is publicly confirmed as a follower of Christ; in most of our cases, this would turn out to be an optimistic declaration.

4. Lewis Mumford, "A Modern Catholic Architect," *Commonweal*, March 2, 1927.

5. See "Barry Byrne (1883–1967)," Church of Christ the King, accessed April 18, 2023, https://turnerscross.com/architecture/barry-byrne/.

6. Mark Burry, "Antoni Gaudí and Frei Otto: Essential Precursors to the Parametricism Manifesto," *Architectural Design* 86, no. 2 (2016): 30–35.

7. See also Christina Cogdell, *Toward a Living Architecture* (Minneapolis: University of Minnesota Press, 2019).

8. See "Explore Sagrada Familia's Interior | Symbolism, Floorplan & Key Elements," Barcelona Tickets, accessed April 18, 2023, https://sagradafamilia.barcelona-tickets .com/sagrada-familia-tower-interiors/.

9. Javier Senosiain, *Bio-Architecture* (New York: Routledge, 2003).

10. I am using "classical" and "traditional" a bit interchangeably in this chapter, though, as this example already makes clear, something can be "traditional" and very much not "classical." Nonetheless, the two approaches share a common relationship to time, and to how we value the styles of previous eras, which forms a sharp contrast with modernism—where, ideologically at least, there has often been a willingness to do away with older styles altogether. It's this contrast that really interests me through the chapter, which is why I will bundle classical and traditional together sometimes.

11. See, for example, the website of the Traditional Architecture Group, which is a society linked to the Royal Institute of British Architects (i.e., the main professional body for UK architects), accessed April 18, 2023, http://traditionalarchitec turegroup.org/about.

12. India Block, "Trump Orders New Government Buildings Must Be 'Beautiful,'" *Dezeen*, December 21, 2020.

13. See "Defence and National Rehabilitation Centre (DNRC) and Replacement for Headley Court at Stanford Hall," John Simpson Architects, March 2020, https://www.johnsimpsonarchitects.com/news-defence-national-rehabilitation -centre-jsa.html.

14. "Handover of the Gift of the Defence and National Rehabilitation Centre by the Duke of Westminster," DNRC, June 21, 2018, https://www.thednrc.org.uk /facts-figures/press-releases/22/Handover-of-the-gift-of-the-Defence-and-National -Rehabilitation-Centre-by-the-Duke-of-Westminster.

15. Donald H. Ruggles, *Beauty, Neuroscience, and Architecture: Timeless Patterns and Their Impact on Our Well-Being* (Norman: University of Oklahoma Press, 2018).

16. Create Streets is an organization that both advocates for an approach to urban design that it calls "gentle density" and provides services to clients broadly based on this approach. Its website says that it exists "to help solve the housing crisis and to help neighborhoods, communities, landowners, councils and developers create and manage beautiful, sustainable places of gentle density that will be popular, are likely to be correlated with good wellbeing and public health outcomes and which are likely to prove good long term investments based on the historical data of value appreciation and maintenance costs." ("Our Story," Create Streets, accessed April 18, 2023, https://www.createstreets.com/front-page-2/about-us/our-story.) Create Streets is by no means a simplistic or dogmatic "traditionalist" organization—and I think would understand itself to be led by evidence for what people want in planning and design. But I don't think it does great violence to this definition to say that it is a rather conservative (small "c") organization. In 2021, indeed, the Conservative government appointed its founder, Nicholas Boys Smith, as chair of the new Office for Place—a public body intended, according to the then housing minister, Robert Jenrick, to correct "post-war mistakes" and put "beauty back at the heart of how we build" (speech by Robert Jenrick, Office for Place Launch, July 21, 2021, https://www.gov.uk/government/speeches/office-for-place-launch).

17. See "Our Story," https://www.createstreets.com/front-page-2/about-us/our-story/.

18. These themes have been at the center of a range of public and government reports in the UK in recent years, as the housing market has badly failed to keep up with demand and a sense of anxiety has set in about the quality and range of new-build communities. See, for example, the Royal Institute of British Architects report "The Ten Primary Characteristics of Places People Want to Live," December 3, 2019, published in response to a government report on making Britain's new housing development less grimly homogeneous (https://www.architec ture.com/knowledge-and-resources/resources-landing-page/ten-characteristic s-of-places-where-people-want-to-live). See also "Living with Beauty," January 30, 2020, the final report from the government's Building Better, Building Beautiful Commission—co-chaired by Nicholas Boys Smith—on improving the design of new homes and neighborhoods (https://www.gov.uk/government/groups/building-better -building-beautiful-commission).

19. I actually put this argument to Boys Smith over email. He replied, in fairness, that we don't have to take people's word for it—that we can also use pricing data as a guide to what economists call "revealed preferences" (this is the idea that what people actually buy, and will pay more for, is a good guide to what they really value). I'm not convinced by this—the idea that behavior is a reliable guide to desire is a typical economist's fallacy, in my view—but for more on this, see his report "Beyond Location," with Alessandro Venerandi and Kieran Toms, in the April/May 2018 issue of *Land*.

20. Roger Scruton, *Beauty: A Very Short Introduction* (Oxford, UK: Oxford University Press, 2009).

21. Roger Scruton, *The Aesthetics of Architecture* (1979; repr., Princeton, NJ: Princeton University Press, 2013).

22. David Watkin, *Morality and Architecture* (Chicago: University of Chicago Press, 1984).

23. Alice Coleman, *Utopia on Trial: Vision and Reality in Planned Housing* (London: Hilary Shipman, 1985).

24. Alex Potts, "The New Right and Architectural Aesthetics," *History Workshop* 12 (1981): 159–162.

25. "Americans' Preferred Architecture for Federal Buildings," National Civic Art Society, October 2020, https://www.civicart.org/americans-preferred-architecture-for-federal-buildings.

26. Martyn Brown, "New Homes Need to Be Built in Keeping with Traditional Architectural Styles," *Express*, July 21, 2021.

27. Ann Sussman and Justin B. Hollander, *Cognitive Architecture: Designing for How We Respond to the Built Environment* (New York: Routledge, 2014).

28. Matthias Schmelzer, "'Born in the Corridors of the OECD': The Forgotten Origins of the Club of Rome, Transnational Networks, and the 1970s in Global History," *Journal of Global History* 12, no. 1 (2017): 26–48.

29. Ian McHarg, *Design with Nature* (1969; repr., Hoboken, NJ: Wiley, 1995).

30. Anne Whiston Spirn, "Ian McHarg, Landscape Architecture and Environmentalism: Ideas and Methods in Context," in *Environmentalism in Landscape Architecture*, ed. Michael Conan (Washington, DC: Dumbarton Oaks, 2001).

31. Ian McHarg, *Man: Planetary Disease* (Washington, DC: US Agricultural Service, 1971).

32. Peder Anker, *From Bauhaus to Ecohouse: A History of Ecological Design* (Baton Rouge: Louisiana State University Press, 2010).

33. Douglas Murphy, *Last Futures: Nature, Technology and the End of Architecture* (New York: Verso, 2016).

34. Nicholas Wade, "New Alchemy Institute: Search for an Alternative Agriculture," *Science*, February 28, 1975.

35. D. C. Wahl, "Bionics vs. Biomimicry: From Control of Nature to Sustainable Participation in Nature," in *Design and Nature III: Comparing Design in Nature with Science and Engineering*, ed. C. A. Brebbia (Southampton, UK: WIT Press, 2006).

36. Julian Vincent, "Biomimetic Patterns in Architectural Design," *Architectural Design* 79, no. 6 (2009): 74–81.

37. O. Maksimov and T. G. Leighton, "Pattern Formation on the Surface of a Bubble Driven by an Acoustic Field," *Proceedings of the Royal Society* (2012): 46857–46875.

38. Philip Ball, "Beijing Bubbles," *Nature* 448 (2007): 256.

39. See "A Form Inspired by the Natural Formation of Soap Bubbles," ARUP, accessed April 18, 2023, https://www.arup.com/projects/chinese-national-aquatics -center.

40. Achim Menges, "Biomimetic Design Processes in Architecture: Morphogenetic and Evolutionary Computational Design," *Bioinspiration & Biomimetics* 7, no. 1 (2012): doi 10.1088/1748-3182/7/1/015003.

41. See the introduction in Michael Hensel and Achim Henges, *Morpho-Ecologies: Towards a Discourse of Heterogeneous Space in Architecture* (London: AA Publications, 2006).

42. Christina Cogdell, *Toward a Living Architecture? Complexism and Biology in Generative Design* (Minneapolis: University of Minnesota Press, 2018).

43. Matias del Campo and Neil Leach, "Can Machines Hallucinate Architecture? AI as Design Method," in *Machine Hallucinations: Architecture and Artificial Intelligence*, ed. M. del Campo and N. Leach (London: Wiley, 2022).

44. Patrik Schumacher, "Parametricism as Style—Parametricist Manifesto," 2008, http://www.patrikschumacher.com/Texts/Parametricism%20as%20 Style.htm.

45. Patrik Schumacher, "Patrik Schumacher on Parametricism—'Let the Style Wars Begin,'" *Architects Journal,* May 6, 2010.

46. Patrik Schumacher, "Introduction: Parametricism 2.0—Gearing Up to Impact the Global Built Environment," 2016, https://www.patrikschumacher .com/Texts/Parametricism%202_0_Gearing%20up%20to%20Impact%20the%20 Global%20Built%20Environment.html.

47. Aaron M. Renn, "Interview: Architect Patrik Schumacher: 'I've Been Depicted as a Fascist,'" *Guardian,* January 17, 2018.

48. Vincent L. Michael, "Expressing the Modern: Barry Byrne in 1920s Europe," *Journal of the Society of Architectural Historians* 69, no. 4 (2010): 534–555.

49. Lewis Mumford, "A Modern Catholic Architect," *Commonweal* 5, March 2, 1927.

INDEX

ABOUT THE AUTHOR

Rob Coombe

DES FITZGERALD is professor of medical humanities and social sciences at University College Cork. He has been named a "New Generation Thinker" by the BBC and the Arts and Humanities Research Council. He lives in Cork, Ireland.